Imagining New York City

Imagining New York City

LITERATURE, URBANISM, AND
THE VISUAL ARTS, 1890–1940

Christoph Lindner

OXFORD
UNIVERSITY PRESS

OXFORD
UNIVERSITY PRESS

Oxford University Press is a department of the
University of Oxford. It furthers the University's objective
of excellence in research, scholarship, and education
by publishing worldwide.

Oxford   New York

Auckland   Cape Town   Dar es Salaam   Hong Kong   Karachi
Kuala Lumpur   Madrid   Melbourne   Mexico City   Nairobi
New Delhi   Shanghai   Taipei   Toronto

With offices in

Argentina   Austria   Brazil   Chile   Czech Republic   France   Greece
Guatemala   Hungary   Italy   Japan   Poland   Portugal   Singapore
South Korea   Switzerland   Thailand   Turkey   Ukraine   Vietnam

Oxford is a registered trade mark of Oxford University Press
in the UK and certain other countries.

Published in the United States of America by
Oxford University Press
198 Madison Avenue, New York, NY 10016

Library of Congress Cataloging-in-Publication Data
Lindner, Christoph, 1971–
Imagining New York City : literature, urbanism, and the visual arts, 1890–1940 / Christoph Lindner.
pages   cm
Includes bibliographical references and index.
ISBN 978-0-19-537514-5 (cloth)—ISBN 978-0-19-537515-2 (paper)—
ISBN 978-0-19-970518-4 (ebook)
1. City and town life—New York (State)—New York—History.
2. New York (N.Y.)—Social conditions.   3. New York (N.Y.)—In motion pictures.
4. New York (N.Y.)—In literature.   5. New York (N.Y.)—In art.
6. Space (Architecture)—Social aspects—New York (State)—New York—History.
7. Public spaces—Social aspects—New York (State)—New York—History.
8. Buildings—Social aspects—New York (State)—New York—History.
9. Sidewalks—Social aspects—New York (State)—New York—History.
10. Social change—New York (State)—New York—History.   I. Title.
HN80.N5L49   2015
303.409747′1—dc23   2014023869

1 3 5 7 9 8 6 4 2

Printed in the United States of America
on acid-free paper

{ CONTENTS }

{ ACKNOWLEDGMENTS }

This book has been long in the making, spanning three transatlantic moves, four jobs, and two sabbaticals. It is with pleasure that I am able to acknowledge here the various forms of encouragement, support, and constructive critique that the project has received over these years.

At Aberystwyth University, Peter Barry, Helena Grice, Andrew Hadfield (now at Sussex), Claire Jowitt (now at Southampton), Sarah Prescott, and Tim Woods were instrumental in helping to kick-start the book in both practical and intellectual ways. At Northern Illinois University, William Baker and Keith Gandal (now at CUNY) were key partners for talking about modernism and New York City. At the University of Amsterdam, my research group, the Cities Project, provided both a context and a community within which to develop the book's core ideas about urban modernity. Many more opportunities for intellectual exchange, which shaped, challenged, and extended my thinking, were provided by the cosmopolitan intellectual community of the Amsterdam School for Cultural Analysis (ASCA).

A significant portion of this book was written during a visiting professorship at New York University in 2013, and I would like to thank both the Department of Social and Cultural Analysis and the Institute for Public Knowledge at NYU for hosting my visit. Jessica Coffey, Sam Carter, Candice Golys, Caitlin Zaloom, and Erik Klinenberg were among the many people at NYU who helped to make this time productive and stimulating. I am also grateful to the New School for Public Engagement for appointing me as a visiting scholar during the last months of my research stay in New York and for providing not only a superb work space but also access to a highly engaged faculty and student community. For other, equally important forms of hospitality and insider knowledge about New York, I thank Douglas and Jolie Glickman, John and Rani Londoner, Andre and Ana Appignani, Erica Rutt Gale, Tom Polley, and Theodore Ross. Final revisions to the manuscript were made during a visiting scholar appointment at the Institute for Urban and Regional Development at the University of California, Berkeley—a uniquely inspiring place for research and writing on cities.

My thinking has benefited from conversations and exchanges with many scholars in the fields of American studies, architecture, art history, cultural analysis, geography, media studies, sociology, and urban studies, including, among others, Nezar AlSayyad, Gary Bridge, Peter Brooker, Hugh Campbell, Ben Campkin, Deborah Cherry, Yiu-Fai Chow, Stanley Corkin, Jeroen Dewulf, Stephanie Hemelryk Donald, Isabel Gil, Derek Gregory, Sue Harris, Joseph Heathcott, Andrew Hussey, Shirley Jordan, Jeroen de Kloet, Barabara Korte, Janet Kraynak, Bill Marshall, C.J. Lim, David Pinder, Jennifer Robinson, Eric Sandeen, David Scobey, Maren Stange, Edward Soja, Douglas Tallack, José Van Dijck, Ginette Verstraete, Sophie Watson, Richard J. Williams, and Sharon Zukin. I am also indebted to the book's two anonymous reviewers for their detailed and insightful comments.

A number of institutions and funding bodies generously provided support for this project, beginning with the British Academy, who funded the first archival visit to New York City. I am also grateful to the Graduate School at Northern Illinois University for providing a summer research grant at a crucial stage in the book's development. For awarding a much-needed publication grant, I am grateful to the Graham Foundation for Advanced Studies in the Fine Arts. Almost every image in this book was made possible by the Graham Foundation. The University of Amsterdam funded a crucial research leave that made it possible to work on the project in situ. For stepping in as acting directors of ASCA during my sabbatical in New York, I owe Robin Celikates and Jeroen de Kloet much more than I can repay. Pedram Dibazar and Miriam Meissner were outstanding research assistants and important intellectual collaborators.

The opportunities to road-test various sections of the book in the form of invited talks and public lectures were invaluable, and I am grateful to the organizers of these events and the audiences who participated at the following institutions: Brown University, Ca' Foscari University of Venice, Catholic University of Portugal, Institute for Advanced Studies in the Humanities–Essen, Massachusetts Institute of Technology, Radboud University of Nijmegen, The New School, New York University, Queen Mary University of London, University of California–Berkeley, University of Copenhagen, University of Greenwich, University of Edinburgh, University of Freiburg, University College London, and the University of London Institute in Paris.

Parts of this book incorporate material revised from the following journal articles, and I am grateful to the publishers involved for permission to draw on this work: "Willa Cather, Daniel Libeskind, and the Creative Destruction of Manhattan," *Journal of American Culture* 28.1 (2005); "New York Vertical: Reflections on the Modern Skyline," *American Studies* 47.1 (2006); "New York Undead: Globalization, Landscape Urbanism, and the Afterlife of the Twin Towers," *Journal of American Culture* 31.3 (2008); and "After-Images of the Highrise City: Visualizing Urban Change in Modern New York," *Journal of American Culture* 36.2 (2013).

This book is dedicated to Becky, Joseph, and Hannah for our time together in Brooklyn.

Christoph Lindner
Berkeley, 2014

{ LIST OF FIGURES }

Imagining New York City

The Mutable City

A hundred times I have thought: New York is a catastrophe, and fifty times: it is a beautiful catastrophe.

—Le Corbusier, *When the Cathedrals Were White*[1]

The Metropolis is an addictive machine from which there is no escape.

—Rem Koolhaas, *Delirious New York*[2]

Archive City

This book is the result of another book that was never written. Some years ago, I spent a sabbatical researching in the urban-related archives of the New-York Historical Society and New York Public Library as part of a planned book titled *Urban Narrative from Dickens to Film Noir*. By the time I emerged from the archives at the end of the research stay, however, my interests had shifted radically and irrevocably to focus on New York City—on its interrelating histories, spaces, practices, and lived experiences. The book initially conceived as *Urban Narrative from Dickens to Film Noir* had turned into *Imagining New York City*.

What happened inside the archives was, of course, something people have been experiencing for centuries in their everyday en-counters with the city. As a place, but also as an idea, New York City had hijacked my imagination. This study is both an expression of and an investigation into that process as it has occurred in critical thinking about urban phenomena, as well as in cultural production and creative practice concerned with New York. So although its gen-esis resides in an immersive, seductive encounter with the city's ar-chival memory of itself, the project completed here is much wider in scope and seeks to intervene in broader, ongoing discussions about how and why we study New York City, particularly in relation to literature, urbanism, and the visual arts.

Changing New York

In this respect, *Imagining New York City* belongs to an extended critical tradition of outsider writing about the city. This claim is not meant apologetically. Rather, I wish to acknowledge here the way in which commentators frequently construct subject positions in relation to New York along insider/outsider lines, even if the city itself frequently blurs and complicates such distinctions. Indeed, New York changes so constantly—so relentlessly—that even insiders frequently find themselves in outsider positions, as the novelist Henry James famously discovered in the early 1900s when returning home to New York after traveling in Europe only to find himself a disoriented stranger in a once-familiar city undergoing rapid architectural transformation.[3] For entirely different reasons related to ethnicity and socioeconomic inequality rather than architecture and urban design, many ethnic minority writers similarly portray New York as a place that can make its inhabitants experience profound and paradoxical feelings of unbelonging, such as in Ralph Ellison's parable of black nationalism in *Invisible Man* (1952) or Piri Thomas's gangster memoir of Spanish Harlem in *Down These Mean Streets* (1967).[4] Given the city's origins as a European colonial outpost, it can even be claimed that New York has always been framed to some degree by outsider views.

Within the existing body of outsider writing about New York one particular critical text is important to cite here, partly because of what it has contributed to our understanding of the city, but mostly because of its background influence on this book. Although not discussed at length in the following sections, *Delirious New York*, by Dutch architect and urbanist Rem Koolhaas, is an essential reference point. First published in 1978 at a time of crisis and introspection in American urbanism when the city itself was struggling to reverse its slide into urban decay, *Delirious New York* offers a playful, upbeat counterpoint to the gloomy vision of the postindustrial city as a broken space of garbage and crime, which, as Stanley Corkin has written about in relation to urban cinema, dominates popular representations of New York in the long 1970s.[5] Rather than being drained, fatigued, or nauseated by New York, Koolhaas derives energy, pleasure, and creativity from the city, including from its provocations, contradictions, and excesses.

Billed as a "retroactive manifesto" for Manhattan, *Delirious New York* revisits the city's modernist experiment in architecture and planning, which Koolhaas sees as inaugurating an entire "culture of congestion," and which he reads as an extension of the ludic transgressions that produce spectacular spaces of amusement and diversion like Coney Island.[6] For Koolhaas, New York is thus a delirious playground, the dreamlike product of a collective hallucination:

> Not only are large parts of its surface occupied by architectural mutations (Central Park, the Skyscraper), utopian fragments (Rockefeller, UN Building) and irrational phenomena (Radio City Music Hall), but in addition each block is covered with several layers of phantom architecture in the form of past occurrences, aborted projects and popular fantasies that provide alternative images to the New York that exists.
>
> Especially between 1890 and 1940 a new culture (the Machine Age?) selected Manhattan as a laboratory: a mythical island where the invention and testing of a metropolitan lifestyle and its attendant architecture could be pursued as a collective experience, where the real and the natural ceased to exist.[7]

Koolhaas understands New York in terms that recognize—even embrace—the messy, chaotic, blurry, overlapping, derealized conditions of being that prevail in his experience of the city, seeing its spaces and structures as something resembling an urban palimpsest—that is, as Andreas Huyssen defines the concept in *Present Pasts*, "lived spaces that shape collective imaginaries" and that can be "read historically, intertextually, constructively, and deconstructively" and are "at the same time woven into our understanding of urban spaces."[8] This book shares this palimpsestic sensibility toward New York City and, in particular, the openness of such an approach to the city's jumbling of memory, space, and meaning and the multiple, shifting valences of these layerings.

Also significant is Koolhaas's argument in *Delirious New York* that that the period between 1890 and 1940 corresponds to a transformative moment in the cultural history and architectural development of the city. As I will discuss at length, this period marks the distinctive and dynamic moment when "Old New York" was dramatically transformed into an iconic modern metropolis. Working loosely within the historical bracket of 1890 and 1940, I focus on precisely this transformative moment, and do so in order to examine the place and significance of the modern city in the urban imaginary.

Modern City, Urban Imaginary

It is therefore important to articulate what I mean by the terms "modern" and "urban imaginary." By "modern" I specifically refer to the city produced during the modernist moment in art and urbanism, and under the capitalist condition of urban modernity, which so profoundly shaped aesthetic sensibilities from the 1890s through the first half of the twentieth century. It is a period in New York's cultural history in which, as William Scott and Peter Rutkoff suggest in *New York Modern*, the city and the arts developed a particularly intimate bond:

> Frequently expressed abstractly and at times radically so, the subject of New York Modern remained urban life, in all its elusive complexity and variety.
>
> In the modern arts...New York artists reflected, analyzed, and helped to construct their city. The locales and details of New York, with its bustling economy, diverse peoples, and incipient egalitarianism, offered a vast array of subjects, which its artists depicted from a variety of perspectives—narrative and expressionist, factual and mythical, rhythmical and dissonant, formal and improvisational. Across styles and mediums, New York artists addressed modern urban life. They listened and responded to the cacophony of voices that echoed through the city's bars and cafés, tenements and town houses, and skyscrapers and docks. They deemed New York the quintessential modern city, a microcosm of the contemporary world.[9]

In developing the concept of "New York Modern" Scott and Rutkoff have in mind a longer historical span than the term might first appear to suggest, and are referring to what they see as a continuous—if eclectic and diverse—artistic culture stretching from the late 1880s to the 1970s, when the city's dominance of the international art world wanes. Although this span takes us into what art historians and cultural theorists generally understand as the era of postmodernism, the view that New York produced an artistic culture reflecting the city's distinct urban conditions in the late nineteenth century, and that this culture in turn helped to shape those conditions in the twentieth century, is shared by this study and informs my formulation of "modern New York."

This is not to disregard the much broader historical span, reaching back to the city's early-modern colonial roots as well as ahead toward its neoliberal globalization, that can also be encompassed by the idea of a modern city. Indeed, like various other studies of modern New York—ranging from Samuel Zipp's forward-thinking history of postwar urban renewal in *Mahattan Projects* to William Sharpe's defamiliarizing take on the city after dark in *New York Nocturne*, to Max Page's tracing of fantasies of New York's destruction in *The City's End*[10]—this book stretches the time and space associated with the modern city beyond their conventional boundaries. So although the central focus of this book is the historical period loosely corresponding to the relatively short-lived moment of modernism in art and urbanism, my discussion also seeks to place the modern city itself, as both a concept and an object of analysis, in the broader context of New York's urban development from seventeenth-century colonial settlement to twenty-first-century global city.

Such a project necessarily requires a degree of temporal oscillation. I wish to emphasize this point because, at regular intervals throughout the book, my discussion makes strategic jumps in time, either moving back to New York's premodern past or ahead to its global future. The idea is to make explicit certain key connections between modern New York and the expansive cultural-historical terrain both preceding and succeeding it. For instance, it is difficult to write about the cultural history of the New York skyline and its various transformations without addressing, to some degree, the impact of 9/11 on the city and its relationship with vertical architecture. Or, to cite another example, my discussion of New York's sidewalk culture is enriched not only by tracing its roots back to promenade practices inherited from the grand boulevards of European capitals like Paris but also by following that sidewalk culture forward into the twenty-first century, where it becomes nostalgically enmeshed in postindustrial urban design experiments like the High Line elevated park. The value to such temporal excursions is that they make visible the long history of modern New York and the resonant ways in which it continues to shape the city.

In using the term "urban imaginary" I refer to a concept adapted from spatial thinking in urban studies and philosophy to describe the interpretive frameworks through which we give meaning to our urban environments. Emerging from the work of urban-spatial thinkers like Henri Lefebvre and Kevin Lynch in the 1950s and 60s,[11] and later refined by critical spatial theorists like Edward Soja, the urban imaginary can be understood in Soja's terms as "the mental or cognitive mappings of urban reality and the interpretive grids through which we think about, experience, evaluate, and decide to act in the places, spaces, and communities in which we live."[12] In *Other Cities, Other Worlds*, Andreas Huyssen draws on such formulations to argue that the urban imaginary is not just a "cognitive and somatic image" but also "an embodied material fact and thus part of any city's reality,"[13] adding:

> All cities are palimpsests of real and diverse experiences and memories....An urban imaginary marks first and foremost the way city dwellers imagine their own city as the place of everyday life, the site of inspiring traditions and continuities as well as the scene of histories of destruction, crime, and conflicts of all kinds. Urban space is always and inevitably social space involving subjectivities and identities differentiated by class and race, gender and age, education and religion.

My thinking in this book is informed by Huyssen's assertion that the urban imaginary has an embedded material existence, as well as by Soja's closely related notion that this "city-centric consciousness"[14] has a strong basis in spatial practice and is rooted in the lived experience of the city.[15]

Soja and Huyssen develop their ideas about the urban imaginary in response to the late-capitalist phenomenon of the global city and the various forms of generic, neoliberal, networked, and amnesiac urbanism associated with urban postmodernity. Yet their insights into what constitutes the urban imaginary and the ways in which that imaginary registers, materializes, and intervenes in urban spaces and everyday practices apply much more widely in both geographic and historical terms; and, as I wish to demonstrate, those insights are as relevant for the modern city as they are for the global city. Cultural production, I argue, is one place where the modern city and the interpretive frameworks through which we give that condition meaning coalesce.

Skylines and Sidewalks

Seeking to understand the processes and conditions through which modern New York both shapes and is shaped by the urban imaginary, this book works at the intersections of literary, visual, and material culture. In particular, it considers how and why certain city spaces—such as the skyline, the sidewalk, the grid, the slum, and the subway—have come to emblematize key aspects of the modern urban condition. To this end, the book examines the diverse ways in which the metropolis has been represented across a wide range of cultural production that includes literature, film, visual art, architecture (treated both as a structure that is represented and as a form of representation), and urban planning and design.

The book is organized into two parts: "Skylines" and "Sidewalks." The two parts derive their thematic focus and spatial perspective on the city from the way New York itself is frequently—although not exclusively—constructed, experienced, and imagined along vertical and horizontal lines, a dynamic that was particularly conspicuous during the boom years of architectural and infrastructural modernization in the late nineteenth and early twentieth centuries and that registers profoundly in cultural responses to the rise of the modern city. As urban historian Thomas Bender observes in *The Unfinished City* in his discussion of the construction of the Brooklyn Bridge: "Just as the aesthetic movement of the Brooklyn Bridge is at once vertical and horizontal, so the dynamism and energy of New York City during the half century following the opening of the bridge was both horizontal and vertical. These two movements expressed the urbanity of the city; they represented two intertwined ways of grasping the metropolis."[16] Bender sees the Brooklyn Bridge as both embodying and activating New York's vertical and horizontal movements. This is achieved not only through the bridge's architecture but also through its public perception and user experience. The height and visibility of the bridge, particularly when it was completed in

1883 before skyscrapers blossomed in Manhattan, draw the eye upward and establish the structure as a towering, vertical presence in the city. Meanwhile the mobility enabled by the bridge, which allows traffic (including pedestrians) to flow between Brooklyn and Manhattan, aligns the structure with New York's horizontality. While remaining alert to the ways in which New York's two modes of movement and spatial orientation interrelate, as in the case of the Brooklyn Bridge, the book's two halves focus, respectively, on the vertical and horizontal dimensions of the city, thus enabling each of those dimensions to be explored in depth.

The first part, "Skylines," examines the emergence of the modern skyline and the ways in which it acquired symbolic and cultural significance between 1890 and 1940. The discussion takes the post-9/11 city as a point of departure to bring into focus the cultural and architectural significance of the New York skyline as a site (and source) of anxiety. It then circles back to the early high-rise architecture of pioneers like Cass Gilbert and Ernest Flagg to focus on the rise of the modern skyscraper, cityscapes, panoramas, verticality, and imaginations of the vertical city. The main argument here is that the modern skyline of New York figures across a diverse body of cultural production as a highly unstable space to read and interpret. In works ranging from the immigrant stories of Abraham Cahan and Willa Cather to the social realist paintings of the Ashcan School, the high-rise photography of Alfred Stieglitz and Alvin Langdon Coburn, and the vertiginous flickerings of urban actuality films and avant-garde cinema, the skyline hovers between the sublime and the uncanny, ultimately figuring as a site of instability and change that invites yet resists interpretation.

The second part, "Sidewalks," examines the city from its street-level intimations, considering the architectural history and cultural significance of iconic avenues like Broadway and the Bowery as well as spaces of public intersection like the slum and the subway. From the emergence of the Manhattan grid and the modernist phenomenon of grid art, to the nocturnal streetwalkers of Nella Larsen's Harlem and Stephen Crane's Lower East Side, and from the sidewalk recordings of early documentary and narrative cinema to the mean streets of Jacob Riis's slum photography and the isolated passengers of Mark Rothko's underground abstractions, Part II explores the diverse cultural manifestations and spatial reconfigurations of the modern sidewalk and its conditions of speed, movement, and dislocation. The principal line of argument here is that both the modern sidewalk itself (as an urban form) and the experiences it generates (as a public space) are anything but marginal or subsidiary. Rather, as demonstrated in relation to a rich variety of examples, the modern sidewalk emerges— and endures—as an active site of contestation and experiment.

Given that the subway features prominently in part II, it is worth explaining why this subterranean space is included in a discussion focused on streets and sidewalks, and not addressed in a separate part focused, for instance, on the cultural underground or New York's mass transit system. The reason is that I am interested in exploring the ways in which the subway—as a social and cultural space—can be understood as a reformulation of the street, including its everyday sidewalk practices. Such an approach to thinking about the interrelations of the subway and the street is facilitated by analyzing the two spaces together. As I argue, the underground space of the subway has been central to New York's urban imaginary precisely because of its intimate connections to, and simultaneous departures from, the street. Because of this centrality, my discussion of the subway is related less to the cultural history of transit or the significance of the underground as an alternative dimension of the city (although both of these topics are addressed) and more to the sidewalk as a formative feature of a modern urban sensibility that extends below ground.

What connects the book's two halves are not just the interconnections and overlaps between the urban spaces and practices under analysis. The book also coheres around a central argument. My contention is that the representation of New York between 1890 and 1940 is dominated by much more than a stress on the iconographic appearance of the city and the new forms of visuality and aesthetic encounter associated with urban modernity, which has been the standard account of modern art and culture in New York, and one that has been developed in broad historical studies such as Scott and Rutkoff's *New York Modern* or Bender's *The Unfinished City*, as well as in more conceptual or thematic studies, such as Douglas Tallack's *New York Sights*, Maria Balshaw's *Looking for Harlem*, or Angela Blake's *How New York Became American*.[17] Drawing on such works, but also seeking to extend their insights in new theoretical and empirical directions, I argue that New York's urban imaginary is also dominated by a stress on the way new forms of city space were being organized, experienced, and, above all, imagined.

In this respect, the book shares the orientation of philosophers like Michel Foucault and Henri Lefebvre, whose work stresses the spatiality of social life and urban form. In Foucault's work, for example, this registers in his concept of heterotopia and the attention it brings to the interplay of space, knowledge, and power in both producing and resisting hegemony.[18] In Lefebvre's work, it registers in his theory of the social production of space, in which social and spatial relations are understood as mutually constructed.[19] This book does not seek to rehearse Foucault and Lefebvre on space and society, but it does mobilize the idea, developed in their writing, that spatiality is a powerful, shaping force in the life and culture of cities. More to the point, my discussion finds that a similar spatial sensibility—what I would describe as a heightened alertness to the spatiality of urban life—informs creative practice across the fields of literature, urbanism, and the visual arts in the rapidly transforming environment of modern New York.

After City

In his conclusion to *Modernity and Metropolis: Writing, Film, and Urban Formations*, Peter Brooker confronts the end of the modern metropolis: "The city is at an end, announced Rem Koolhaas as we approached the millennium. . . . We seem to be pitched into a future 'no-place' beyond ourselves. . . . The type of city at issue is the 'modern' American or American inspired twentieth-century city."[20] According to such apocalyptic declarations, the subject of this book and one of the most elaborate and visible expressions of the American metropolis—New York City—would appear to be vanishing or dying in the form in which we have known it over the course of the twentieth century. Yet as Brooker immediately points out, such alarmist claims, while effective at grabbing attention, obscure the more complicated situation involved in twenty-first-century urban restructuring. It is a situation, he suggests, that involves "a double condition of simultaneous decline and emergence: in short, a reflexive transformation."[21]

This reflexive transformation is one that both encapsulates the modern metropolis and yet dissolves its forms of urbanism and spatial organization into a new set of patterns, connections, and orders:

"The story of this critical transition is less a movement towards one type of city or post-city than of uneven local and global development, of sharp disparities and loss of definition in both amoebic postmodern urban complexes and the layered 'modern' global cities which have themselves entered upon a dynamic transnational life."[22] In sketching this picture of uneven, distributed urban restructuring, Brooker is drawing on the work of thinkers like David Harvey, Rob Shields, and Edward Soja, who all associate twenty-first-century urban transformations with the emergence of new spatial orders reflecting globalization's post-Fordist, neoliberal orientation.[23]

In the decade following the publication of Brooker's book in 2002, the idea that we live in a new urban age that is somehow distinct from urban modernity has not only gathered momentum but also become something of a cliché. This has been reinforced by explicitly paradigm-forming publications like Ricky Burdett and Deyan Sudjic's *The Endless City* and its companion volume *Living in the Endless City*, which both present findings from the London School of Economics' "Urban Age" project and seek to highlight the newness of twenty-first-century urban conditions.[24] Yet as Brooker rightly stresses, and as I have argued elsewhere in relation to postcolonial urbanism and global cities,[25] the modern city—as space, form, experience, and idea—persists in the era of globalization, even if it is being transformed.

This is not to claim that the global city—including its terminological variations and conceptual spin-offs such as the postmetropolis, the generic city, or the overexposed city[26]—is just a linear, historical successor to the modern city. Nor am I attempting to downplay the scope and scale of urban restructuring that has been taking place under intensified globalization processes. Rather, my point is that the modern city does not disappear or perish in the era of globalization, but is subsumed and reconfigured. As Soja has acknowledged in relation to the phenomenon of regional urbanization, which many recognize as the major form that urbanization has taken in the early twenty-first century,[27] "what's happening now is an extended form of what's been happening to the modern metropolis."[28]

This is one of the reasons why, at a time of profound urban change worldwide, this book refocuses attention on an earlier moment in the cultural life of the metropolis, a moment that sets into motion the rise of the global city and the epochal shift toward "planetary urbanization" that has grown out of the capitalist industrialization process of the last two centuries.[29] Within modern New York, I argue, literature, urbanism, and the visual arts make vital contributions to the formation of an urban imaginary that, in dispersed and reconfigured forms, feeds directly into twenty-first-century perceptions and interpretations of the city and the critical culture through which we seek to understand the mutability of urban life.

PART I

Skylines

Manhattan. In the middle of the night sometimes, above the sky-scrapers, across hundreds of high walls, the cry of a tugboat would meet my insomnia, reminding me that this desert of iron and cement was also an island.

—Albert Camus, "The Rains of New York"[1]

And [New York] is the most beautiful city in the world? It is not far from it. No urban nights are like the nights there. I have looked down across the city from high windows. It is then that the great buildings lose reality and take on their magical powers. They are immaterial; that is to say one sees but the lighted windows. Squares after squares of flame, set and cut into the ether. Here is our poetry, for we have pulled down the stars to our will.

—Ezra Pound, *Patria Mia*[2]

New York Vertical

This part of the book addresses the modern skyline of New York. To bring the subject into focus, I start by commenting briefly on Horst Hamann's 2001 book of photography from which I have borrowed the phrase "New York vertical."[3] Reminiscent in many ways of Berenice Abbott's urban photography of the 1930s—and in particular of her WPA project *Changing New York*[4]—Hamann's black and white city images stress not only the vertical components of New York's modern architecture but also the interconnected geometry of those forms (figure 1). The result is a collection of photographs that constructs and defines the city almost exclusively in terms of its verticality. Such a vision of New York is of course nothing new; and this is precisely what interests me about Hamann's photography. His work does more than reinforce a century-old image of New York as a city of extreme verticals. It also underlines in creative and often surprising ways the extent to which those verticals continue even today to dominate the cultural imagination of urban space. In this sense, Hamann's images highlight an important feature of the New York skyline. Its hypermediated silhouette contains what has become the most graphic and emblematic expression of the vertical city.

FIGURE 1. *Horst Hamann*, Steel Triangle, Rockefeller Center, *1998. (Courtesy Horst Hamann)*

Pursuing this idea, I want to consider the ways in which the modern skyline has been represented and imagined at several key moments in its vertical history. New York's cityscape has, of course, been the subject of a great deal of scholarly interest, particularly in the aftermath of the terrorist attacks of September 11, 2001. For instance, in his historical study of New York's metropolitanism, *The Unfinished City*, Thomas Bender devotes considerable attention to the symbiotic relationship between skyscraper and skyline, reasserting the long-standing argument that Manhattan's modern cityscape registers the near-total domination of the architecture of corporate capitalism over public space and culture.[5] Similar scrutiny of the cityscape has also preoccupied a number of other, more mainstream studies of New York, including James Sander's lavishly illustrated *Celluloid Skyline: New York and the Movies* and Jan Seidler Ramirez's wide-ranging *Painting the Town: Cityscapes of New York*.[6] More recently, Douglas Tallack's *New York Sights: Visualizing Old and New New York* shows the full extent to which visual culture—ranging from high art to ephemera—turned to the panoptic perspective of the cityscape view to register the seismic urban changes shaking Manhattan during the transitional years of the early 1900s.[7]

One feature shared by these books is an emphasis on the visual dimensions of New York's modernity. Such an emphasis is arguably deserved, not least because of the continuing interpretive challenges posed by the modern city's visual heterogeneity. While still engaging with issues of visuality, my aim is to broaden the scope of discussion beyond the visual to stress in addition the importance of the textual and the material to the critique of cityscape. Specifically, my argument in part I is that the modern skyline of New York figures across a full range of cultural production as a highly unstable space to read and interpret, and that this site of instability and change is further distinguished by visions of the city that remain ambivalently caught between the sublime and the uncanny.

To develop this line of thought, my discussion opens by revisiting a familiar view of the vertical city by Michel de Certeau in *The Practice of Everyday Life*, before considering a somewhat controversial commentary on the New York skyline by Jean Baudrillard in his "Requiem for the Twin Towers." The related argument here is that, far from being new or unique, the city musings of Baudrillard and de Certeau belong to a long line of cultural critique extending back to the shoreline meditations of writers like Walt Whitman, Henry James, and Willa Cather, the urban iconography of artists like John Sloan, Alfred Stieglitz, and Paul Strand, the utopian architectural visions of urbanists like Hugh Ferriss and Le Corbusier, and the grainy high-rise vistas of early cinema classics like *Metropolis* (1927) and *King Kong* (1933).

The City from Above

In *The Practice of Everyday Life* Michel de Certeau begins his chapter on "Walking in the City" by reflecting on the experience of visiting the observation deck at the World Trade Center in the late 1970s. For de Certeau, the vertical journey to the top of a soaring skyscraper is one of liberation from the chaos and confinement of the city street:

> To be lifted to the summit of the World Trade Center is to be lifted out of the city's grasp. One's body is no longer clasped by the streets that turn and return it according to an anonymous law; nor is it possessed...by the rumble of so many differences and by the nervousness of New York traffic. When one goes up there, he leaves behind the mass that carries off and mixes up in itself any identity of authors and spectators.[8]

Significantly, this euphoria of release from the city street is linked in de Certeau's thinking to the somewhat erotic pleasure of voyeurism—the pleasure, that is, of "seeing the whole."[9] For what the observation deck provides through its sheer elevation is not only distance from the city but also a new visual perspective from which the urban expanse below appears as a whole, graspable image, a viewpoint impossible to achieve at the muddled and meandering level of the street.

Seen from above, the city is thus laid bare—revealed and exposed—to the prying curiosity of the urban gaze. The visitor is "transfigured into a voyeur."[10] And it is precisely in the guise of the voyeur that de Certeau, skimming and scanning the undulating surfaces of the city, describes his aerial view of Manhattan:

> Seeing Manhattan from the 110th floor of the World Trade Center. Beneath the haze stirred up by the winds, the urban island, a sea in the middle of the sea, lifts up the skyscrapers over Wall Street,

sinks down at Greenwich, then rises again to the crests of Midtown, quietly passing over Central Park and finally undulates off into the distance of Harlem. A wave of verticals. Its agitation is momentarily arrested by vision. The gigantic mass is immobilized before the eyes. It is transformed into a texturology in which extremes coincide—extremes of ambition and degradation, brutal oppositions of races and styles, contrasts between yesterday's buildings, already transformed into trash cans, and today's urban irruptions that block out its space.... A city composed of paroxysmal places in monumental reliefs. The spectator can read in it a universe that is constantly exploding.... On this stage of concrete, steel and glass, cut out between two oceans (the Atlantic and the American) by a frigid body of water, the tallest letters in the world compose a gigantic rhetoric of excess in both expenditure and production.[11]

De Certeau's urban panorama is marked by several distinctive features. Not least among these is the perception of the rigid geometry of New York's modern architecture in terms of motion and fluidity. Manhattan's two principal clusters of skyscrapers—the vertical constellations of the downtown and midtown business districts—appear as "waves of verticals" surging up between the troughs of Greenwich Village, Central Park, and Harlem. Another distinctive feature of this aerial view is that the sense of motion is simultaneously countered by an effect of immobilization. New York's "gigantic mass" is "momentarily arrested by vision," stressing the city's contrasts and extremes. Equally striking are the images of violent energy. Everywhere, the city is convulsed by spasms, agitations, paroxysms, eruptions, and explosions. But perhaps the most distinctive feature of de Certeau's urban panorama is the transformation of the skyline into a text to be read. Most notably, the Twin Towers of the World Trade Center become "the tallest letters in the world," spelling out a message of capitalist excess that is engraved throughout and across the skyline.

Today, it is no longer possible to see and experience New York from exactly the same perspective as Michel de Certeau in *The Practice of Everyday Life*. The terrorist attacks of September 11, 2001, that destroyed the Twin Towers of the World Trade Center also destroyed this unique vantage point. And while the loss of this vantage point is meaningless when compared to the very real human tragedies of

9/11, it has nonetheless had a profound impact on the way people look at and relate to the city.

One small example of this impact occurred in Brooklyn Heights just across the river from Manhattan. On the waterfront promenade facing out toward the prow of Lower Manhattan, local residents in the immediate wake of 9/11 attached photographs of the skyline to the iron railings in an attempt to guide viewers in their observation of the city. The photographs all featured silhouettes of Manhattan that still included the distinctive profile of the Twin Towers, showing the location and appearance of the absent skyscrapers. The assumption—and indeed the reality—was that many visitors and residents came to the promenade precisely in order to see the alteration to the skyline. In a way, they came to experience an absence, to gaze upon an urban view that no longer existed. And in this abstract sense the Twin Towers of the World Trade Center have not entirely disappeared from the New York skyline. Rather, haunting the contemporary imagination, the two skyscrapers continue even now to exert a spectral presence over the city.

Requiem for the Twin Towers

The very fact that people were drawn to vantage points such as the Brooklyn Heights promenade in the wake of the terrorist attacks because of what could no longer be seen in the urban panorama comments forcefully on the symbolic significance of both the Twin Towers themselves and the skyline to which they belonged. In his short, contemplative essay, "Requiem for the Twin Towers," cultural theorist Jean Baudrillard discusses exactly this subject while attempting to disentangle the Twin Towers in historical and architectural terms from the rest of New York's skyscrapers. Interspersed between reckless remarks about how the collapse of the towers resembled a form of suicide and how their aesthetic of "twin-ness" invited a violent return to "a-symmetry" and "singularity,"[12] Baudrillard does offer some critical insight:

> All Manhattan's tall buildings had been content to confront each other in a competitive verticality, and the product of this was an architectural panorama reflecting the capitalist system itself—a

pyramidal jungle, whose famous image stretched out before you as you arrived from the sea. That image changed after 1973, with the building of the World Trade Center.... Perfect parallelipeds, standing over 1,300 feet tall, on a square base. Perfectly balanced, blind communicating vessels.... The fact that there were two of them signifies the end of any original reference. If there had been only one, monopoly would not have been perfectly embodied. Only the doubling of the sign truly puts an end to what it designates.... However tall they may have been, the two towers signified, none the less, a halt to verticality. They were not the same breed as the other buildings. They culminated in the exact reflection of each other.[13]

Like de Certeau some twenty years before him, Baudrillard similarly sees the contours of New York's modern architecture in terms of energy and chaos. In addition, he also stresses the legibility of the city when seen from a distance, reading into its verticality an expression of the capitalist spirit of competition. The difference is that Baudrillard locates a schism in the skyline—one that de Certeau, standing on top of the source of that rupture, seems to overlook. Baudrillard's thinking is that, in architectural terms at least, the Twin Towers mark a departure from the city's competitive verticality precisely because of their structural solipsism, what I would call their uncanny doubleness. As perfect mirror images of each other, the two towers constitute their own self-referential system, no longer competing for height and visibility with the other buildings around them but instead endlessly reflecting their own identical images back at each other. De Certeau calls the Twin Towers "the tallest letters in the world" and Baudrillard, picking up on the same idea, refers to them as "signs."

For Baudrillard, however, those signs designate a slightly different moment in the cultural history of capitalism than New York's other, older skyscrapers, such as the Woolworth, Empire State, and Chrysler Buildings. In their semiotic and architectural "reduplication,"[14] the Twin Towers represent powerful and highly visible symbols of the late-capitalist age of globalization. As the architectural historian Mark Wigley similarly suggests in *After the World Trade Center*, "the key symbolic role of the World Trade Center...was to represent the global marketplace. In a strange way, supersolid, supervisible, super-located buildings stood as a figure for the dematerialized, invisible, placeless market."[15] Baudrillard concludes that this symbolism is the

reason the Twin Towers were destroyed: "the violence of globalization also involves architecture, and hence the violent protest against
it also involves the destruction of that architecture."[16]

In the case of the World Trade Center, however, the link between
architecture and violence is far more complicated than Baudrillard's
comments would suggest. Given the global impact of the events of
9/11, it is important to remember and acknowledge that the attacks
on the Twin Towers were brought about by a highly complex set of
political, historical, and cultural factors—factors that included but
also exceeded the symbolic dimensions of the Twin Towers. For instance, as Stephen Graham argues in *Cities, War, and Terrorism*, the
WTC attacks were also connected to New York's cultural and ethnic
heterogeneity:

> The 9/11 attacks can be seen as part of a fundamentalist, transna-
> tional war, or Jihad, by radical Islamic movements against pluralistic
> and heterogeneous mixing in (capitalist) cities. Thus it is notable
> that cities that have long sustained complex heterogeneities, reli-
> gious pluralism, and multiple diasporas—New York and Istanbul,
> for example—have been prime targets for catastrophic terror at-
> tacks. Indeed, in their own horrible way, the grim lists of casualties
> that bright New York day in September 2001 revealed the multiple
> diasporas and cosmopolitanisms that now constitute the often
> hidden social fabric of "global" cities like New York.[17]

While the argument that New York's cultural and ethnic heterogeneity rendered the city a terrorist target may be oversimplifying the
impetus behind the attacks, Graham does highlight an important dimension of New York's globalism that is too often overlooked. Baudrillard is therefore partially right in saying that the Twin Towers
were party to their own destruction, but not in the way—or for the
reasons—he proposes.

Whether or not we agree with Baudrillard's reading of the Twin
Towers, and in particular with his idea that the skyscrapers were
somehow separate and distinct from all others in New York, his reflections do touch on one of the city's most striking and enduring
features. Manhattan has one of the most visually compelling and
symbolically charged skylines in the world today.

In their philosophical musings on Manhattan, Baudrillard and de
Certeau respond in broadly similar ways to the sprawl and spectacle
of the urban panorama by presenting the skyline as a text to be read.

In the process, I would argue, they both see the skyline as sublime—in the Burkean sense of an aesthetic marvel that awes and overwhelms. I would also argue that they both depict the skyline as uncanny—in the Freudian sense of an unnerving encounter with the familiar rendered newly strange and alien. And finally, I would suggest that, through various metaphors of motion, they both identify the skyline as a site of instability and change that invites yet resists interpretation—creating the sort of tension between movement and stasis rendered so visible in Hiroshi Sugimoto's artfully blurred photograph of the World Trade Center (figure 2).

Far from being exclusive to the present global metropolitan age, however, such perspectives on New York have in fact dominated the cultural representation of the city's skyline from its first great moment of verticality onward. Specifically, as I discuss next, the cultural history of the skyline in the late nineteenth and early twentieth centuries is similarly marked not only by expressions of ambivalence but also by an emerging consciousness of the discursive dimensions of urban space. The results are graphic and enduring visions of the city as a sprawling urban text that mesmerizes and inspires yet also agitates and disturbs. In short, my argument is that, since the rise of the modern skyscraper, Manhattan has always been caught somewhere between the sublime and the uncanny.

Building the Skyline: A Brief Architectural History

Urban skylines are not static or immutable. Rather, their individual shapes and appearances continuously shift with every change to the built environments that produce them. In this sense skylines are animate reflections—or manifestations—of the material lives of cities. Sometimes, as the collapse of the Twin Towers reminded us, radical alterations to the skyline can occur violently, unexpectedly, and almost instantaneously. Other times, as demonstrated by the uniformly modern architectural development of *La Défense* business park on the edge of central Paris, those changes can occur deliberately, gradually, and at the peripheries of vision. In the case of early twenty-first-century New York, the skyline has perhaps been most notably punctuated and controversially renewed by the construction of the Freedom Tower, later renamed One World Trade Center, on

FIGURE 2. *Hiroshi Sugimoto,* World Trade Center, *1997. (Courtesy Hirshhorn Museum and Sculpture Garden, Smithsonian Institution, Joseph H. Hirshhorn Purchase Fund, 2004. Photo by Lee Stalsworth)*

the Ground Zero site—the very existence of which recalls the inherent mutability of the city.

Significantly, the "convulsions of urbanization"[18] that culminated in New York's vertical architecture first took hold of the city in the second half of the nineteenth century, before reaching their highest intensity between 1890 and 1940. During this period of rapid urban growth and development, encompassing the consolidation of the five boroughs in 1898, New York's physical appearance and character were radically transformed by the widespread construction of sky-scrapers. As late as 1883, the neo-Gothic spire of Trinity Church on Broadway and Wall Street in Lower Manhattan remained the tallest completed structure in the city (figure 3). The spire is 284 feet tall.

By 1900, however, more than ten new buildings exceeded this height, including the prominent Park Row and St. Paul office build-ings, which were both completed in 1899 at heights of 391 and 315 feet respectively.[19] Within two more years, as many as fifty additional buildings towered above the spire of Trinity Church. And by the time the city's first great skyscraper boom tapered off in the 1930s—capped by the conspicuous speculative venture of the Empire State Building in 1931—New York had become home to literally thousands

FIGURE 3. *Prevertical New York: aerial view of Lower Manhattan, with the spire of Trinity Church visible along the "spine" of Broadway, c. 1876. (Courtesy Picture Collection, the New York Public Library, Astor, Lenox and Tilden Foundations)*

of skyscrapers.[20] It is this scramble for the sky, involving the demolition, construction, and reconstruction of countless numbers of buildings, that produced the first distinctive silhouettes of New York's modern skyline.

For many throughout the world, as David Ward and Olivier Zunz note in *The Landscape of Modernity*, New York's "dense lines of skyscrapers" quickly came to represent "the most graphic statement of modernity,"[21] a sort of collective architectural expression of what Robert Hughes, in reference to modern art, has called "the shock of the new,"[22] and what David Nye, writing about the social construction of technology, has called the "American technological sublime."[23] Yet New York was not the world's first vertical city. Rather, the modern components of New York's emerging skyline were derived and developed from the pioneering vertical architecture of another city altogether: the midwestern American boomtown of Chicago.

As Marco d'Eramo reminds us in *The Pig and the Skyscraper*, Chicago is where the skyscraper was invented. So in this sense, it is also the original vertical city:

> Chicago is the city that invented the skyscraper—and it shows. The forms of these massive buildings leap catlike towards the clouds, curving in the azure dome of the sky, bold silhouettes looming bizarrely overhead, possessed of an incomparable lightness, a levity made possible by the concrete infusion of billions of dollars.... Once more you find yourself meditating.... It was only a century ago, during the 1880s, that the Chicago School laid the foundations of modern architecture. Among the school's greatest exponents were Dankmar Adler, Daniel H. Burnham and John W. Root, William Le Baron Jenney and Louis Sullivan, Frank Lloyd Wright, William Holabird and Henry Hobson Richardson. Influenced by the ironwork construction of European railway stations, they conceived of the skyscraper as a structure borne not by supporting walls but by an internal ironwork frame.[24]

D'Eramo's lively description of Chicago in terms of levity and feline agility recalls Michel de Certeau's aerial view of Manhattan in *The Practice of Everyday Life*. Certainly, d'Eramo sees the city through metaphors of motion as an exhilarating spectacle of the sublime and the uncanny. And although he may not read a "texturology" into the skyline in quite the same manner as de Certeau, he does similarly experience the meditative effects of city gazing.

The more important point to note here, however, is that a key architectural innovation enabling the upward rush of the modern city was, as d'Eramo stresses, the revolutionary introduction of the ironwork frame in Chicago during the 1880s. Up to this point, structural dependence on load-bearing external walls had severely limited building height. By shifting the weight of buildings onto metal skeleton frames manufactured from substantially stronger and lighter material than masonry walls, the Chicago School effectively unlocked the skyscraper's potential to shoot ever higher into the sky. The pressure to build upward that had been mounting for several decades in rapidly growing cities like Chicago, Minneapolis, and New York at last found an outlet for release. And although the first generation of these new steel giants retained quite a lot of the squat, heavy look of earlier brick-and-mortar attempts at the high-rise, they paved the way for generations of successively taller skyscrapers, including today's glass-faced corporate monoliths.

In Chicago this unlocking of the skyscraper's vertical potential began with such notable constructions as the Home Insurance Building, widely considered by architectural historians as the prototype of the skyscraper.[25] Completed in 1885 by the architect William Le Baron Jenney, the ten-story Home Insurance Building was the first tall building in Chicago to use skeleton frame construction (figure 4). Others soon followed, and by the mid-1890s the city's scramble for the sky had produced a wide array of new high-rises, including the Monadnock Building (1893), Fisher Building (1895), Reliance Building (1895), and, tallest of all at 302 feet, Burnham and Root's record-breaking twenty-two story Masonic Temple (1892).

In New York the rush to build upward was similarly enabled by the arrival of skeleton construction in the early 1880s, though the question of whether the technique was imported from Chicago or reinvented in New York remained hotly debated well into the twentieth century. In 1899, for example, this architectural rivalry was registered quite literally on the exterior of New York's Tower Building, which had been completed a full decade earlier in 1889. An engraved plaque was fixed to the building featuring the following bold and controversial statement:

> This tablet placed in 1899 by the Society of Architectural Iron Manufacturers of New York, commemorates the erection during 1888–89, in this, the Tower Building, of the earliest example of the

FIGURE 4. *Home Insurance Building, Chicago. (Courtesy Frances Loeb Library, Graduate School of Design, Harvard Library)*

skeleton construction, in which the entire weight of the walls and floors is borne and transmitted to the foundation by a framework of metallic posts and beams. Originated and designed by Bradford Lee Gilbert, architect, Jackson Architectural Iron Works, contractors for the steel and iron work.[26]

Such proprietorial claims over the skeleton frame were rife in New York throughout the 1880s and 1890s, and understandably so given the potential profits at stake in the city's vertical building boom. As Sarah Landau and Carl Condit suggest in *Rise of the New York Skyscraper*, these discrepancies of creative ownership derived from varying technical definitions of what exactly constituted skeleton construction as well as from issues of patenting and intellectual property. The fairest conclusion to be drawn is that, following innovations such as Jenney's Home Insurance Building, "architects, engineers, and builders in New York, Chicago, and Minneapolis were simultaneously and independently developing the iron skeleton system."[27]

In 1893 Chicago's skyscraper fever was severely cooled by the introduction of a city ordinance limiting building height to 130 feet. Another cooling factor was the major architectural, cultural, and economic distraction of the 1893 World's Columbian Exposition, which temporarily diverted both attention and resources away from the continuing development of Chicago's Loop district. In New York, however, where no such height restrictions existed, skeleton construction continued to thrive unabated throughout the 1890s. The technique's potential to produce increasingly taller buildings offered the most practical solution to the ever-growing pressure being placed on the city's limited office space. The result was the creation of the largest, tallest, and densest conglomeration of tall buildings in the world, as Landau and Condit outline:

> The proliferation of skyscrapers in the 1890s completely changed the appearance of Manhattan's central business district, still largely confined to a small triangle below Wall Street. By the middle of the decade no other city even remotely approached New York in its concentration of sheer commercial splendor.... By 1890, just as the descriptive appellation "sky-scraper" was coming into common parlance, the New York high-rise commercial building was rapidly approaching maturity. The final technical components were being developed: the steel frame fireproof covering of all framing members, wind bracing, the curtain wall, electrically operated elevators, central heating, incandescent electric lighting throughout the building, forced-draft ventilation in all enclosures, and automatic controls. And the New York skyscraper's distinctive towerlike form... was evolving.[28]

Together, these advances in architecture, engineering, design, and technology not only made it possible to build ever higher into the sky, but also helped to transform the office building from an essentially inert form into an efficient, high-tech machine geared toward the dynamic needs—both symbolic and functional—of modern commerce and corporate capitalism. Among the more notable examples of this rapidly evolving urban machine were the vertical upsurges of

the World (1890; figure 5), Decker (1893), Manhattan Life (1894), and
American Tract Society (1895) Buildings as well as the conspicuous
towers of the American Surety (1896), Gillender (1897), Commercial
Cable (1897), St. Paul (1898), and Park Row (1899) Buildings.

So although Chicago invented the skyscraper, New York is where
the form matured. By the first decade of the twentieth century, New
York architects had not only advanced and refined skyscraper design
far beyond the boxlike productions of early skeleton high-rises but
had also established a distinct urban aesthetic in the soaring form of
the office tower. That form was to dominate commercial real estate

FIGURE 5. *City Hall and World Building, 1905. (Courtesy Library of Congress,
Prints and Photographs Division)*

development in Manhattan to 1916, when the city's new setback law prompted the next significant phase in the evolution of the New York skyscraper.

The most prominent of these early twentieth-century towers were the Singer, Metropolitan Life, and Woolworth Buildings—each the tallest in the world on completion, at heights of 612, 700, and 792 feet respectively. Completed in 1908 (and demolished in 1968), the earliest of these three was Ernest Flagg's Singer Tower, which stood out prominently on the skyline not only because of its unprecedented height but also because of its slender tower and unusual lantern top. In 1909, however, the Singer Building was topped by LeBrun and Sons' newly completed Metropolitan Life Building, which featured a campanile-style tower inspired by the Bell Tower of Venice's Piazza San Marco. But by far the most domineering presence on the prewar skyline was the massive neo-Gothic tower of the Woolworth Building, completed in 1913 by architect Cass Gilbert and financed in cash by five-and-dime tycoon Frank W. Woolworth. Famously described as a cathedral of commerce at its dedication ceremony, the Woolworth Building fused a modern vertical aesthetic with ornamental elements lifted from medieval religious architecture and design. This unusual combination of the medieval and the modern proved so visually stunning that the building quickly became a defining city landmark alongside such established New York icons as the Brooklyn Bridge (figure 6).

Together, the elevated spires of the Singer, Metropolitan Life, and Woolworth Buildings marked the vertical culmination of American Beaux Arts architecture—the eclectic neoclassical style prevalent in major American cities throughout the early 1900s and so named for its French intellectual influence. In addition, as Carol Willis notes in *Form Follows Finance*, these branded skyscrapers also signaled in brash and public ways "the growing presence and power of corporations in the modern city."[29] But perhaps the most enduring legacy of these three skyscrapers is that they inextricably and permanently tied the city's identity to its modern skyline. Chicago may have been the original vertical city, but New York had now become its most exuberant embodiment.

By the 1910s, however, New York's frantic race for the sky was creating some serious problems at ground level. One side effect of building upward was the phenomenon of the canyon street : the straight vertical walls of tall buildings created a claustr

FIGURE 6. *Brooklyn Bridge and Woolworth Building, 1921. (Courtesy Picture Collection, the New York Public Library, Astor, Lenox and Tilden Foundations)*

canyon-like effect blocking out sunlight and sky. In the financial district of Manhattan, where laissez-faire skyscraper development was at its most pronounced, open space was rapidly disappearing at street level. The situation had been worsening throughout the early twentieth century as the number and density of tall buildings continued to increase.

As a countermeasure, the city passed zoning legislation in 1916 that strictly regulated the height and shape of tall buildings. The implications for the future of skyscraper design were profound, as Carol Willis details:

> The passage in 1916 of New York's first zoning legislation changed the rules of the game for skyscraper design. In addition to regulating uses by districts (commercial, residential, and unrestricted), the law limited the height and bulk of tall buildings with a formula called the *zoning envelope*. Designed to protect some measure of light and air for Manhattan's canyons, it required that after a maximum vertical height above the side-walk (usually 100 or 125 feet) a building must be stepped back as it rose in accordance with a fixed angle drawn from the center of the street. A tower of unlimited height was permitted over one-quarter of the site.[30]

Importantly, the zoning envelope did not stop or even slow down the city's upward climb; it just controlled certain aspects of it. The impact on skyscraper design was immediate and long-lasting, leading to the "setback" style of skyscraper that came not only to dominate but also to distinguish New York's vertical architecture until the 1950s (figure 7).

The high point of the setback style spanned the Roaring Twenties and the early years of the Great Depression. During this chaotic period of reckless speculation and runaway development, Manhattan experienced yet another sudden surge of skyscraper construction. New additions to the skyline included the towerless ziggurats of the Paramount Building (1927) and 120 Wall Street (1930); the slender slabs of the Chanin (1929), Lincoln (1930), Daily News (1930), and RCA (1932) Buildings; and the needlepoints of the Bank of Manhattan (1930), General Electric (1931), and Cities Service (1932) Buildings. Sharing the same sculptural setback look, these skyscrapers registered in visible and indelible ways the influence of the zoning envelope formula on architectural design, generating an aesthetic and geometric homogeneity that continues even today to interconnect New York's extended cityscape.

Among these art-deco giants of the late 1920s and early 1930s, two buildings stood out above the rest. The first was the Chrysler Building, designed by William Van Alen and completed in 1930. In addition to its phenomenal height (1,048 feet), the midtown skyscraper was distinguished by its enormous stainless steel spire, modernist gargoyles, and elaborately decorated setbacks. At a height of 1,454 feet, the other rival presence on the skyline was the even taller Empire

FIGURE 7. *RCA Building at the Rockefeller Center, 1933. (Courtesy Library of Congress, Prints and Photographs Division)*

State Building, designed by Shreve, Lamb and Harmon Associates and completed in 1931 (figure 8). Breaking records not only for height but also for speed of construction, the Empire State Building represented a remarkable and improbable achievement of high-rise architecture, extreme engineering, and creative financing.[31] "Standing in lonely dignity in the midriff of Manhattan, a sentinel by land, a reassuring landmark by air," as George E. Kidder Smith so emotively describes it, "the quadri-faced pharos of the city"[32] was crowned by a spectacular glass-and-metal mooring mast immortalized in the 1933 film *King Kong*.

FIGURE 8. *Empire State Building at night, 1937. (Courtesy Library of Congress, Prints and Photographs Division)*

With the construction of the Chrysler and Empire State Buildings in the early 1930s, New York's first great moment of verticality, begun some fifty years earlier, reached its zenith. As the architectural critic Lewis Mumford noted in a 1933 "Sky Line" article for *The New Yorker*:

> The skyscraper period is fast coming to an end, and the skyscraper as we knew it during the past fifty years, has now pretty well reached the peak of its development. By a turn of the wheel, we are back at the point where we started; no sensible person would say that our present buildings are fundamentally better than the old Monadnock Building in Chicago, but as a result of the architects' building classic colossi and Gothic pinnacles and Byzantine battlements till their scrapbooks were exhausted, they are now back once more to the essential form, cleaned and clarified.[33]

For Mumford, who never was an advocate of the skyscraper solution to modern urbanism, the cyclical decline of New York's "orgy of tall building"[34] in the grip of the Great Depression comes as something of a relief. "Psychologically speaking," he writes in response to the newly completed Empire State Building, "the aesthetics of skyscrapers have long passed the point of diminishing returns; there is nothing to say about a new skyscraper except that it is another skyscraper tower."[35]

In an earlier "Sky Line" article from 1932 Mumford even goes as far as to welcome the city's downturn in skyscraper construction as an opportunity for New York architects to engage in some much-needed critical reflection:

> One of the fortunate results of the depression is that New York architects will at least have a little time to think over what they have been doing; they may even have a chance to visit and inspect, with whatever mingled feelings of triumph and nausea the occasion may demand, the buildings that were designed in their offices during the past ten years. Not for nothing did the story go the rounds a few years ago about Mr. X, the senior partner of one of the most famous architectural firms, who on a ferryboat one day, coming back to the city with a party of clients, roundly denounced the betrayal of the sacred cause of architecture in one particularly bad new skyscraper on the horizon—only to discover that the building had been done by his own office a year or so before.[36]

As the ironic vignette of Mr. X suggests, part of Mumford's objection to the vertical city lies in the blind speed of its rise, enabling what he describes elsewhere as an unthinking or "unconscious" architecture.[37] Another part of his objection lies in the aesthetic negligence he discerns in the ubiquitous form of the modern skyscraper tower. Mumford may be overstating the case here, but his broader architectural critique is significant in that it calls attention to how the spiky silhouette of the early twentieth-century skyline represents the culmination of the city's most extreme and transformative phase of architectural production.

During this fifty-year period, as Thomas Bender and William Taylor argue, New York changes from an urban space governed by "civic horizontalism" to one overtaken and defined by "corporate verticality."[38] This dramatic shift not only from the horizontal to the vertical but also from the civic to the corporate generated the first bold shapes of today's capitalist cityscape, creating what Roland Barthes describes in an essay on Bernard Buffet's New York paintings as "a city of geometric heights, a petrified desert of grids and lattices, an inferno of greenish abstraction under a flat sky, a real Metropolis from which man is absent by his very accumulation" (figure 9).[39]

FIGURE 9. *City of geometric heights: Carl Van Vechten,* Lower New York, *1938. (Courtesy Library of Congress, Prints and Photographs Division)*

More importantly, Mumford's architectural critique also illustrates the way New York's verticals tend to produce extreme and often paradoxical responses. Like Barthes's dehumanized urban vista, Mumford's Manhattan is a space of beauty and exhilaration yet also horror and discomfort. In his own words, the city's vertical architecture is an occasion for both "triumph" and "nausea." As such strong and mixed reactions suggest, the emergence of the modern skyline had a profound and lasting impact on the urban imaginary.

In the case of Mumford, whose comments come at the height of New York's first major phase of vertical development, the impact on the urban imaginary leads to a vision of the skyline strangely marked by expressions of both rapture and repulsion. But Mumford is not alone in this ambivalence. For as we see next, the invention of the modern skyline has left similarly deep and troubled imprints across a wide range of cultural production, including literature, visual art, film, and urban architecture and design. The ways in which a diverse body of writers, artists, filmmakers, architects, and designers confronted, interpreted, and ultimately attempted to give meaning to the rise of vertical New York is the subject of the remainder of this part.

Text and the City

The ever-changing skyline of New York has preoccupied writers ever since the city's low-rise beginnings as a Dutch trading post in the early seventeenth century. Even before that, the first European explorer to venture into New York Bay was moved to describe the scene in writing. In 1524 the Florentine navigator Giovanni da Verrazano chanced upon a "beautiful harbour" containing an "island of triangular form" during an expedition along the North American coast.[40] His account of the voyage in a letter to the king of France contains the earliest recorded description of the geographic location that eventually becomes home to the five-borough sprawl of New York City:

> After proceeding one hundred leagues, we found a very pleasant situation among some steep hills, through which a very large river, deep at its mouth, forced its way to the sea.... But as we were riding at anchor in a good berth, we would not venture up in our vessel, without a knowledge of the mouth; therefore we took the boat,

and entering the river, we found the country on its banks well peo-
pled, the inhabitants not differing much from the others, being
dressed out with the feathers of birds of various colours.... All
of a sudden, as is wont to happen to navigators, a violent contrary
wind blew in from the sea, and forced us to return to our ship,
greatly regretting to leave this region which seemed so commo-
dious and delightful, and which we supposed must also contain
great riches.[41]

Despite the conspicuous absence of the city, this early skyline still
has a powerful effect on the imagination of the observer. In this respect Verrazano's account shows how the draw of the New York skyline not only predates the city itself but also grows out of a much
earlier encounter with the site's natural landscape. Indeed, it is this
landscape—and in particular the unusual topography and wealth of
natural resources noted by Verrazano—that underlies and enables
the European colonization of the region and, through this process, the
eventual growth of the city. It is also interesting to note that, in this
first ever written description of New York Bay, Verrazano observes
the land from the exact perspective that comes to dominate its cultural representation in the centuries that follow. Specifically, in what
becomes the prevalent city view from the seventeenth century
onward, the site is seen from the harbor looking northward toward
the prow of Lower Manhattan (figure 10).

FIGURE 10. *Early skyline of Lower Manhattan: bird's-eye view of New
Amsterdam, 1635. (Courtesy Picture Collection, the New York Public Library,
Astor, Lenox and Tilden Foundations)*

By the nineteenth century, as the transition from landscape to cityscape accelerates and New York begins to acquire its modern urban
character and appearance, the skyline becomes a firmly established
literary motif. For example, in *Domestic Manners of the Americans*
(1832), the sensational precursor to Charles Dickens's *American Notes*
(1842), the English novelist and travel writer Frances Trollope begins
her account of visiting New York with this panoramic view of the
city:

> [M]y imagination is incapable of conceiving any thing of the kind
> more beautiful than the harbour of New York. Various and lovely
> are the objects which meet the eye on every side, but the naming
> of them would only be to give a list of words, without conveying
> the faintest idea of the scene. I doubt if ever the pencil of Turner
> could do it justice, bright and glorious as it rose upon us. We
> seemed to enter the harbour of New York upon waves of liquid
> gold, and as we darted past the green isles which rise from its
> bosom, like guardian sentinels of the fair city, the setting sun
> stretched his horizontal beams farther and farther at each moment,
> as if to point to us some new glory in the landscape.[42]

Like Verrazano some three hundred years earlier, Trollope is powerfully moved by the beauty of the harbor view. But although that view
now contains one of the world's largest and most densely developed
cities, the urban is almost completely glossed over in the language of
the passage by the heavy stress on nature. There is even a certain re-
luctance on Trollope's part to see or acknowledge the expanding
presence of the city. Moreover, her refusal to name the urban sights
combined with her explicit reference to J. M. W. Turner, the British
Romantic landscape painter, further underlines this point, effectively inviting the reader to imagine the unnatural cityscape in terms
of a natural landscape. Thus filtered through the ecocentric lens of
pictorial Romanticism, Trollope's sensuous vision of the skyline
transfigures the blooming metropolis into an aesthetic wonder derived from and connected to the natural world that, in an ironic
twist, New York's urban expansion was rapidly supplanting.

While Frances Trollope clearly responds with exuberance to New
York's nineteenth-century skyline, other writers of the period are far
less enthusiastic and forgiving about the city's horizontal spread.
Most notably, for the transcendentalist Henry David Thoreau,
who spent six months living on Staten Island in 1843,[43] the sight of

Manhattan's confused jumble across the water presented a hideous and unwelcome sight. As he complains in a letter to Ralph Waldo Emerson:

> I don't like the city better, the more I see it, but worse. I am ashamed of my eyes that behold it. It is a thousand times meaner than I could have imagined. It will be something to hate,—that's the advantage it will be to me.... The pigs in the street are the most respectable part of the population. When will the world learn that a million men are of no importance compared to *one* man? But I must wait for a shower of shillings, or at least a slight dew or mizzling of sixpences, before I explore New York very far.[44]

Such extreme expressions of disdain for the urban panorama are hardly surprising coming, as they do, from the future author of *Walden* (1854) in a letter to the outspoken author of *Nature* (1836). Yet it is revealing to learn that part of Thoreau's revulsion at the sight of Manhattan derives from a larger anxiety concerning the relation of the individual to the urban crowd. That anxiety, also explored by Edgar Allan Poe in his city story "The Man of the Crowd" (1840),[45] is one that the philosopher Walter Benjamin specifically links to the social experience of modernity when he remarks on "the obliteration of the individual by the big-city crowd."[46] For Thoreau, who seeks to reclaim the individual from the anonymity of the crowd, the skyline represents precisely that process of obliteration and therefore becomes "something to hate." And while we can only speculate about how far such urban experiences contributed toward Thoreau's decision to retreat to nature in 1845, it is fair to say that his visual confrontation with the New York skyline does prompt him to begin commenting, however cursorily, on the issues of individualism and self-knowledge that go on to preoccupy his later writing.

Furthermore, Thoreau's closing remark about needing more money to explore the city comments on more than just the expense of urban tourism. It also touches on one of his underlying reasons for visiting New York in the first place. As his letters from Staten Island reveal, Thoreau was driven by financial need to make frequent trips into Manhattan in search of a market for his planned writing. So although he is repelled by the city on one level, the budding writer is nonetheless drawn to it on another one entirely. And in this reluctant attraction to the object of his disgust, Thoreau experiences yet another distinct urban phenomenon observed by Benjamin in his critique of modernity:

in the era of high capitalism, the writer needs the city. "The true situation of the man of letters," writes Benjamin, is that "he goes to the marketplace as a *flâneur*, supposedly to take a look at it, but in reality to find a buyer."[47] Benjamin may be writing about Baudelaire and Paris, but the comment equally applies to Thoreau and New York. After all, in his exploratory excursions into the city, Thoreau assumes the double role of sightseer and commodity in the urban marketplace.

In "Manhattan from the Bay," a short fragment from his experimental prose memoir *Specimen Days* (1882), Walt Whitman recalls a view of the city encountered while pleasure sailing around New York Bay on a lazy summer day in 1878:

> And rising out of the midst [of sloops and schooner yachts], tall-topt, ship-hemm'd, modern, American, yet strangely oriental, V-shaped Manhattan, with its compact mass, its spires, its cloud-touching edifices group'd at the centre—the green of the trees, and all the white, brown and gray of architecture well blended, as I see it, under a miracle of limpid sky, delicious light of heaven above, and June haze on the surface below.[48]

The emergence of this modern, skyrocketing, and strangely "othered" metropolis is what the transitional cityscapes of Trollope and Thoreau begin to register. For as Peter Brooker suggests, "the future of New York City could already be seen" by the 1850s.[49] And in glimpsing that future, writers like Trollope and Thoreau not only seem to anticipate the rise of the vertical city but, in the process, prefigure the even more extreme urban visions of late nineteenth- and early twentieth-century writers. Indeed, once New York turns vertical, the experience of wonder and estrangement already evident in the prevertical narratives of Trollope and Thoreau becomes significantly accentuated in literary and other artistic representations of the skyline.

One such representation occurs in Henry James's early twentieth-century travelogue *The American Scene* (1907). Returning home to the United States in 1904 after some twenty years spent living in Europe, James finds that the low-rise New York of his childhood has been replaced with a "strange vertiginous" city.[50] As he seeks to come to terms with this radical transformation, James offers this piercing critique of the modern skyline:

> [T]he multitudinous sky-scrapers standing up to the view, from the water, like extravagant pins in a cushion already overplanted,

and stuck in as in the dark, anywhere and anyhow, have at least the felicity of carrying out the fairness of tone, of taking the sun and the shade in the manner of towers of marble.... You see the pincushion profile, so to speak, on passing between Jersey City and Twenty-third Street, but you get it broadside on, this loose nosegay of architectural flowers, if you skirt the Battery, well out, and embrace the whole plantation.... Such growths, you feel, have confessedly arisen but to be "picked," in time, with a shears.[51]

Seen here from the perspective of the harbor, Manhattan figures first as an overstuffed pincushion and then as a disorderly bouquet of overgrown flowers waiting to be sliced apart by shears. In addition to the theme of excess, what links the two metaphors is the imagery of discomfort and incision: needlepoints, sharp edges, and even the threat of decapitation. Moreover, this skyline also suffers from an absence of order. In James's terms, the constellation of skyscrapers conforms to no visible pattern, suggesting a perceived need for some degree of rationality and restraint to be imposed on the city's upward growth.

For Henry James, then, the effect of gazing at the skyline after returning home from his extended stay in Europe is to experience both wonder and unease: wonder at the vertical excess and extravagance; and unease at the unfamiliarity of this new and animated urban spectacle. Here, as in the much later narrations of Baudrillard and de Certeau, the result is a dual sense of excitement and estrangement. The difference, however, is that in James's text the uncanny ultimately comes to dominate much more forcefully over the sublime. One reason is that, as Morton and Lucia White argue in *The Intellectual versus the City*, James's response to the modern cityscape is colored by a Eurocentric nostalgia for prevertical New York.[52] In a letter to Emerson from 1843 Thoreau mentions visiting James's father at his home in Washington Square and reports that "[James] has naturalized and humanized New York for me."[53] It is interesting, if not a little ironic, that some sixty years later the son of the only person capable of making Thoreau feel at ease in New York cannot naturalize and humanize the new face of the city for himself.

In his 1919 essay on the uncanny Sigmund Freud suggests that the *unheimlich* (literally, the unhomely) "is in reality nothing new or alien, but something which is familiar and old-established in the mind and which has become alienated from it only through the process of repression."[54] Building on Freud's formulation, the architectural historian Anthony Vidler suggests that this "propensity of the familiar to turn on its owners, suddenly to become defamiliarized,"[55] is a phenomenon connected not only to the interior spaces of the psyche as per Freud but also to the exterior spaces of the modern city as per Benjamin: "the uncanny, as Walter Benjamin noted, was also born out of the rise of the great cities, their disturbingly heterogeneous crowds and newly scaled spaces."[56] Vidler calls this "condition of modern anxiety" the "architectural uncanny,"[57] and defines it as an aesthetic mode of estrangement endemic to capitalist modernity and closely linked to the spatial formations and social experiences of the city. In such terms, Henry James's skyline in *The American Scene* can be understood as a manifestation of the architectural uncanny in the full sense that Vidler gives to the term. For what James ultimately reads into the text of the defamiliarized skyline is, quite literally, the *unhomeliness* of the modern city (see figure 11). The old and familiar is suddenly made new and strange.

A similarly fraught narration of the New York skyline appears in Henry Adams's fictionalized autobiography *The Education of Henry Adams* (1918). Paralleling James's homecoming in *The American Scene*,

FIGURE 11. *New York skyline, 1913. (Courtesy Library of Congress, Prints and Photographs Division)*

the passage in question features the experience of another wandering American returning to the city after a long absence. Interestingly, the year is also 1904 and the skyline is observed from the same location and perspective as James's earlier text:

> As he came up the bay again, November 5, 1904,...he found the approach more striking than ever—wonderful—unlike anything man had ever seen—and like nothing he had ever much cared to see. The outline of the city became frantic in its effort to explain something that defied meaning. Power seemed to have outgrown its servitude and to have asserted its freedom. The cylinder had exploded and thrown great masses of stone and steam against the sky. The city had the air and movement of hysteria, and the citizens were crying, in every accent of danger and alarm, that the new forces must at any cost be brought under control.[58]

As Adams describes it, the skyline comes uncannily alive in the imagination of the observer, creating powerful feelings of awe, hysteria, and confusion, and also generating uneasy visions of movement, violence, and eruption. Like Henry James, moreover, Adams similarly expresses both anxiety over the cityscape's visual disorder and a desire to exert control over the seemingly autonomous urban machine.

More significantly, Adams goes slightly further than James to suggest in an explicit way that the defamiliarized skyline contains some kind of meaning. The problem, as he makes a point of stressing, is that the ever-shifting text of the new city resists interpretation: "the outline of the city became frantic in its effort to explain something that defied meaning." But although Adams fails on this occasion to decipher the meaning he senses in the urban landscape, he does demonstrate an emerging consciousness of the discursive dimensions of urban space—the "gigantic rhetoric of excess in both expenditure and production"[59] that de Certeau, following Henri Lefebvre, much later comes to call the "immense texturology" of the city.[60]

Willa Cather also foregrounds this texturology in "Behind the Singer Tower" (1912), an urban disaster story in which she not only stresses the legibility of the city but also suggests that a close reading of the futuristic skyline can offer insight into the form of modern urbanism she enigmatically refers to as "the New York idea."[61] In a morbid prefiguring of the skyscraper explosions of 9/11, "Behind the Singer Tower" takes place in the smoldering aftermath of a high-rise hotel fire that traps and kills hundreds of people on the upper floors of the building.

Though based on the real-life disasters of the Windsor Hotel fire of 1899 and the Triangle Waist Company fire of 1911, Cather's story also has parallels with one of the twentieth century's most haunting maritime disasters: the sinking of the *Titanic*, an event that occurred less than a year after Cather wrote the story in 1911 and only a month before its first publication in *Collier's* magazine in May 1912. Robert K. Miller explains the connection in his transatlantic reading of the story:

> When "Behind the Singer Tower" was first published on May 18, 1912, American readers had good reason to receive with interest a story about a major disaster in which hundreds of prominent people lost their lives at a time when they felt safely protected by modern engineering and opulent furnishings. The *Titanic* had sunk the previous month, and journalists were still reporting the news of what had gone wrong on that April night in the North Atlantic.... In choosing to write about the vulnerability of an exceptionally large object devoted to housing people in transit and in which lives are suddenly and sensationally consumed, Cather seems to have been remarkably prescient. Although Leonardo DiCaprio is unlikely to star in a multimillion dollar production of "Behind the Singer Tower," Cather's "night to remember" can, like the sinking of the *Titanic*, help us to better understand the cultural anxieties running beneath the surface of the century we have so recently left behind.[62]

While Miller is probably right about the actor Leonardo DiCaprio, he is not entirely accurate in saying that "Behind the Singer Tower" is unlikely to become a Hollywood blockbuster. For in many ways it already did with the 1974 sensation *The Towering Inferno*, starring Steve McQueen and Paul Newman. Like Cather's story, the film features a massive skyscraper fire caused by faulty cabling and cost-cutting construction.

More to the point, however, the resonance between Cather's towering inferno and the sinking of the *Titanic* hinges on the way both disasters involve a misplaced confidence in modern technology and engineering, resulting in the destruction of two prominent icons of modernity: the skyscraper and the ocean liner. As Miller's analysis suggests, the poignancy of "Behind the Singer Tower" lies in the way Cather brings the cultural anxieties surrounding the *Titanic* much closer to home. Her disaster occurs not in the middle of the Atlantic

Ocean but in the dead center of the modern city—in the shadow, as her title specifies, of one of the world's tallest buildings at that time (figure 12). As it happens, the Singer Tower itself has since succumbed to the destructive energy of the city. In 1968, the early New York skyscraper was demolished to make way for the U.S. Steel Building, an imposing black monolith known simply as One Liberty Plaza.[63]

FIGURE 12. *Singer Tower, 1908. (Courtesy Library of Congress, Prints and Photographs Division)*

The plot of "Behind the Singer Tower" centers on a group of male professionals who take a nocturnal boat ride around New York Bay in order to observe the effect of the skyscraper fire on the urban panorama. Interestingly, Cather uses the boat ride partly to offer a gendered critique of postdisaster spectatorship. In particular, she repeatedly calls attention to the way the men fixate on the size of the skyscrapers: "Zablowski pointed with his cigar toward the blurred Babylonian heights crowding each other on the narrow tip of the island.... [A]mong them rose the colossal figure of the Singer Tower."[64] As the subtle phallic imagery of this passage begins to insinuate, Cather's urban observers exhibit a kind of "edifice complex" in which their concerns about skyscraper safety can be linked in a classic Freudian turn to a more unconscious and distinctly male fear of castration.

This idea certainly appears to inform this passage in which Cather's description of the skyline not only emphasizes the phallic dimensions of the vertical city but also culminates in an excruciating image of mutilation:

> There was a brooding mournfulness over the harbor, as if the ghost of helplessness and terror were abroad in the darkness.... The city itself, as we looked back at it, seemed enveloped in a tragic self-consciousness. Those incredible towers of stone and steel seemed, in the mist, to be grouped confusedly together, as if they were left after a forest is cut away. One might fancy that the city was protesting, was asserting its helplessness, its irresponsibility for its physical conformation, for the direction it had taken. It was an irregular parallelogram pressed between two hemispheres, and, like any other solid squeezed in a vise, it shot upward.[65]

Here, the traumatized skyline acquires self-consciousness in the imagination of the observer, communicating strong feelings of terror, disorientation, and helplessness. In many ways Cather's urban panorama shares the imagery of pain and discomfort found in Henry James's earlier text. James' overstuffed pincushion now becomes Cather's emasculated city squeezed in a vise. In Cather's version, however, the threat of dismemberment looming over James's skyscrapers is gruesomely realized. The subtle effect is to question the male-inflected aura of power, competition, and achievement hanging over the modern skyline and, in the process, to expose the potential vulnerability of New York's vertical project.

Looking beyond Cather's commentary on modernity and masculinity, it is worth noting that her somber vision of the early twentieth-century skyline resonates eerily with the appearance of downtown New York on September 11, 2001—a day when the city, enveloped in the smoke, dust, and debris of the collapsed WTC towers, experienced the real trauma of a real skyscraper catastrophe. This resonance is further amplified by Cather's attention to the human dimension of her urban disaster. In the following passage Cather is writing about the fictional "Mont Blanc Hotel"—an Alpine reference designed to conjure up images of high altitude—yet her words could just as easily be describing what happened at the Twin Towers:

> On the night of the fire the hotel was full of people from everywhere, and by morning half a dozen trusts had lost their presidents, two states had lost their governors, and one of the great European powers had lost its ambassador. So many businesses had been disorganized that Wall Street had shut down for the day. They had been snuffed out, these important men, as lightly as the casual guests who had come to town to spend money, or as the pampered opera singers who had returned from an overland tour and were waiting to sail on Saturday. The lists were still vague, for whether the victims had jumped or not, identification was difficult, and, in either case, they had met with obliteration, absolute effacement, as when a drop of water falls into the sea.[66]

Among the many haunting images that emerged from New York on 9/11, one controversial photograph stood out for the way it so intimately revealed the horror of that day. Taken from street level by photojournalist Richard Drew only moments before the first skyscraper collapse, the still shot captured the image of an unknown man free-falling past the perfectly straight vertical lines of the Twin Towers. In a 2003 article for the *Los Angeles Times* Drew movingly describes the image as "a photographic record of someone living the last moments of his life," adding that "every time I look at it, I see him alive."[67] As Drew's comments suggest, part of what makes the photograph so disturbing to view is the way it raises some very difficult questions about the nature of suicide, death, and human agency. These are the same questions raised by Cather's story and its own horrific images of high-rise leaping, including one of an opera singer fatally plunging from his hotel window "toward the cobwebby life nets stretched five hundred feet below."[68] Such uncanny parallels between Cather's 1912 story and Drew's 2001 photograph are more than just a simple case of fiction foreshadowing reality. They reveal deep-rooted cultural anxieties about the fallibility of skyscraper technology and the dangers of placing too much faith in technological progress.

In *Welcome to the Desert of the Real*, a thought-provoking series of essays on the events of 9/11, the freewheeling philosopher Slavoj Žižek notes the similarities between the real images of mass destruction in New York and the fantasy disaster spectacles of Hollywood blockbusters like *Escape from New York* (1981), *Independence Day* (1996), and *The Matrix* (1999). Žižek proceeds from this often-made observation to argue that

> the unthinkable which happened was the object of fantasy, so that, in a way, America got what it fantasized about, and this was the biggest surprise.... We should therefore invert the standard reading according to which the WTC explosions were the intrusion of the Real which shattered our illusory Sphere: quite the reverse.... It is not that reality entered our image: the image entered and shattered our reality.[69]

Žižek makes a compelling point about the way in which the events of 9/11 inverted our experience of the conventional relationship between the reality of urban disaster and its popular cultural representation. Yet the history of that representation reaches back much further than the action films cited by Žižek. In "Behind the Singer Tower" Cather's preoccupation with towering infernos, high-rise leaping, and postdisaster spectatorship shows that the fantasy rehearsal of New York's architectural destruction has been ongoing ever since the city's first moments of verticality. In short, Cather's story illustrates how the image that crashed into and shattered our reality on 9/11 has been in circulation for as long as the form of the skyscraper itself.

Together, the textual cityscapes of Henry James, Henry Adams, and Willa Cather construct a vision of the New York skyline in which the soaring verticals of the city function primarily as symbols of corporate capital, and this symbolism is one source of their shared anxiety about the skyrocketing development of the city. However, in the imagination of many immigrant and ethnic American writers, the New York skyline also functions in a slightly different way as a powerful symbol of social opportunity, albeit a frequently problematic one. As it happens, this other symbolism is integral to the architectural vision behind the post-9/11 redevelopment of the Ground Zero site in Lower Manhattan, and I would like briefly to address this point before considering the conflicted optimism found in the strange and dreamy cityscapes of the writers Abraham Cahan, James Weldon Johnson, and Theodore Dreiser.

New York Dreamscapes

In his architect's statement for the WTC redevelopment project (figure 13), Daniel Libeskind cites the immigrant experience of sailing into New York Harbor and seeing the city's skyline for the very first time as a source of inspiration for his master-plan design, revealing in the process just how forcefully that singular urban scene can capture the imagination:

> I arrived by ship to New York as a teenager, an immigrant, and like many millions of others before me, my first sight was the Statue of Liberty and the amazing skyline of Manhattan. I have never forgotten that sight or what it stands for. This is what this project is all about.... Now everyone can see not only Ground Zero but the resurgence of life.... The sky will be home again to a towering spire of 1776 feet high, the "Gardens of the World." Why gardens? Because gardens are a constant affirmation of life. A skyscraper rises above its predecessors, reasserting the pre-eminence of freedom and beauty, restoring the spiritual peak to the city, creating an icon that speaks of our vitality in the face of danger and our optimism in the aftermath of tragedy. Life victorious.[70]

In contrast to James, Adams, and Cather who see high-rise New York in terms of congestion and deformity, Libeskind presents the skyline as a space of liberation and renewal. His vertical vision contains none of the imagery of unhomeliness we have encountered so far. Rather, the form of the skyscraper emerges as a natural, regenerative presence in the city, an idea reinforced in Libeskind's design by the incorporation of hanging vertical gardens in the translucent glass spire of the tower (one of many flamboyant features that did not survive David Childs's later revision of the design). The implication is that, in contemporary global cities like New York, the skyscraper has

FIGURE 13. *Design study for Freedom Tower and WTC site, 2004. (Courtesy Studio Daniel Libeskind and Archimation)*

now become such a domesticated and mentally internalized form that, as in the case of the Twin Towers, its absence can be far more uncanny than its presence.

A key point that Libeskind makes in his rhetoric of renewal is that what his twenty-first-century skyscraper symbolizes is nothing less than the democratic ideal of freedom that he originally read into the skyline as an immigrant arriving in New York back in the 1950s. Not only does he refer to the skyscraper as an icon of opportunity and optimism, but he also sees its presence on the skyline as a reassertion of the American spirit of liberty. Indeed, the idea of freedom is so integral to Libeskind's design that it has been inscribed into virtually every dimension of the building. Most obviously, there is the building's intended name: Freedom Tower (later formalized as One World Trade Center). But there is also the building's height of 1776 feet, a number that explicitly references one of the most important dates in American history: the year of the Declaration of Independence. Finally, and perhaps most subtly, there is the building's form. The asymmetrical tower and soaring offset spire are deliberately designed to evoke the gently twisting profile of the Statue of Liberty, thereby setting the skyscraper into dialogue with the city and its immigrant history.

Coming as they do from the deeply philosophical and politically attuned architect of such difficult memorial projects as the Jewish Museum in Berlin and the Imperial War Museum in northern England, Libeskind's grand symbolic claims for the Freedom Tower may seem a little oversimplified. For example, his statement almost completely elides the sinuous and contentious history of "freedom" as a concept in multicultural America, including immigrant New York. It also remains to be seen whether the building can be sustained as the city's "spiritual peak" over the long term. These equivocations aside, however, it is at least fair to say that, through sheer height, the building's design does succeed in "recapturing the skyline," to cite a loaded phrase often used by the New York press and in a more proprietorial capacity by the Lower Manhattan Development Corporation.

As discussed earlier, Jean Baudrillard has argued that, in their uncanny doubleness, the Twin Towers put a stop to New York's "competitive verticality."[71] With the Freedom Tower design, Libeskind restarted the city's race for the sky on the very site where it was temporarily suspended. Libeskind even acknowledges the building's competitive vertical function in his architect's statement when he stresses that the tower rises triumphantly above all predecessors, including the Twin Towers it replaces. In this respect, what Libeskind's design registers is the tenuous yet deeply embedded ideological connection in the American public mind between democracy and the vertical form of the skyscraper, a connection that the urban planner Thomas Adams already had identified back in 1931 when he wrote that, for many people, "New York is America, and its skyscraper a symbol of the spirit of America."[72]

This perceived link between America and skyscrapers is one that, from the turn of the twentieth century onward, many immigrant New York writers consciously address in the material of their fiction. For example, the skyline's power to act as a symbol of nation is stressed quite heavily in *The Rise of David Levinsky*, published in 1917 by Abraham Cahan, a Lithuanian-born Jewish writer, newspaper editor, and trade unionist who arrived in New York from Russia in 1882. In this fictional rags-to-riches autobiography about Jewish-American life in turn-of-the-century New York, Cahan pursues a concern that recurs throughout his creative and political writing. That concern is the transformative effect of the urban American experience on New York's immigrant population.

In this respect, Cahan's perspective on the city differs substantially from that of affluent, American-born writers like Henry James, whose nostalgic urban reflections often bemoan the passing of an exclusive and predominantly monocultural version of Old New York. As Shaun O'Connell notes in his literary history of New York, in contrast to James, who "worried about the ways immigrants would change America," socially conscious immigrant writers like Abraham Cahan "examined the ways America transformed the immigrant."[73] This difference of perspective registers in Cahan's alternative version of the skyline, where the panoramic spectacle of New York, now filtered through the immigrant gaze, represents no longer an encoding of capital but instead a space of unbounded possibility:

> The immigrant's arrival in his new home is like a second birth to him. Imagine a new-borne babe in possession of a fully developed intellect. Would it ever forget its entry into the world? Neither does the immigrant ever forget his entry into a country which is, for him, a new world in the profoundest sense of the term....I conjure up the gorgeousness of the spectacle as it appeared to me on that clear June morning: the magnificent verdure of Staten

Island, the tender blue of sea and sky, the dignified bustle of passing craft—above all, those floating, squatting, multitudinously windowed palaces which I subsequently learned to call ferries. It was all so utterly unlike anything I had ever seen or dreamed before. It unfolded itself like a divine revelation. I was in a trance or in something closely resembling one.... My transport of admiration, however, only added to my sense of helplessness and awe. Here on shipboard, I was sure of shelter and food, at least. How was I going to procure my sustenance on those magic shores? I wished the remaining hour could be prolonged indefinitely.... When I say that my first view of New York Bay struck me as something not of this earth it is not a mere figure of speech.[74]

In Cahan's narrative of renewal, which strongly resonates with Libeskind's patriotic recollections, the immigrant's arrival in New York is depicted in terms of spiritual rebirth. The significance of the moment proves so overpowering that the visual experience of the landscape leaves the observer in a trancelike state of ungrounded delirium akin to religious ecstasy. The result is the transformation of the scene—at least in the narrator's imagination—into a fantastical, otherworldly apparition.

This sort of sublime, revelatory vision is characteristic of Cahan's long-distance views of New York. In another arrival moment from one of his earliest immigrant stories, "The Imported Bridegroom" (1898), Cahan offers a similar scene of sublimity and enchantment: "Can there be anything more beautiful, more sublime, and more uplifting than the view, on a clear summer morning, of New York harbor from an approaching ship? Shaya saw in the enchanting effect of sea, verdure, and sky a new version of his vision of paradise.... Yet, overborne with its looming grandeur, his heart grew heavy with suspense."[75] As in *The Rise of David Levinsky*, the immigrant gaze once again sees the cityscape of New York in terms of an earthly paradise. In both cases, the distortion leads to a mental projection that sets impossibly high expectations for the immigrant's new life in America. This contrast between reverie and reality is of course the point of these quasi-supernatural skylines, both of which are also accompanied by a sense of foreboding and anxiety. Using the innocent, unknowing perspective of the arriving immigrant, Cahan deliberately sets up an ideal image waiting to be undermined by the lived experience of the city.

In *The Rise of David Levinsky*, this process of disillusionment begins almost immediately as the narrator disembarks into the carceral space of the "big Immigration Station,"[76] and continues in the city itself where, standing lost beneath the "hurtling and panting" elevated railway, "the active life of the great strange city" causes him to "feel like one abandoned in the midst of a jungle."[77] "The Imported Bridegroom" follows a similar pattern of estrangement and disorientation. Upon arrival in the city, Shaya, the titular object of "importation," is taken directly to a fine clothing store on Broadway where, in an attempt to make him look "Americanized," his importer decks him out in the trendiest "garb of Gentile civilization" and parades him along the street.[78] The humiliating experience leaves him feeling "tied and fettered"[79] and deeply unsure of his new identity. It also contributes to his growing sense of objectification.

Despite these critiques of the urban experience, Cahan's New York panoramas do not in themselves offer the sort of explicit treatment of the built environment of the city dominating the textual cityscapes of most other writers of the late nineteenth and early twentieth centuries. Skyscrapers, for instance, remain conspicuously absent, though almost everything else surrounding the vertical city, from the natural landscape to the maritime traffic, makes an appearance. The same also holds true in *Yekl* (1896), Cahan's earliest novel about immigrant New York, suggesting that the conspicuous absence of the city's most visible vertical elements is related to the nature of Cahan's interest in the skyline. In order to show the misplaced optimism of the immigrant gaze at the precise moment of arrival in the city, as well as to establish an ideal image of the city, Cahan presents a blinkered long-distance view in which the architectural uncanny of the modern metropolis is completely glossed over. To compensate for this oversight, however, Cahan does make a point of juxtaposing his sublime long-distance views with uncanny urban close-ups.

Fantasy Island

The paradox of New York's double significance as a symbol of liberation and estrangement is perhaps most graphically illustrated by the Harlem Renaissance writer James Weldon Johnson, in whose work the skyline's power to enchant acquires a far more sinister overtone.

In his groundbreaking novel about the double consciousness of black life in America, *The Autobiography of an Ex-Coloured Man* (1912), Johnson offers an alternative narrative of arrival in the vertical city that not only counterbalances Libeskind's unbridled optimism but also problematizes the skyline's function as a ubiquitous symbol of opportunity. One of Johnson's central concerns in *The Autobiography* is "the dread power of the city"[80] and the way large urban centers such as New York operate on the imagination of inexperienced newcomers. It is precisely this concern that underscores Johnson's description of the narrator's first encounter with New York. The event relates the modern African-American experience not of immigration but of migration—in this case from the rural South to the urban North:

> We steamed up into New York Harbour late one afternoon in spring. The last efforts of the sun were being put forth in turning the waters of the bay to glistening gold; the green islands on either side, in spite of their warlike mountings, looked calm and peaceful; the buildings of the town shone out in reflected light which gave the city an air of enchantment; and, truly, it is an enchanted spot. New York City is the most fatally fascinating thing in America. She sits like a great witch at the gate of the country, showing her alluring white face and hiding her crooked hands and feet under the folds of her wide garments—constantly enticing thousands from far within, and tempting those who come from across the seas to go no father. And all these become the victims of her caprice. Some she at once crushes beneath her cruel feet; others she condemns to a fate like that of galley-slaves; a few she favors and fondles, riding them high on bubbles of fortune; then with a sudden breath she blows the bubble out and laughs mockingly as she watches them fall.[81]

Here, as in the urban vistas of James, Adams, Cather, and Cahan, the New York skyline continues to figure as an exhilarating spectacle of the sublime and the uncanny. A slight difference, however, is that Johnson places more emphasis on the play and significance of color. Reminiscent of Frances Trollope's description of low-rise New York in terms of Romantic landscape painting, Johnson's penumbral urban panorama is framed by "green" scenery and bathed in "glistening gold" light. Rising from the center of this gilded composition is the "white-faced" city, ominously perceived by the narrator as a cruel

Sphinxlike enchantress guarding the entrance to a world of wealth and opportunity.

The trope of New York as "gateway" to America has been a recurring metaphor for the city ever since its colonial beginnings. In Johnson's version, however, the symbolically charged interplay between black observer and white metropolis subtly reshapes that familiar metaphor in terms of racial and ethnic difference. The clear message is that this "white-faced" gatekeeper does not grant equal access to all, and certainly not to African-American migrants like Johnson's narrator. In this sense, the skyline functions as a false icon of opportunity. It seduces the unsuspecting victim into a life of economic hardship and social inequality—into the very condition of urban alienation that Johnson goes on to write about so powerfully in *Black Manhattan* (1930), his countercultural history of "the black metropolis within the heart of the great Western white metropolis."[82]

Johnson's representation of the New York skyline as both gateway and dead end reveals what Maria Balshaw describes in *Looking for Harlem* as "the paradoxical attitude to the city one finds structuring African American urban literature throughout the twentieth century."[83] Like many other writers of the Harlem Renaissance, Johnson presents a double image of the modern metropolis that, in Balshaw's terms, not only contains a "passionate urbanism" in which "the city stands for the future, and in particular the future of the race" but also "paints the city as the site of deprivation, squalor and discontent."[84] The result is "the paradox of the city of heaven that it also the city of hell."[85] For Johnson, that urban paradox—so dramatically enunciated by the modern skyline—is what makes New York "the most fatally fascinating thing in America" (figure 14). It is a source of the city's aura of enchantment yet also a cause of its everyday horror.

The skyline's illusory and dreamlike qualities are also a recurring concern for the American naturalist writer Theodore Dreiser. In his 1926 collection of New York sketches, *The Color of a Great City*, Dreiser opens the volume with this sublime urban dreamscape:

It was silent, the city of my dreams, marble and serene, due perhaps to the fact that in reality I knew nothing of crowds, poverty, the winds and storms of the inadequate that blow like a dust along the paths of life. It was an amazing city, so far-flung, so beautiful, so dead. There were tracks of iron stalking through the air, and streets that were as cañons, and stairways that mounted in vast

FIGURE 14. *Midtown Manhattan skyline, looking south, 1931. (Courtesy Library of Congress, Prints and Photographs Division)*

flights to noble plazas, and steps that led down into deep places where were, strangely enough, underworld silences.... And then, after twenty years, here it stood, as amazing almost as my dream, save that in the waking the flush of life was over it. It possessed the tang of contests and dreams and enthusiasms and delights and terrors and despairs.[86]

Blurring the distinctions between the imaginary and the real, Dreiser depicts the city even more emphatically than James Weldon Johnson as a fantastical, illusory space of contradictions and extremes. Foreshadowing Fritz Lang's cinematic vision of the two-tiered city in *Metropolis* (1927), Dreiser's New York is polarized between majestic, vertiginous heights and gloomy, subhuman depths. More disturbingly, the city is described as being both dead and alive, as if suspended in an indeterminate and uncanny state of undeath. The overall effect is to project a deeply conflicted image of vertical New York as enticing, beautiful, and familiar yet also frightening, strange, and unhomely.

It is significant, moreover, that Dreiser presents the city specifically in terms of a waking dream. Not only does this situate the meditative experience of city gazing on the threshold between the conscious and unconscious minds, it also reinforces the importance of image and illusion to the construction of the city's modern urban identity. In short, like most of Woody Allen's films, Dreiser's urban dreamscape reminds us that New York is not just a physical place; it is also a state of mind.

Dreiser further develops this idea in "The Rivers of the Nameless Dead," a later sketch from *The Color of a Great City* in which he sees the skyline of Manhattan as a potentially deceptive image capable of luring the unsuspecting viewer into a false sense of the city:

> There is an island surrounded by rivers, and about it the tide scurries fast and deep. It is a beautiful island, long, narrow, magnificently populated, and with such a wealth of life and interest as no island in the world before has ever possessed....Enormous buildings and many splendid mansions line its streets....If you were to...see the picture it presents to the coming eye, you would assume that it was all that it seemed....A world of comfort and satisfaction for all who take up their abode within it—an island of beauty and delight. The sad part of it is, however, that the island and its beauty are, to a certain extent, a snare. Its seeming loveliness, which promises so much to the innocent eye, is not always easy of realization.[87]

Like James Weldon Johnson in *The Autobiography*, Dreiser makes a point of emphasizing the importance of distinguishing between the harsh, everyday realities of urban life and the glossy, idealized image of the city projected by the skyline. In Dreiser's terms, problems arise when the "innocent eye" fails to make that distinction and, as a consequence, inaccurately reads into the distant silhouette of the "beautiful island" a false promise of wealth and opportunity. The implication is that gazing at the modern cityscape requires certain interpretive skills in order to see beneath or beyond the surface. Without these, the viewer is liable to be seduced by the superficial "beauty" and "delight" of the spectacle.

While Dreiser may be overstating the skyline's power to exert control over the imagination of the casual observer, he does make a significant point concerning the cityscape itself. It is the same point that has underscored not only my own argument but also, as we have seen, the urban narratives of writers as diverse as Henry James, Henry Adams, Willa Cather, Abraham Cahan, and James Weldon Johnson, as well as the critical reflections of thinkers like Baudrillard and de Certeau. Namely, Dreiser suggests that to gaze upon the cityscape of vertical New York is to confront one of capitalist modernity's most emblematic and volatile urban texts.

In *The Skyscraper in American Art*, Merrill Schleier argues that, despite the exuberant urban optimism of artists like Charles Sheeler and Hugh Ferriss, New York's visual imagination most often responds to the rise of the vertical city in "ambivalent terms."[88] Surveying a diverse body of literature, we have seen how New York's literary imagination is similarly dominated by a profound ambivalence toward the city's first great moment of verticality. For many early twentieth-century writers, the most discernible place where this ambivalence registers is in the tension between the sublime and the uncanny underpinning their narrative treatments of the modern skyline.

For Henry James, Willa Cather, and Henry Adams, who see Manhattan in terms of congestion and deformity, this tension arises out of an anxiety over the rapid pace of capitalist urbanization and, in particular, the consequent explosion of unfamiliar and ungainly urban sights. For Abraham Cahan and James Weldon Johnson, who identify New York as a problematic icon of opportunity, the tension is created by the skyline's power to enchant and mislead the immigrant and migrant gaze. And finally, for Theodore Dreiser, whose imaginative city sketches take the dreaminess of the skyline to conceptual extremes, the tension derives from the gap between the elusive city of the imagination and the lived city of everyday life.

In their shared ambivalence, these early twentieth-century literary treatments of the skyline reveal the extent to which New York's shape-shifting verticals have been a recurring concern for writers seeking to encapsulate and even dramatize the tensions, dreams, and possibilities of life in the modern city. It is important to emphasize, however, that the tension between the sublime and the uncanny evident in these urban reflections is not merely confined to literary representations of New York's first great moment of verticality. Looking beyond literature to other representational fields, as I do next, it is clear that a similar tension also permeates other creative treatments of the city's modern skyline, including those of photography, painting, film, and urban design.

After-Images of New York

From Jonathan Crary's *Techniques of the Observer* to James Donald's *Imagining the Modern City*, cultural criticism has long emphasized the importance of questioning traditional notions of imaginary representation.[89] Doing just that in *After-Images of the City*, Joan Ramon Resina advances the concept of "after-image" in order to develop "new ways to approach the subject of cities from a broad cultural point of view" while avoiding the "static or simply seriatim scrutiny of images" that frequently accompanies "classic image-of-the-city studies."[90] As he defines it, the after-image is "a visual sensation that lingers after the stimulus that provoked it has disappeared, and opens up the idea of 'image' to a cluster of theoretical possibilities based on temporal displacement, sequentiality, supersession, and engagement."[91] Crucially, the concept of after-image "does not suggest one transcends and leaves behind the imaginary."[92] Rather, the image is "fully retained, but is now a temporalized, unstable, complex image brimming with the history of its production."[93] In other words, the image invoked by the term after-image is "not to be conceived in a narrowly optic sense but in a larger visual one."[94]

By stressing the material, temporal, and mental workings of images, the concept of after-image offers a helpful way to approach the visual culture of cities. This is especially true in the case of New York in the late nineteenth and early twentieth centuries, where the abrupt emergence of a modern metropolis positively requires thinking about images in terms that are alert and receptive to the destabilizing effects of spatial reordering and aesthetic change on the urban imaginary. Mary Woods argues exactly this point in her essay "After-Images of the 'New' New York,"[95] and cites the avant-garde work of Alfred Stieglitz and his circle of photographers, who were most active in the city between the early 1900s and the mid-1930s:

> The photographic process itself (involving exposure, development, and printing of the still or moving image at separate and discrete moments in time) is what Resina characterizes as an after-image at its most basic level.... But the Stieglitz circle of photographers engage the question of after-image on a much more profound level. Their photographs of the "new" New York, a city of skyscrapers, also involve temporal dimensions Resina discovers in after-image.... The experience and comprehension of time articulated in Resina's conceptualization of the after-image are crucial not only for the forms and compositions of these photographs but also for the processes of their making, presentation, and interpretation.[96]

As Woods's comments suggest, there is an important dynamic at work in the city images produced by the Stieglitz circle, which included such notable figures as Alvin Langdon Coburn, Edward Steichen, Paul Strand, and Charles Sheeler. It is a dynamic that not only foregrounds an interplay between image, time, memory, and place but that does so in the specific context of vertical New York and in direct response to the city's modernization. For this reason, I want to look more closely at the ways in which members of this group of photographers represent the skyscraper in the material of their art.

Perhaps more than any other artist, as Woods describes, Alfred Stieglitz led the way in "developing the techniques and the aesthetics of photographing New York skyscrapers and the vertical city they created."[97] This is not to say that Stieglitz was among the first to photograph skyscrapers. From the construction of the earliest skyscrapers in the 1880s onward, high-rise architecture has been the subject of a great deal of photographic and other pictorial representation. Prior to 1900, however, the majority of skyscraper photography was commercially oriented, appearing in newspapers, magazines, postcards, and guidebooks, effectively servicing a voracious public appetite for documentary images of a new urban-architectural phenomenon. While the mass production, dissemination, and consumption of commercial skyscraper imagery has continued unabated ever since, the turn of the century saw the emergence of another mode of skyscraper photography: the art image. This was one of Stieglitz's many contributions to New York's budding modern art scene of the early 1900s. Through his numerous photographs of skyscrapers and skylines, which sought not just to document urban change but also to develop a new urban aesthetic, Stieglitz helped to establish New York's vertical architecture as a subject of artistic study.

The skyscraper that most powerfully captured Stieglitz's imagination in the early years of the new century was the Flatiron Building, which he began photographing soon after its construction. Designed by Daniel Burnham's Chicago-based architectural firm in the Beaux Arts style and built on a triangular lot at the intersection of Broadway and Fifth Avenue, the twenty-one-story Flatiron emerged as a New York icon even before its completion in 1903 (figure 15). One reason was the building's unusual shape. By 1900, the geometric tyranny of the New York grid, with its uniformly rectangular lots, was already exerting a homogenizing effect on skyscraper design. In its triangularity, the Flatiron represented a rare departure from this design constraint, producing a visually arresting and distinctive wedgelike form that has been attracting visitors to the site from the moment of its ground-breaking onward. Another reason for the building's popularity with the public was its location within the city. The Flatiron not only stood at the intersection of two important and busy New York thoroughfares, it also faced out over Madison Square, one of Manhattan's few open spaces. This location both ensured a steady stream of passersby and, even more importantly, provided an uninterrupted view of the skyscraper from street level. Such views were a rarity in the densely developed heart of the city, and the significance was not lost on Stieglitz, who worked and exhibited in the vicinity of the Flatiron.

FIGURE 15. *Flatiron Building, c. 1905. (Courtesy Library of Congress, Prints and Photographs Division)*

In his earliest photograph of the skyscraper, *The Flatiron* (1903), Stieglitz captures the building from Madison Square on a snowy winter morning (figure 16). Unlike the many commercial artists working around the Flatiron at this time, Stieglitz does not foreground or even focus on the skyscraper in his photograph, choosing instead to distance and destabilize his architectural subject. The foreground is dominated by a Hiroshige-like tree trunk rising parallel to the vertical lines of the skyscraper located across the square. Toward the top of the photograph, the trunk forks into two branches, creating a triangle that not only echoes the Flatiron's defining characteristic but also gestures at a certain geometrical affinity between the natural and urban worlds. The middle distance contains a row of empty park benches, two small, indistinct human figures, and a band of snow-covered trees rising up to block the view of the bottom half of the skyscraper. Towering alone in the left background—almost as if floating weightless in space—is the slender vertical structure of the Flatiron, its ornate neoclassical façade slightly out of focus and bathed in a dull, grey light.

Countless critics and art historians have commented on this renowned and frequently reproduced photograph. In her comprehensive reevaluation of Stieglitz's career, for example, Katherine Hoffman suggests that the image conveys a sense of balance, order, and tranquility:

> The photograph emphasizes a decorative, harmonious whole as man-made structure and the world of nature balance each other. The building does not seem like an office building in an urban center. Rather there is a sense of wholeness and idealism in the photograph that speaks not of commercialism, or materialism, or of any of the chaos that is part of urban and modern life, but of harmony, peace, and an aesthetic spirit, set in a moment of silence.[98]

Hoffman is right to stress the photograph's juxtaposition of natural and urban elements, as well as its eliding of the surrounding city and the wider urban context. However, her view that Stieglitz presents a picture of wholeness and harmony overlooks a series of tensions that animate the otherwise placid image.

Alert to these tensions, Mary Woods offers a more compelling and nuanced reading of Stieglitz's Flatiron photography:

> The challenge to Stieglitz was to make visible the collision of the present with the past and future in a two-dimensional medium.

FIGURE 16. *Alfred Stieglitz, The Flatiron, 1903. (Courtesy Georgia O'Keeffe Museum/Artists Rights Society, New York)*

He and his protégés Steichen and Coburn did so by abstracting the building and absorbing it into fugitive effects. In their images, the Flatiron was neither inert nor fixed; it partook of the contingencies of time, weather, light, and shadow. Stieglitz found a way to depict the building as becoming, not simply being.... In his photography...the skyscraper is poised between lightness and solidity; it is emerging and dissolving; natural and man-made; modern and timeless.[99]

The crucial distinction between this reading and Hoffman's is that Woods sees Stieglitz's Flatiron photography as actively seeking balance, not as already having achieved it. Interpreted in this way, Stieglitz's juxtaposition of the natural and urban worlds—particularly in light of the foregrounding of nature—calls into question the relationship between the two even as it equates them. It also posits the skyscraper as an intrusion into the landscape, albeit one that appears to belong in this setting.

More importantly, in this reading, the skyscraper is suspended in a state of indeterminacy. It remains caught between motion and stasis, between absence and presence, between old and new New York, and—to interject the terms of my own broader argument—between the sublime and the uncanny. Indeed, combined with the blurring of the distinctions between nature and the city, Stieglitz's distancing, defamiliarizing treatment of the Flatiron produces effects of strangeness and wonder. The peculiar commingling of these spatial, temporal, and aesthetic tensions is what prompts Woods to describe the photograph as both icon and after-image—a lingering visual sensation that is at once spectacle and art.[100]

Stieglitz's own account of the genesis of the photograph complements such a reading. Particularly interesting are his comments on the emotions aroused by the Flatiron as well as his view on what the building symbolizes:

One day there was a great snowstorm. The Flat-Iron Building had just been erected on 23rd street, at the junction of Fifth Avenue and Broadway. I stood spellbound as I saw that building in the storm. I had watched the building in the course of its erection, but somehow it had never occurred to me to photograph it in the stages of its evolution. But that particular snowy day, with the trees of Madison Square all covered with snow, fresh snow, I suddenly saw the Flatiron Building as I had never seen it before. It looked, from where I stood, as if it were moving toward me like the bow of a monster ocean steamer, a picture of the new America that was still in the making....

And when I saw the Flatiron again after many years of having seen other tall buildings in New York City suddenly shooting into the sky, the Woolworth Building and then still others, the Flatiron Building did seem rather ugly and unattractive to me. There was a certain gloom about it. It no longer seemed handsome to me; it no longer represented the coming age. It did not tempt me to photograph it.... But the feeling, the passion I experienced at that earlier time for the Flatiron still exists in me. I can feel the glory of those many hours and those many days when I stood there on Fifth Avenue lost in wonder, looking at the Flat-Iron Building.[101]

Significantly, Stieglitz confesses to developing an interest in the Flatiron only after its completion and only when the building is made newly strange by the transformative effects of a snowstorm. His interest in the skyscraper does not stem from the architectural accomplishment, or even the spectacle of construction. Rather, his interest derives from the building's aesthetic possibilities, from its power to capture the visual imagination, to leave him lost in awe and wonder. His description of the Flatiron as a "monster ocean steamer" cutting through the city not only ascribes motion to the static structure, suggesting a certain anxiety about its looming presence, but also links the skyscraper to another oversized icon of modernity, much as we saw with the Singer Tower and the *Titanic* in the case of Willa Cather's short story. And it is precisely as a symbol of an emerging modern culture of "time and space"[102]—a new America still in the making—that Stieglitz sees and presents this early New York skyscraper.

Given Stieglitz's initial enthusiasm for the Flatiron, it is worth noting that his enchantment with the building eventually fades. As his comments reveal, the Flatiron's ability to fire his imagination is directly connected to the way its height and verticality represent the "coming age." This symbolic power, however, is eroded by the rapid construction of successively taller skyscrapers throughout the city, such as the soaring neo-Gothic tower of the Woolworth Building, completed in 1913. In just over a decade, the Flatiron changes in Stieglitz's mind from a hypervisible symbol of New York's burgeoning future into an overshadowed monument to the city's past. And with this transformation, the triangular novelty of the Flatiron ceases to be an energizing, mesmerizing sight, with the result that Stieglitz no longer feels compelled to photograph it, even though the memory of his early flirtations with the building still stirs emotions. Stieglitz's changing response to the Flatiron also highlights a broader urban phenomenon that architects and city planners already understood and exploited to full effect by this time—namely, the extent to which the ephemeral cultural significance of skyscrapers is tied into competitive questions of size.

Although Stieglitz's passion for the Flatiron fades, his photographic interest in New York's vertical architecture does not. Rather, his interest moves on to other, newer, vertical scenes, constantly changing and evolving alongside the urban landscape he photographs. Indeed, the theme of change—in both subject matter and visual perspective—proves to be a dominant concern in Stieglitz's work well into the 1930s, when the proliferation of slender, setback skyscrapers led to visual affirmations of their crisp, clean lines and ultrabalanced geometry in photographs like *Looking Northwest from the Shelton* (1932) and *New York from the Shelton* (1935). And while the guarded urban optimism discernible in Stieglitz's early Flatiron images comes and goes in his subsequent cityscape photography, his ambivalence toward the vertical city remains a constant—albeit frequently subtle—feature throughout.

In *Old and New New York* (1910), for example, Stieglitz contrasts the industrial, skeletal appearance of a new skyscraper under construction with the nostalgic low-rise charm of traditional nineteenth-century brownstones, stressing the temporal disjunction created by the coexistence of the two types of building, each of which embodies a different historical moment in the life of the city. Here again, the skyscraper is relegated to a hovering, otherworldly apparition haunting the background of the photograph. The foreground contains an uneven row of brownstones lining a street alive with people and traffic. In the very front, a lone male figure in a hat—possibly the artist Max Weber[103]—stares across the street at one of the old buildings. Nobody is looking directly at the skyscraper. And yet this architectural specter literally overhangs the scene, its incompleteness suggesting further upward growth and the city's shift toward an increasingly vertical orientation.

Another of Stieglitz's photographs from the same year, *City of Ambition* (1910), offers a broader cityscape view (figure 17). Taken from a pier jutting out into the East River, it presents the skyline of Lower Manhattan as a barricade of modern architecture dominated by the dark silhouettes of vertical towers. Rising highest of all is the Singer

FIGURE 17. *Alfred Stieglitz,* City of Ambition, *1910. (Courtesy Georgia O'Keeffe Museum/Artists Rights Society, New York)*

Tower, its distinctive lantern-top profile proudly capped by a soaring flag. The cityscape is framed by a cloudy sky at the top and the bright, shimmering surface of the water at the bottom, both of which contrast against the dark, dull mass of industrial and corporate buildings. In this arrested vision of New York, where all signs of life and movement are dehumanized, the modern metropolis emerges as both an aesthetic object and an alienating presence. Like James Weldon Johnson's sepulchral city or Henry Adams's exploding urban dynamo, Stieglitz's city of ambition is beautiful yet strange.

Mary Woods suggests that it is the nature of the photographic after-image to weave "time and change back into the two-dimensional spaces" of the medium.[104] This is certainly what Stieglitz seeks to achieve in his skyscraper photography, which places particular stress on the temporality and transience of the city. It is also what distinguishes his work, especially in the early years of the twentieth century, from New York's overflow of commercial skyscraper imagery. For these reasons, Stieglitz's photography marks a major artistic development, and one that has produced some of the most memorable images of the vertical city.

The influence of these images on other artists is another of Stieglitz's lasting contributions to urban visual culture. It is an influence discernible not just in the Flatiron frenzy of close associates, such as Coburn and Steichen, but also in the work of generations of later artists ranging—in the medium of photography—from the skyscraper imagery of Berenice Abbott and Margaret Bourke-White in the 1930s to the vertical mania of Horst Hamann and the fuzzy, ghostly architectural images of Hiroshi Sugimoto in the 1990s.

Stieglitz's influence can even be traced as far as Michael Wesely's *Open Shutter* project, which takes the engagement with time and change evident in Stieglitz's New York cityscapes to new technical and conceptual extremes. A German artist best known for making photographs of urban construction sites with exceptionally long exposures (some as long as three years), Wesely was invited to record the rebuilding of New York's Museum of Modern Art between 2001 and 2004 (figure 18). Sarah Hermandson Meister, the museum's associate curator in photography, explains the resulting work:

> In the Spring of 2000, The Museum of Modern Art invited Wesely to respond to Yoshio Taniguchi's design for its renovation and expansion, taking advantage of this unique opportunity to capture this turning point in the Museum's history. For nearly three years.... Wesely's cameras were trained on the realization of Taniguchi's design, recording the emergence of a new museum within its immediate urban environment.
>
> It takes patience and close attention to read Wesely's long exposures, and that is part of their meaning. In midtown New York, tourists and taxis are a constant presence, yet their movements were too

fleeting to be recorded.... The surrounding buildings appear as solid forms, but only because the face they presented daily to the cameras was unchanged. Most of the structures that were demolished or built during the exposure have a ghostlike presence, evoking simultaneously a vanishing and an emerging vista.[105]

FIGURE 18. *Michael Wesely, 9.8.2001–2.5.2003* The Museum of Modern Art, New York. (*Courtesy Michael Wesely/Artists Rights Society, New York*)

Like Stieglitz in his treatment of the rising vertical city, Wesely is concerned in his long-exposure museum photographs not just with recording the emergence of new urban architecture but also, as Meister notes, with registering "the structure and fabric of urban change."[106] Wesely's technique for creating these long exposures, however, enables him to capture both the passage of time and processes of change in ways that were not available to Stieglitz. The result is the ultimate series of New York after-images: still photographs of an ever-changing cityscape in which time is layered, allowing myriad visual impressions from countless moments to coexist in a single representational space. It is therefore interesting that the tensions animating Stieglitz's work persist in Wesely's *Open Shutter* series, where the city remains caught in an even more accentuated and indeterminate way between motion and stasis, presence and absence, old and new.

Revisioning the Skyscraper

Following Stieglitz, Alvin Langdon Coburn and Edward Steichen produce Flatiron photographs that refine but also extend Stieglitz's urban vision. In both Coburn's *Flatiron-Evening* (1905) and Steichen's *Flat Iron Building* (1912), the vertical form of the skyscraper continues to be distanced and defamiliarized, looming in the background like some spectral apparition. Further paralleling Stieglitz, Coburn and Steichen shoot the Flatiron from Madison Square, using trees and branches in a similar way to foreground nature and place the building and the park into dialogue. An important difference, however, is that Coburn and Steichen do not crop the city from their photographs, but instead widen their scope to include adjacent buildings, traffic, crowds, streets, and lampposts. Another difference is that the photographs are taken in the early evening when the streetlights first begin to glow, adding further contrast to the darkening scene. Although still presented as wondrous and strange, the Flatiron is far more integrated into the everyday life of the city in the work of Coburn and Steichen.

The ambivalence underscoring these crepuscular Flatiron scenes, where the skyscraper is a source of both inspiration and anxiety, leads to a far more conflicted vision of vertical New York in Coburn's

The House of a Thousand Windows (1912). Taken as part of a series of photographs depicting high-rise office buildings, *The House of a Thousand Windows* shows Liberty Tower from the top of the nearby and even taller Singer Tower (figure 19). By looking down on the skyscraper from above instead of looking up at it from the ground, Coburn does more than simply shift the visual perspective dominating skyscraper photography at this time. He also records successive waves of modern high-rise construction and the unrelenting upward growth of the city, blending the architectural past, present, and future of New York in one disorienting photographic composition.

More significant, however, is Coburn's thematic focus on a rather unremarkable office building, which displays his intention, as Merrill Schleier asserts, "to interpret the skyscraper as a symbol of business and commerce."[107] Although hardly new or surprising, this equation of skyscrapers with capitalism acquires heightened significance given the treatment of the office building in the photograph. Coburn's elevated perspective gives the skyscraper the awkward appearance of being top-heavy and, in a further inversion of expectation, the base of the structure (and not the top) gets pushed into the distance, becoming difficult to discern in the shadows below. The overall effect is one of abstraction in which the building's myriad windows appear as a stack of uniform black squares offset against a harsh, rectilinear urban landscape. Coburn himself described the photograph as "a cubist fantasy,"[108] suggesting not only that *The House of a Thousand Windows* bears the influence of European modernism but also that it marks a conscious move toward abstract photography.

There is a certain irony, then, in the photograph's title, *The House of a Thousand Windows*, in the sense that this "house" is anything but homely. Rather, as Tamara Follini notes, the office building emerges as "an ominous dwelling" thrusting itself "menacingly towards the viewer."[109] This foreboding atmosphere is reinforced by the dark, blank window panes that obscure, rather than illuminate, any traces of human life. This is the realm of the architectural uncanny: a space of estrangement marked, in Nicholas Royle's theoretical elaboration of Freud, by "a sense of homeliness uprooted,"[110] and distinguished, in Anthony Vidler's account of "unhomely houses," by "the disturbing unfamiliarity of the evidently familiar."[111] Coburn's presentation of the mundane, functional office tower as a site of vertigo, spatial incarceration, and relentless conformity serves to critique both

FIGURE 19. *Alvin Langdon Coburn, The House of a Thousand Windows, 1912.*
(Courtesy International Museum of Photography at George Eastman House)

the reifying influence of modern business on architectural design
and the growing insignificance of humanity within the urban and
corporate systems.

Such a reading of *The House of a Thousand Windows* appears to
run counter to an account of the image made by Coburn at an exhibition of his work at London's Goupil Gallery in 1913. Commenting

on a group of New York photographs, which also included images of the Woolworth and Municipal Buildings and aerial views of Madison Square and Trinity Church, Coburn expressed his enthusiasm for skyscraper photography: "These five pictures were made from the towers of New York's highest buildings. How romantic, how exhilarating it is in these altitudes, few of the denizens of the city realize, they crawl about in the abyss content upon their own small concerns, or perhaps they rise to the extent of pointing with pride to 'the tallest building in the world' the Singer."[112] There is an odd tension in this passage between Coburn's desire to communicate the vertiginous pleasures of the skyscraper and his apparent disdain for the oblivious masses subsisting at ground level. Looking beyond this uncomfortable insight into the artist's condescending attitude toward the everyday inhabitants of New York, it is interesting that Coburn describes his high-rise experiences as energizing encounters with the urban sublime. While such feelings of being enamored and awed are easier to discern in more celebratory skyscraper photographs like *The Woolworth Building* (1912), they nonetheless inform *The House of a Thousand Windows*, where the office tower is rendered in terms of a mesmerizing wonder of geometry despite—or perhaps because of—its deeply unhomely qualities. More than any other photograph from this period, *The House of a Thousand Windows* captures Coburn's enthusiasm for shooting the city from above, his efforts to develop a new urban aesthetic in response to the skyscraper form, and, most importantly, his concomitant anxiety over capitalism's dehumanizing effects on the urban environment.

As the work of artists like Stieglitz, Steichen, and Coburn illustrates, capturing and interpreting the vertical form of the skyscraper posed both technical and aesthetic challenges to early twentieth-century photography. One common solution to engaging the rise of vertical New York, most visible in the Flatiron series of the Stieglitz circle, was to shoot a specific tall building in isolation, singling it out from an increasingly crowded skyline for detailed, individual study. In this mode, the skyscraper is typically treated as emblematic of broader developments in architecture and society. Another approach to engaging the rise of vertical New York was to employ the panoramic perspective offered by the cityscape view, such as in Stieglitz's *City of Ambition*. In this mode, which effectively replicates the distancing, estranging effects of the aerial view from a horizontal rather than a vertical orientation, the skyscraper does not emerge in isolation but, instead, figures as an integral part of the urban landscape and the wider spectacle of the modern city.

Cinema and the Vertical City

Many of the visual strategies employed in early skyscraper photography recur in early film as well. Such crossover is hardly surprising given that quite a few early twentieth-century photographers were also experimenting with film, and that the medium of film itself developed out of the technology of still photography. Indeed, as Nancy Mowll Mathews compellingly demonstrates in *Moving Pictures*,[113] film was initially treated by both practitioners and the public alike more as an extension of photography than as an autonomous art form. Like photography, moreover, film quickly rose to the challenge of shooting the vertical city, and skyscraper films—particularly those produced for mass consumption in peep-show machines like Edison's Kinetoscope—became an early cinematic genre and a mainstay of American commercial filmmaking beginning in the late 1890s.

In turn-of-the-century New York, these peep-show screenings, which often consisted of short fragments of urban footage, served a double function as both entertainment for the masses and an indoctrination into a shared perception of the modern city: a dynamic image of New York as a futuristic site of urban change and wonder. For a brief period and a small amount of money, New Yorkers and visitors alike could not only experience the strange flickerings of this new, animated medium but in the process visually consume the city as never seen before. It is therefore significant that early New York cinema frequently showcased the city's vertical architecture, offering documentary-style shorts ("actuality" films) that ranged from gliding panoramas of the skyline filmed from boats skirting the Manhattan shoreline to vertiginous scenes of high-rise construction in progress, to candid shots of everyday life in and around skyscrapers, such as the American Mutoscope and Biograph Company's highly popular two-minute short *At the Foot of the Flatiron* (1903), which captures the comic effects of the building's notorious wind tunnel on passersby. By being associated with the vertical city in this way, film helped to popularize skyscrapers in the public mind at a crucial early stage in their development. Similarly, as a recurring subject of early cinema, skyscrapers helped in turn to establish film as an integral part of modern urban culture. From the very beginning, film delivered what people wanted to see, which included feeding a growing public appetite—in large part created by the budding film industry itself—for urban spectaculars centered on the theme of verticality. Film seemed like the perfect new medium to capture the new modern world, including the urban phenomenon of the skyscraper. After all, film and skyscrapers emerged at almost exactly the same time in the late nineteenth century, and both marked significant innovations in engineering and technology. It seemed somehow appropriate, then, for the moving images of the nascent cinema to capture the speed, scale, and scope of change wrought to the city by the accelerated rise of the skyscraper.

What perhaps most distinguishes New York films of this era is an almost uniform attempt to portray the city in realistic terms, instinctively seeking to obscure or at least downplay film's inherent mediation of its subject. Well into the 1910s, the cinematic city was typically treated by filmmakers—and received by the public—as a mirror to the real city. For example, in *Skyscrapers of New York City, from the North River*,[114] a three-minute actuality produced by the Edison Company in 1903, the camera slowly tracks the skyline of Lower Manhattan from a cruising riverboat (figure 20). The entire film consists of detached "factual" imagery, a sort of filmic urban reportage, and displays little to no aesthetic or narrative consideration. Even so, the result is richly suggestive, as Murray Pomerance comments in his reading of the film:

> As we pass wharf after wharf, seeing steamers and ferries and tugs in their moorings, a long array of striking buildings graces the skyline, each a kind of silent cache holding the lives, stories, and fates of thousands of New Yorkers. While in the foreground the waterfront is busy with smoking ships, railway cars drawn up at piers, and some pedestrians, the buildings in their majestic silence and stolidity constitute together an elaborate wall of potentiality.[115]

In addition to offering an evocative prose counterpoint to the film's urban panorama, Pomerance's description identifies several noteworthy features. Most significant is that the film treats its subject from a distance, superficially recording the appearance of New York without actually engaging the city or penetrating its facade. The drama of the film, therefore, does not derive from any story it tells

FIGURE 20. *Frame enlargements,* Skyscrapers of New York City, from the North River, *1903. (Courtesy Library of Congress, Motion Picture, Broadcasting and Recorded Sound Division)*

but rather from its oblique, incidental gesturing at the myriad untold stories embedded within the skyline's "wall of potentiality." So although the modern skyline figures as a source of visual fascination, it is left tantalizingly uninterpreted for the viewer. In this respect, *Skyscrapers of New York City, from the North River* is representative of the cinematic treatment of the vertical city in the period leading up to the feature-length theatrical releases of the 1910s and 1920s.

Following the rise of narrative cinema and the relocation of the American film industry to Hollywood in the 1910s, the narrative potential of New York—so vividly suggested by the modern skyline—starts to become realized in films like *Traffic in Souls* (1913), *The Shock Punch* (1925), *New York* (1927), and *Speedy* (1928), leading to the creation of a mythic, cinematic version of the city that continues even today, through the films of Woody Allen, Spike Lee, and Martin Scorsese, to dominate the popular perception of New York worldwide. So powerful and widespread is this cinematic city that Jean Baudrillard, writing in the 1980s about the artificial nature of urban America, suggests that "to grasp its secret you should not begin with the city and move inwards to the screen; you should begin with the screen and move outwards to the city."[116] Beyond articulating his broader theory of hyperreality, in which the real has been replaced by a mass-mediated simulation that conceals its disappearance, Baudrillard's comment identifies the enormously influential role that film has played in shaping, sustaining, and disseminating the dominant, globalized image of New York. This is why Baudrillard and others controversially maintain that the true identity of the city is to be found on-screen, not on the streets. Such a displacement of the real metropolis by its hyperreal mediation has become a commonplace feature of postmodern culture, but the process began over a full century earlier with the rudimentary screen sensations of New York's first nickelodeon parlors.

An influential film that builds on the skyscraper actualities and high-rise melodramas of the silent era is *Manhatta* (1921), a short experimental reel collaboratively made by painter-photographer Charles Sheeler and photographer Paul Strand, who both had close ties to Stieglitz. *Manhatta* marks a turning point in American filmmaking not only because it bridges the gap between cinema and modernist art but also because, as Juan Suárez argues in *Pop Modernism*, it helped to inaugurate "the American experimental film tradition as well as one of its most prolific and international genres, the 'city film' or 'city symphony.'"[117] While some film historians would contest the notion that the genre of the symphonic city film originated in the United States before spreading to Europe (where it is best exemplified by Walter Ruttmann's 1927 masterpiece *Berlin: The Symphony of the Great City*), most would concede that *Manhatta* does at least represent one of the first avant-garde films made in America and, for this reason alone, stands out among the glut of New York films produced in the 1920s.

Manhatta derives inspiration and structure from Walt Whitman's *Leaves of Grass* (1855), a collection of fervently sensual poems thematically and symbolically grounded in the lived experience of New York. Just as Whitman's work prefigures American literary modernism, so too does his mid-nineteenth-century vision of the city seem to anticipate the growth and development of the modern metropolis. Sheeler and Strand begin each segment of *Manhatta* with an urban epigraph from *Leaves of Grass*, effectively inviting viewers to interpret the film's vision of the city through the lens of Whitman. By creating this intertextual dialogue, Sheeler and Strand do more than imply that the writer's earlier insights into New York continue to hold true in the twentieth century. They also align themselves with a poet acclaimed for radically breaking with convention and boldly reinventing an art form. Accordingly, the use of Whitman's poetry as both a framing and structuring device tacitly signals the filmmakers' avant-garde intentions. It also suggests that, on some level, the film can be understood as a modernist screen adaptation of Whitman's literary New York—a "de(re)composition," to use Kamilla Elliott's concept of adaptation, in which literature and film "decompose, merge, and form a new composition."[118]

Thus haunted by Whitman's "proud and passionate city" of "tall facades of marble and iron,"[119] *Manhatta* chronicles a working day in the life of New York. The film opens with a series of approach shots of Lower Manhattan from the Staten Island ferry taken in the early morning, and it ends with a hovering aerial view of the bay from the top of a skyscraper at sunset. In between, the film roams through Lower Manhattan, focusing on the corporate and business districts and their dense agglomeration of tall buildings. Throughout, Sheeler and Strand strive not just to capture the appearance of New York's vertical architecture but in the process to incorporate the unique visual perspectives on the city offered by that architecture. To this end, most of the shots are taken from elevated positions, either looking out across the horizon toward other skyscrapers or looking down from unusual (and often awkward) angles at the streets, people, and traffic below. The main effect is to stress the disconnection in scale between humanity and the new urban environment. Another effect is to stress the dominance of the skyscraper in everyday life in New York, from its prominence in the skyline to its proliferation throughout the city, to its multiple functions as a site of commerce, work, domesticity, and leisure.

Seeking to reveal what they saw as the inherently photographic nature of the modern city, Sheeler and Strand minimize camera movement throughout *Manhatta* and employ many meticulously composed shots that emphasize stillness and abstraction in ways that are evocative of their own high-rise photography. Even in the few scenes featuring human figures, movement appears reluctant, involuntary, or automated. For example, there is a short scene showing the disgorging of morning commuters at the ferry port in Lower Manhattan. Looking down over the constricted gangway, the camera shows passengers disembarking as one faceless, almost lifeless mob, bringing to mind T. S. Eliot's famous description of London commuters in *The Waste Land* (1922) as a spectacle of the undead: "A crowd flowed over London Bridge, so many / I had not thought death had undone so many."[120] Later, the film offers a short montage of bird's-eye views of city streets in which the anonymous, antlike pedestrians are brutally dwarfed by the architectural gigantism of the modern city. In these and other similar moments, *Manhatta* emphasizes "abstract patterns and collapsed perspectives" that, as Suárez argues, stand in opposition to the "Whitmanesque romanticism" framing the film.[121]

The resulting vision of vertical New York is one that fluctuates ambiguously between celebration and critique and that ultimately remains more concerned with using film to bring the multiple, subjective perspectives of pictorial modernism to bear on the skyscraper city than in articulating the place of the individual within the vast urban machine. Even so, *Manhatta* does succeed in visually communicating something of the automatism of modern city life, and, in so doing, connects American cinema to a larger, transatlantic current in visual art—ranging from the cubism of Georges Braque and Pablo Picasso to the surrealism of Max Ernst and René Magritte—seeking to understand and express what it means to be modern.

The City from Greenwich Village

From Stieglitz's spectral skyscrapers and Sheeler and Strand's sprawling urban machine to the jumbled cubes of John Marin's Manhattan watercolors or the threatening black blocks of Georgia O'Keeffe's high-rise vistas, the representation of vertical New York in American modernist art is often characterized by abstraction and, to a certain degree, detachment. By contrast, New York's Ashcan School of realist painters developed a more socially engaged approach to the same subject, and one that foregrounds, rather than displaces, the human element. Most active in the city between 1908 and 1914, but not directly implicated in the modernist movement, the Ashcan artists, who included Robert Henri, George Bellows, and John Sloan, rejected the genteel impressionistic style popular at the turn of the twentieth century in favor of a hard-edged, rapid-fire "new realism" focused on urban subject matters and, in particular, the daily lives of New York's working class and poor.

While the majority of the Ashcan artists' paintings portray human figures engaged in mundane, everyday activities, such as Bellows's compassionate slum depiction *Cliff Dwellers* (1913) or Sloan's intimate rooftop scene *Sunday, Women Drying Their Hair* (1912), a number of their works contain broader, more panoramic views of New York that deliberately engage the built environment of the city and its vertical architecture. Among these is Sloan's *The City from Greenwich Village* (1922), a nostalgic nighttime view of the city as seen from the artist's Washington Place studio overlooking Sixth Avenue (figure 21). The center foreground is dominated by the snaking track of the elevated railway and the thin, elongated body of an approaching train. On the street below, the smudgy forms of a few lone pedestrians and vehicles are visible. Most of the painting shows huddled rows of rather unremarkable low-rise residential and mixed-use buildings receding into the distance. In the right foreground the sharp wedge of a tall, triangular loft building—reminiscent of the Flatiron—protrudes severely toward the viewer. In the left foreground an advertising billboard, illuminated by the glow of the street lamps, displays the lone word "moonshine," serving not just as a reference to the commercialization of urban space but also as a subtle comment on the aesthetic effects of the city's electric lighting. Hovering in the left background and radiating a bright golden glow, the skyline of Lower Manhattan, crowned by the dramatic protuberance of the Woolworth Building, rises sharply above the cozy Greenwich Village scene.

In his reading of this painting, Thomas Bender connects its vision of Lower Manhattan to the "City of Ambition" depicted in Stieglitz's photographic skylines, but stresses that, in Sloan's case, "the unmistakable location of the creator of the image is that of a local, neighborhood observer," so that "we are drawn to Sixth Avenue at West Third Street in Greenwich Village, not to Wall Street in the distance."[122] This

FIGURE 21. *John Sloan,* The City from Greenwich Village, *1922. (Courtesy National Gallery of Art, Washington, DC)*

idea is articulated in the painting's title, *The City from Greenwich Village*, which not only places emphasis on the location from which the city is seen but also establishes a spatial and thematic divide between downtown and the Village. Part of what this reveals is the extent to which Ashcan artists like Sloan remained rooted in the working-class neighborhoods and immigrant communities of New York, with the result that their representations of the modern skyline—as an architectural expression of wealth and influence—are typically rendered from outsider perspectives and removed locations.

Accordingly, *The City from Greenwich Village* is more than what Bender describes as a "warm, soft, and slightly nostalgic" mood piece celebrating "the romance of the modern city"[123]—although it is still that. The painting is also a comment on the place of the skyscraper district of Lower Manhattan within New York's wider urban landscape. Seen here from across the tenement rooftops of Greenwich Village, the vertical city is not only distanced but also disconnected from the main space of the painting, as if to suggest that this radiant apparition, like the new social and economic opportunities it signals, lies beyond the reach of the city's ordinary inhabitants. The one point of connection between the painting's two disparate worlds resides in the meandering form of the elevated train which, as an icon of mass transit, implies free, rapid movement across the different spaces of the city. Such a reading of the train is tenuous, however, since the elevated tracks disappear from view well before they reach downtown. It would be just as easy to interpret the painting's train as circumventing the financial district as it would be to see it as a conduit into that exclusive space of capital and power.

Despite these darker undercurrents, however, *The City from Greenwich Village* conveys an overall feeling of optimism about New York and, in particular, the anachronistic charm of close-knit neighborhoods like the Village. Even the estranging qualities of the distant skyscrapers are mitigated by the warm, golden glow emanating from the beacon-like cluster. Sloan's New York may be divided but, partly due to its aesthetic appeal, it is also a place of possibility.

Metrotopia

The theme of New York as a place of possibility is, of course, a common one in the city's cultural production during the late nineteenth and early twentieth centuries, much as it continues to be today. While some artists like John Sloan remain cautiously optimistic about what those possibilities are, others such as Hugh Ferriss take that optimism to extremes and see in the emerging skyscraper city the potential for a new metropolitan utopia. Trained as an architect and specializing in architectural rendering, Ferriss was instrumental following the 1916 zoning ordinance in creating the ordered, geometric look of the setback style of skyscraper, which found its zenith in the Empire State Building. The series of skyscraper drawings he produced in 1922 in collaboration with architect Harvey Wiley Corbett provided a ready-made design solution to the new zoning restrictions that other architects could and did adapt. The drawings also formed the basis of a more substantial design study, published in 1929 under the title *The Metropolis of Tomorrow*, in which Ferriss set out his vision for the future of the skyscraper city.[124]

The Metropolis of Tomorrow is a monumental work of utopian fantasy that combines copious illustrations of imagined skyscrapers and sprawling high-rise developments with a running commentary on the requirements for creating the ideal city that occasionally spills over into manifesto, poetry, and philosophy. The result is both a playful dreamscape of vertical architecture and a serious critical intervention in the field of urban planning and design. For Ferriss, who believed not only in the need for rationality and order to be imposed on the modern city but also in the importance of creating awe-inspiring architecture with the power to lift the human spirit, the modern skyscraper appeared to offer the perfect solution. Hence the double inflection of the skyscraper in Ferriss's work as a symbol of both rationality and transcendence, as Merrill Schleier argues:

> Ferriss's utterly romantic city views were meant to convince the spectator to accept both the new urban sphere and a new cosmological order. Inherent in his metropolis of the future is the simultaneous belief in the superiority of controlled technology and the triumph of a new spirituality. At the same time, Ferriss developed a highly rational approach to urban planning.... Ferriss's imaginative visualizations were not only conceived as a pragmatic solution to zoning restrictions, but as a universal panacea for urban problems in general.... Ferriss believed that his images would encourage thoughtful city planning. Most urban problems could be corrected if architecture would only adopt his orderly approach.[125]

Ferriss's faith in the skyscraper's potential to improve the quality of life in cities, combined with his view that aggressively ordered planning held the key to unlocking a utopian urban future, parallels the thinking of some other prominent architects and planners of the 1920s, including the Swiss-born guru of architectural modernism Le Corbusier, whose own vision of the ideal skyscraper city, elaborated in his 1925 plan for a contemporary city for three million inhabitants, bears a striking resemblance to Ferriss's high-rise metrotopia (figure 22).

It is not surprising that similarities exist between the imagined cities of Ferriss and Le Corbusier. Not only did both architects advocate rationality and order in urban planning, they were also directly inspired by their personal experiences of the New York skyline and the city's existing skyscrapers. In the case of Le Corbusier, as Mardges Bacon points out, the carefully spaced-out high-rise blocks envisioned in his Contemporary City reflect an "admiration for the aesthetic of the isolated business tower, particularly the Woolworth Building."[126] Le Corbusier himself makes the link explicit in his 1926 *Almanach d'architecture moderne*, in which he places an iconic pho-

FIGURE 22. *Le Corbusier,* Plan Voisin for Paris, *1925. (Courtesy Fondation Le Corbusier c/o Pictoright Amsterdam)*

tograph of the Woolworth Building alongside two other images of
skylines, one real and one imagined. The first is an aerial photograph of Lower Manhattan's dense cluster of vertical architecture
dating from the early 1920s and bearing the inscription "The skyscraper foments disorder." The second is a drawing from his Contemporary City showing symmetrically spaced-out rows of identical
towers, bearing the inscription "The skyscraper must bring order."
Le Corbusier's point is that, while the Woolworth Building can be
celebrated as a small step toward achieving the rational city advocated in his work, it ultimately fails because of its haphazard placement within the crowded and disorderly layout of Lower Manhattan.

The problem with vertical New York, in other words, is that it does
not take the rationalizing project inherent in the construction of skyscrapers far enough. Or so Le Corbusier maintains. As he writes in
his 1937 American travelogue, *When the Cathedrals Were White*:

> The skyscraper is not a plume rising from the face of the city. It has
> been made that, and wrongly. The plume was a poison to the city.
> The skyscraper is an instrument. A magnificent instrument for the
> concentration of population, for getting rid of land congestion, for
> classification, for internal efficiency. A prodigious means of im-
> proving the conditions of work, a creator of economies and, through
> that, a dispenser of wealth. But the skyscraper plume, multiplied
> over the area of Manhattan, has disregarded experience. The New
> York skyscrapers are out of line with the rational skyscraper.[127]

As this ode to efficiency and organization begins to articulate, Le
Corbusier sees in the New York skyline both the obstacle and the solution to realizing the ideal city. The solution lies in perfecting the
skyscraper-machine and strategically planning its spatial deploy-
ment throughout the city. The obstacle lies in the existing disorder of
the built environment and the way New York's chaotic urban development squanders the skyscraper's ordering possibilities. This is why
Le Corbusier concludes that "the skyscrapers of New York are too
small and there are too many of them," but that "they are proof of the
new dimensions and the new tools; the proof that henceforth everything can be carried out on a new general plan, a symphonic plan—
extent and height."[128] This also explains why Le Corbusier describes
New York skyscrapers as being simultaneously "sublime, naïve, touching, idiotic."[129]

In *The Metropolis of Tomorrow*, Hugh Ferriss adopts almost the same position. Not only does Ferriss condemn the lack of "conscious design"[130] in the development of modern American cities, he also calls for a new order of skyscrapers capable of relieving congestion, easing traffic, facilitating commerce, and generally improving the social and mental lives of inhabitants by restoring reason and order to the spatial organization of the city. An important difference, however, is that Ferriss places far more stress in his urban prophecies on the sublimity of the modern skyscraper—on its capacity to inspire and perturb the imagination through its breathtaking appearance and monumental scale. As a consequence, there is a tension in Ferriss's drawings created on the one hand by his desire to promote a pragmatic approach to urban planning and design characterized by logic, clarity, and precision and on the other hand by his urge to elevate the skyscraper form into the boundless, inscrutable realm of the sublime. His drawings, therefore, are conceived to be not merely functional and informative but also elusive and evocative (figure 23).

FIGURE 23. *Hugh Ferriss, "Looking West from the Business Center," from* Metropolis of Tomorrow, *1929. (Courtesy Avery Architectural and Fine Arts Library, Columbia University)*

Ferriss divides *The Metropolis of Tomorrow* into three parts, each with its own thematic focus. In the first part, "Cities of Today," he engages existing skyscrapers, citing what he sees as notable examples of high-rise design that succeed in creating "lofty presences."[131] Among the buildings he praises are Chicago's neo-Gothic Tribune Tower (1922)—clearly influenced by Louis Sullivan's design for the Woolworth Building—and the New York setback giants, the Chanin (1929) and Chrysler (1930) Buildings, the latter of which was still under construction when Ferriss's book was published. Surveying his contemporary architectural scene, Ferriss suggests that these monumental buildings signal the emergence of a new "species of tower-building" rather "than an assortment of unrelated individual towers," and that "their community lies...in some similarity of proportion, or silhouette, or vertical movement, or organic structure."[132] For Ferriss, the emergence of this new generation of skyscraper is a welcome development, and he closes the book's opening part by expressing his hope that "these giant structures" will "before long be displayed in projects of civic, or even nation-wide, import."[133] Above all, the commentary and images in this part of the book are designed to establish the skyscraper as a positive force in the city and, in the process, to generate enthusiasm for its rapidly growing presence.

In the second part of the book, "Projected Trends," Ferriss steps back from consideration of individual buildings to address broader developments in urban planning and design. At the same time, he also begins to blend the real and the imaginary in his drawings, producing sprawling panoramas of vast high-rise complexes that extrapolate from existing urban conditions. For instance, responding to the outward growth of New York and inspired by a proposal by architect Raymond Hood to incorporate apartments and offices into the framework of a suspension bridge, Ferriss includes a speculative drawing of a hybrid skyscraper-bridge that looks strangely like a cross between the Chicago Tribune Tower (designed by Hood) and the Manhattan Bridge, which was completed in 1909. Mostly, however, Ferriss uses this part of the book to comment on the widespread trend in American cities toward centralization that has resulted "in the tendency to build higher and higher structures."[134] Exploring ways of coping with this trend in future urban development, Ferriss promotes the setback skyscraper as a practical design solution, mainly because the "stepping back" of buildings allows architects to "modify and vary [their] rising mass" thereby allowing more air and light to reach occupants.[135]

Given Ferriss's early involvement in the evolution of the setback style, as well as his rave reviews of various existing setback skyscrapers in the opening part of *The Metropolis of Tomorrow*, this advocacy comes as no surprise. More interesting is that, in making his case for the setback skyscraper, Ferriss rejects the idea of a decentralized city as unrealistic and counter-productive, describing the "dispersal of large centers of population" as "a mere dream."[136] Instead, adhering to the modernist architectural mindset, Ferriss maintains that the challenges of congestion and density posed by centralization can be overcome most effectively by improving the design of buildings and reordering the layout of cities.

What such a redesigned and reordered city might look like is the subject of the book's final part, "An Imaginary Metropolis," in which Ferriss presents his vision of urban utopia. As Carol Willis notes, his city of the imagination not only reworks "the precedents and projections described in the first chapters" but also introduces order and harmony to the "unchecked constructive energy and intense concentrations of buildings depicted in previous sections."[137] Here, the skyline is punctuated by evenly spaced pyramidal towers, each at least one thousand feet in height and all sharing the same sculptured setback look. These vertical giants are interconnected by a complex geometric network of superhighways and interspersed with wide expanses of identical low-rise buildings featuring abundant rooftop gardens. At the center of the city lies a circular park overlooked by three immense high-rise structures. The structures serve as "primary centers"[138]—or minicities[139]—for the city's three main districts: the Business, Science, and Art Zones.

The novelty of Ferriss's plan lies partly in the way he reorganizes the city into three distinct but interconnected districts, each with its own separate identity and function, and partly in the way he radically magnifies the scale of tall buildings while simultaneously spacing them further apart. In his thinking, this results in both practical and aesthetic improvements over existing cities:

> The cities with which we were previously familiar may, in a given area, compare as to total cubic content with the city now below us. In other words, a great number of typical, fairly large skyscrapers, set in very close juxtaposition, may have the same total cube, and house the same population as a few tremendous towers set a wide intervals—with very low buildings in the intervening areas.

In the former cases, however, the close juxtaposition of formidable masses—the monotonous repetition of similar bulks for block after city block—the close store of equally high facades across narrow streets,—all combine to shut the human being away from air, light, and every pleasing prospect. In the city now below us— the same cubic content is so disposed, and high masses so dispersed, that a more human environment seems possible.[140]

Ferriss's concern about rehumanizing the modern city is interesting given that his plan to restore light, air, and beauty to urban residents also involves imposing various new forms of control over them, which include overdetermining how they use and move through the different spaces of the city. Further, as Kevin McNamara points out, "space for unproductive public activity is neglected."[141] There is, for instance, no Leisure Zone to complement or offset the productive space of the Business, Science, and Art Zones. Picking up on this aspect of Ferriss's vision, Willis also calls attention to the way the Imaginary Metropolis is "surprisingly silent and static,"[142] almost devoid of people, traffic, and other signs of human life. This future city may be refreshingly humanizing in some respects, but in its emptiness, stasis, and spatial controls, it is also profoundly dehumanizing.

The Empty City

To address the broader cultural implications of Ferriss's empty city, it is necessary to revisit the field of cinema. The reason is that, in a strange but fascinating twist, images of empty or deserted cityscapes were beginning to emerge as a recurring motif of the urban uncanny in films of the 1920s. Most notably, Fritz Lang's 1927 sci-fi sensation *Metropolis* contains a number of slow, panning shots of a dehumanized, mechanical city similarly devoid of motion and life. In this dystopian, futuristic cityscape, partly conceived as a warning against the geometric tyranny of modernist urban design, the human population is reduced to invisibility and insignificance. Lang's vision of a monstrous metropolis of the future was inspired, or so the publicity myth goes, by his first encounter in 1924 with the skyscraping architecture of Manhattan: "I saw a street, lit as if in full daylight by neon lights and topping them, oversized luminous, advertising moving

turning flashing on and off, spiralling…something which was completely new and near fairy-tale like for a European in those days, and
this impression gave me the first thought of an idea for a town of the
future."[143] It is interesting that, in his fantastical cinematic reimagin-
ing of the skyscraper city, Lang relied on the distancing, depopulat-
ing perspective of the high-rise view to gain a visual purchase on the
modern metropolis, since the same observational technique was also
being used by many documentary and avant-garde filmmakers of
the 1920s concerned with recording the sprawl and spectacle of vertical New York.

Among New York films produced in this period, Sheeler and
Strand's avant-garde screen experiment, *Manhatta*, stands out in this
respect. Although analyzed in some detail earlier in my discussion,
the film is worth citing again because, as it goes about chronicling a
day in the life of the vertical city, *Manhatta* repeatedly employs static
aerial views of deserted cityscapes in order to capture the photographic qualities Sheeler and Strand associated so strongly with the
architecture of the modern metropolis. Here, in what quickly becomes a repeated pattern in urban cinema, the motif of the empty
city is used to immobilize the urban frenzy and scrutinize it in stasis.

As such aesthetic indulgences suggest, images of empty city space
have long been a source of visual fascination in films concerned with
interpreting the unhomeliness of the city.[144] From *Manhatta* to *Metropolis* and beyond, these images have also had a profound and
lasting impact on the urban imaginary. In early twenty-first-century
cinema, for instance, they memorably resurface in the empty Times
Square of *Vanilla Sky* (dir. Cameron Crower, 2001), the frozen Manhattan skyline of *The Day after Tomorrow* (dir. Roland Emmerich,
2004), and the postapocalyptic Gotham of *I Am Legend* (dir. Francis
Lawrence, 2007). In each case, images of empty city space are used to
disrupt a deeply familiar vision of the city and, in the process, to pre-
pare the viewer for the unhinged nature of reality contained within
the world of the film.

These representational strategies are what link the empty cities of
modern cinema to the deserted vistas of Ferriss's drawings, where
images of urban emptiness are similarly used to produce a defamiliarizing, estranging effect. What is more, Ferriss's preference for rendering
the city from high-rise and aerial perspectives further contributes to
the sense of estrangement haunting his drawings by keeping the viewer
distanced and removed. Unfolding far below, Ferriss's Imaginary

Metropolis is depicted from the same panoptic perspective described by Michel de Certeau in his commentary on the view from the Twin Towers—an immobilizing view in which the observer, now positioned as a kind of voyeur-god overlooking the silent, static city, experiences the illusion of knowledge, legibility, and power.[145]

It therefore makes sense that Ferriss would be drawn to the high-rise view, since the images in his book were intended not just to persuade readers of the value of his approach to design and planning but also to generate excitement for the possibility of their implementation. Ferriss's high-rise views have the potential to accomplish both aims by producing vast idealized cityscapes free from the messy realities of life at street level, while simultaneously activating the voyeuristic pleasure de Certeau associates with "seeing the whole" of the city[146]—even if such totalizing images are ephemeral and illusory.

The important difference between Ferriss's elevated views of urban emptiness and those of modern cinema is that Ferriss draws on the urban uncanny—on the familiar city made newly strange—not as an end in itself but as a way to evoke the sublime. So although his Imaginary Metropolis shares a certain aesthetic resonance with the empty cities of cinema—indeed, some of Ferriss's cityscapes look strangely like sketches of film stills from Lang's *Metropolis*[147]—Ferriss is using the defamiliarizing properties of the uncanny not as a strategy for critiquing the alienating effects of modern urbanism but rather as a way of disrupting established visions of the city and replacing them with an alternative that, through its wild extrapolations and aesthetic departures, is at once reassuringly familiar yet terrifyingly new.

The sad irony of Ferriss's Imaginary Metropolis, like that of modernist urban planning more generally, is that attempts to realize such utopian ambitions have proven largely disastrous, which is an outcome that cinema has long predicted and continues to anticipate and dramatize. One relevant example to cite is the widespread development of public housing projects throughout the United States from the 1940s to the late 1960s, in which the high-rise solution advocated by urbanists like Ferriss and Le Corbusier resulted not in liberation or rehumanization but instead in a host of new urban problems, inequalities, and exclusions. A well-documented case is Chicago's Cabrini-Green housing project, one of the most notorious high-rise ghettos in American urban history.[148]

Built between 1942 and 1962 and finally demolished in 2011, the Cabrini-Green housing project on the postindustrial North Side of

Chicago was a high-rise residential community of fifteen thousand residents at its peak in the 1980s. Despite the Chicago Housing Authority's initial intention to improve the lives of the city's poorest residents by building high-density public housing, Cabrini-Green quickly gained a reputation as a vertical ghetto beset by rampant gang violence, crippling poverty, and chronic neglect. So strong was the housing project's public image as a brutal urban nightmare that it was selected as the location for the horror film *Candyman* (dir. Bernard Rose, 1992), which tells the story of a white female graduate student who is supernaturally assaulted by a black male demon while doing ethnographic research in the projects, thus playing on suburban, middle-class fears about inner-city racial and sexual violence.

Now, in the early twenty-first century, the failures as well as the successes of the high-rise solution to urban development are more evident than ever. Although only indirectly, the fallout from Ferriss's vision is present, for example, in the social and economic deprivations of the Parisian banlieues and their architectures of exclusion, in the drug-ravaged wastelands of tower-block estates in Edinburgh and Glasgow, and even in the fortified, carceral urbanism of luxury skyscraper living in Brazilian cities like Rio de Janeiro and São Paulo (figure 24).[149] Such articulations of the high-rise as an instrument or container of inequality are, of

FIGURE 24. *Fortified luxury skyscraper living in São Paulo: Tuca Vieira,* Paraisópolis, *2005. (Courtesy of the artist)*

course, not the intended or direct product of modernist designs themselves. Rather, these extreme examples speak to the wider urban contexts and underlying structural conditions within which the modernist approach to urban planning and design has evolved over time, and from which many of the problems associated with high-rise living flow.

Despite this aspect of its legacy, the modernist vision of the ideal city—as formulated by architects like Ferriss and Le Corbusier—has had a profound and lasting impact on the urban imaginary, as Jane M. Jacobs, Stephen Cairns, and Ignaz Strebel have traced in their reassessment of the high-rise form.[150] Across the world, and especially in the megacities of Asia and the Global South, the skyscraper continues to be deployed as a perceived solution to the challenges of urban development, ranging from population growth and economic stimulation to programs of social integration and urban renewal. The question is why we continue to invest in both material and symbolic ways in the dream of high-rise living. Part of the answer, I suggest, lies precisely in the aesthetic-imaginative draw of the high-rise form, which thanks to the work of Ferriss and others is now inextricably embedded in the urban imaginary as a critical feature of any major metropolis.

New York Undead

Part I of this book began by touching on the events of 9/11 and reflecting on their material and symbolic effects on the New York skyline. Coming full circle, I want to end this "Skylines" part by returning to the specter of the Twin Towers to comment on the cultural afterlife of these iconic buildings in the era of globalization. Specifically, I want to address how, since 2001, the city has emerged as a notorious symbol of the links between globalization and violence. Building on the insights generated by the preceding discussion of vertical New York, my focus is on an urban landscape architecture project called Lifescape. Under construction since 2008, Lifescape is an ambitious, long-term plan to transform the Fresh Kills Landfill on Staten Island into a public park and recreation area. There are two reasons for my interest in a project to rehabilitate a garbage dump, and both are connected to a broader interest in the interplay between the material and symbolic spaces of the global city.

First, Lifescape marks a significant effort to reclaim and reimagine a derelict landscape that is connected in both material and symbolic ways to the lived space of the city. Second, following the events of 9/11, the wreckage from Ground Zero was transported to the Fresh Kills Landfill, which was specially reopened to accommodate the 1.2 million tons of material. As one commentator has noted, "Fresh Kills...is not just the place where, for more than 50 years, the rest of the city sent its potato peels, broken dishes and every kind of household trash. For several months after the terrorist attacks on the World Trade Center, the sad bits of busted buildings and broken lives were sifted on mound 1/9 of Fresh Kills, piece by shattered piece."[151] Crucially, the Lifescape project acknowledges the presence of these remains and envisions a commemoration of the Twin Towers and the recovery effort in the form of a giant earthwork monument. How this monument evokes the memory of the towers and how it connects the park's landscape back to New York's cityscape are significant concerns for the analysis that follows.

Through an analysis of Lifescape's transformative vision and, in particular, its plans for a 9/11 earthwork monument, I want to consider yet another way in which the Twin Towers will continue to haunt the contemporary imagination. My argument is that Lifescape works simultaneously to reveal and conceal the mutability of urban landscape, attesting not only to the extraordinary versatility of urban space but also to the imaginative ways in which—responding to an experience of collective trauma—such space can be recycled, renewed, and remade in the era of "21st-century green, global connectedness."[152]

In working in this versatile manner, the Fresh Kills Landfill relates in a number of interesting ways to New York as a global site. The most obvious connection is that, as the location of the World Trade Center Recovery Operation, Fresh Kills played a key role in the federal investigation of 9/11 and its efforts to understand how and why New York's symbolic center of transnational corporate capitalism succumbed to terrorist attacks. In the process, Fresh Kills also bore witness in a detailed and intimate way to the violence and horror involved in the destruction of the vertical architecture of globalization. Over a ten-month period, during which the landfill was designated a federal crime scene, the debris from Ground Zero was meticulously sifted and sorted in search of human remains, personal effects, and objects of everyday life. The resulting process of inspection and introspection—fueled in the national imagination by both the media and traveling exhibits such as the New York State Museum's WTC Recovery Exhibition—contributed to wider public efforts to work through the trauma of 9/11.

Fresh Kills is also tied to New York's status as a global city in another way entirely. In its function as a dumping ground for New York's household trash, Fresh Kills stood for over fifty years as "the largest symbol of American waste."[153] The overproduction of waste may not be one of the defining processes of globalization, but it is a direct consequence of the culture of runaway consumption that has increasingly come to dominate global (and globalizing) cities worldwide. Indeed, as Harold Crooks, Mike Davis, and others have shown,[154] the politics of waste—which have long gripped cities ranging from New York, London, and Tokyo to Lagos, Jakarta, and São Paulo—are now inextricably tied to the politics of globalization. Fresh Kills represents a poignant reminder of the material excesses of the global metropolitan condition.

Perhaps the most significant connection between Fresh Kills and New York City as a global site, however, is to be found in the Lifescape project. The reason is that, in its radical plans to redefine the space and function of Fresh Kills, Lifescape is part of the "new spatial order" that Peter Marcuse and Ronald van Kempen see as a definitive feature of globalizing cities since the 1970s.[155] While this reordering typically manifests itself in the proliferation and accentuation of spatial divisions between the urban poor and the urban elite, it is also evident in the retreat of the middle class from urban centers into peripheral clusters and secured enclaves.

In such terms, and mainly because of its location on the suburban margins of the city, Lifescape could be seen as a project aimed at meeting the outdoor recreational needs of a spatially segregated exurban middle class, effectively reinforcing an established pattern of separation. At the same time, however, Lifescape could equally be seen in a more positive light as an intervention in the spatial reorganization of the global city that deliberately resists the divisive trend of contemporary urban development by reclaiming an inhospitable, toxic site for new, sustainable public use. In this respect, Lifescape poses a profound challenge to conventional thinking about what constitutes waste (and wasted space) in cities.

Fresh Kills is therefore a critical site within contemporary New York, and one that has been largely overlooked in existing analyses of the city's development in the era of globalization. Yet as a prominent symbol of consumer waste, a repository of late capitalism's most notorious architectural ruins, and an experiment in new spatial order, Fresh Kills is more than just a controversial garbage dump. Alongside the other urban sites and scenes discussed in this book, Fresh Kills is one of New York's extraordinary locations in which the tensions, trends, and possibilities of the city come together in unique and revealing ways.

Michael Bloomberg describes Lifescape in the preface to the project's master plan as "a green oasis for all New Yorkers."[156] The former New York City mayor's endorsement is followed by a series of equally bold and exuberant statements by various city officials. The Staten Island Borough president, for example, declares Lifescape to be a "simultaneous ending and beginning," a "life within a landscape."[157] The New York City Department of Parks and Recreation commissioner in turn suggests that Lifescape is "reminiscent of the popular movements that gave rise to Central Park, Prospect Park and many of our other greatest parks" and that the city's newest green space will become "a tangible symbol of renewal."[158] Commenting on Lifescape's cultural significance, the New York City Department of Cultural Affairs commissioner anticipates that "the expansive parkland will serve as a cultural destination like no other, engaging New Yorkers and visitors in the city's unique and vibrant creative community."[159]

Apart from the positive spin, which is to be expected from politicians and city officials seeking support for a massive expenditure of public funds, this rhetoric of renewal highlights one of the most important features of the Fresh Kills parkland project. Lifescape is not so much about constructing a new space as it is about creatively reviving a dead space and making it, as stated in the master plan, "rejuvenating to the spirit and the environment."[160] Such a project is made all the more difficult yet significant by the presence of the World Trade Center wreckage within the site. As a way of coping with that presence, the 9/11 earthwork monument is a critical element of the park's design, a symbolic centerpiece that will play a key role in the project's potential to rejuvenate the body and soul of New York in the face of urban decay and postdisaster recovery.

Before I examine this symbolic centerpiece, however, it is important to place the earthwork monument in the broader context of the park's recent history and overall design. Fresh Kills Landfill on Staten Island has served as a dumping ground for New York City's household garbage since 1948, and is the largest domestic waste landfill in the world. The site covers an area of twenty-two hundred acres, which makes it approximately two and a half times the size of Central Park. The landfill was closed in early 2001, but briefly reopened later that year to accommodate the 1.2 million tons of wreckage from Ground Zero. The decision to reclaim the land for new public use had already been reached at this point, but the selected design for the transformation of Fresh Kills was not confirmed by the Department of City Planning until later that year. Following a two-stage international design competition to develop a plan for the adaptive end use of the site, Lifescape was announced as the winning entry in December 2001. The first draft of the Lifescape master plan was completed in 2005, and construction on the project began in 2008, with the first major phase due to be completed within ten years. The full transformation of the site, including its environmental recovery, is expected to take thirty years (figure 25).

Lifescape's multidisciplinary design team is led by James Corner and his landscape architecture practice, Field Operations. Interestingly, Field Operations also worked on another, similar effort to reclaim a derelict space within New York City. This other project, the High Line (discussed further in part II), involved redesigning a defunct elevated railway bed on Manhattan's far West Side into a public walkway, garden, and park, which opened in 2009. In the project's

FIGURE 25. *Rendering of Lifescape from the southeast. (Courtesy Field Operations)*

design statement, Corner's team describes the High Line's goal as being "the retooling of an industrial conveyance into a post-industrial instrument of leisure, life, and growth."[161] Corner's team also cites the importance of creating "an experience of slowness, otherworldliness, and distraction."[162] These comments may be directed at the High Line, but they could just as easily be applied to the park at Fresh Kills. This is not entirely accidental. Both Lifescape and the High Line are not only designed by the same practice but also belong to a larger trend in contemporary landscape architecture toward the reclaiming of once-vital pieces of urban infrastructure for new, imaginative, and sustainable forms of public use.

This trend toward creative, sustainable renewal of urban space most clearly registers in Lifescape's vision of transforming a landfill not just into a landscape but into an ecofriendly natural parkland complete with communal gathering spaces, playing fields, pedestrian and cycle paths, wetlands, grasslands, woodlands, and a wildlife preserve. Commenting in a 2005 journal article on the philosophy and values behind the design, Corner explains Lifescape as both a place and a process:

> Lifescape as a place is a diverse reserve for wildlife, cultural and social life, and active recreation. The aesthetic experience of the place will be vast in scale, spatially open and rugged in character, affording dramatic vistas, exposure to the elements, and huge open spaces unlike any other in the New York metropolitan region.
>
> Lifescape as a process is ecological in its deepest sense—a process of environmental reclamation and renewal on a vast scale, recovering not only the health and biodiversity of ecosystems across the site, but also the spirit and imagination of people who will use the new parkland.[163]

This double inflection of Lifescape as place and process—as both sanctuary space and sustainable space—is graphically articulated in the master plan renderings, many of which present idealized scenes of pastoral serenity and utopian moments of sociality and leisure, all enabled by the environmental reconditioning and spatial reorganization of the site.

Given Lifescape's emphasis on spatial and environmental transformation, one of the more interesting elements of the design is that it plans to retain most of the artificial topography created by the undulating mounds of garbage, some of which reach heights of over two hundred feet. These mounds will be sealed beneath a protective polymer lining and topped by a thick layer of soil, facilitating the environmental recovery of the site. On the surface, therefore, Lifescape will be a vibrant and varied natural landscape, an idea reinforced by the word "life" in the project title.

Underlying this natural landscape, however, will be the cumulated waste of one of the world's most excessive cities. So while Lifescape will appear at first to be disconnected from the city—indeed, the parkland is mainly conceived to offer an escape from the conventional experience of urban space—the landscape will nonetheless remain intimately and inextricably connected to the city at a much more fundamental level. In a very real way, this rehabilitated natural landscape will be shaped and sustained by a hidden cityscape of urban waste.

Included in that waste, of course, are the material remains of the Twin Towers, which will be commemorated by the earthwork monument (figure 26). The monument itself will be formed by two inclining landforms that mirror the exact width and height of each tower laid on its side. And in a further commemorative gesture, the monument will be oriented on an axis with the skyline where the towers originally stood. This will allow for a panoramic view of Lower Manhattan in the far distance, a view that now includes One World Trade Center rising from the redeveloped site of Ground Zero. Fittingly, the new tower not only serves in its own right as a monument to urban resilience but, like the two mounds at Fresh Kills, also evokes the incompleteness of New York.

FIGURE 26. *Rendering of 9/11 earthwork monument. (Courtesy Field Operations)*

In this sense, the earthwork monument establishes a strong link back to the lived space of the city. The orientation of the landforms creates direct visual and symbolic connections with the New York skyline, encouraging visitors to gaze at the city from the vantage point of its recycled dumping ground. Meanwhile, the shape of the monument evokes the origins of the urban wreckage contained in the nearby ground. It transforms the landscape into a symbolic burial mound for the urban superstructures that once stood as the world's most prominent icons of globalization.

Putting these aspects of the monument together, it becomes clear that what the earthwork will do is frame an experience that ensures visitors see much more than what is visibly present on the skyline of Manhattan. The monument will also ensure that visitors remember and reimagine the violent urban reshapings that took place on 9/11. Such a meditative experience of city gazing, in which the estranging effects of the high-rise view described by de Certeau in *The Practice of Everyday Life* are effectively replicated from a horizontal rather than a vertical perspective, is exactly what James Corner has in mind when he imagines how visitors will respond to the monument: "the slow, simple durational experience of ascending the incline, open to the sky and vast prairie horizon, will allow people to reflect on the magnitude of loss."[164]

From their new location on Staten Island, and in their new imaginary state, the undead towers will thus continue to engage and disturb the contemporary imagination, dominating both the park and the view of the city through their ghostly reincarnations. With the construction of the earthwork monument, the Twin Towers will thus acquire an undead afterlife. In their new horizontal form, they will once again become landmarks from which to observe the shifting verticals of New York.

In his essay "Scapeland," Jean-François Lyotard suggests that landscape is an excess of presence that leads to an experience of estrangement, what he calls *"dépaysement."*[165] Despite the debatable claim that estrangement is a precondition for landscape, Lyotard's words perfectly capture the dynamic at work in Lifescape's earthwork monument. It is an excess of presence carefully designed to create an experience of wonder and unease—a site of the urban uncanny aimed at the ultimate source of the urban sublime. Remembering the appearance of the Twin Towers in their original location in Lower Manhattan, the architectural historian Mark Wigley describes them

as "a pure, uninhabited image floating above the city, an image for-
ever above the horizon, in some kind of sublime excess, defying our
capacity to understand it."[166] This image of the Towers as a hovering,
otherworldly excess of presence that invites yet resists interpretation
is precisely what the earthwork monument seeks to revive. It is also
the same image, as discussed throughout part I, that has animated
and informed the cultural representation of the New York skyline
from the earliest days of the vertical city.

PART II

Sidewalks

A city sidewalk by itself is nothing. It is an abstraction. It means something only in conjunction with the buildings and other uses that border it.

—Jane Jacobs, *The Death and Life of Great American Cities*[1]

New York was an inexhaustible space, a labyrinth of endless steps, and no matter how far he walked, no matter how well he came to know its neighborhoods and streets, it always left him with the feeling of being lost.

—Paul Auster, *City of Glass*[2]

New York Horizontal

Part I of this book addressed the vertical dimensions of modern New York. Shifting the focus from the vertical to the horizontal, and so from one dominant and culturally engrained mode of perceiving the metropolis to another, part II examines the city from its street-level intimations. Such a shift is important to make, not just to move beyond the paradigm of the vertical city, which has tended to over-determine both popular and critical accounts of modern New York, but also to enable consideration of the street life of the city, which has been integral to New York's urban identity from the beginning.

This reorientation from the vertical to the horizontal also makes sense for another reason. As Thomas Bender reminds us in *The Unfinished City*, New York has been a horizontal city for the majority of its existence, and its architecture and spatial organization have been dominated historically by an "essentially horizontal perception of urban form" that endured well into the nineteenth century.[3] For example, the Commissioners' Plan of 1811, which has arguably had more of an impact on the development of Manhattan than any other planning initiative, and which unintentionally facilitated the rise of the skyscraper city nearly eighty years later, envisioned the grid as a way of ordering the growth of a horizontally oriented metropolis. In short, the rise of vertical New York in the late nineteenth century occurred in the context of an urban environment originally intended for horizontality.

It is therefore important to stress that, although the explosion of skyscraper construction in the 1890s placed new emphasis on New York's vertical dimensions, its horizontal dimensions remained—as they still do today—integral to the life and culture of the city. The ways in which those dimensions register in cultural production in the late nineteenth and early twentieth centuries is the subject of the second half of this book. So although part II is titled "Sidewalks," the following discussion ranges widely over both the surface and subterranean landscapes of the city. Specifically, I consider the cultural significance of iconic avenues like Broadway and the Bowery, historically marginalized neighborhoods like the Lower East Side and Harlem, and spaces of public intersection like the slum, the El, and the underground realm of the subway.

From the immigrant street scenes of John Sloan's painting and Jacob Riis's photography, to the meandering pedestrians of William Dean Howells's fiction and the sidewalk recordings of the American Mutoscope and Biograph Company (the oldest movie company in the United States, founded in 1895), part II considers the ways in which New York's urban imaginary was shaped by the city's street culture, with its emphasis on speed, movement, and dislocation. To this end, particular attention is paid to the treatment of three dominant sidewalk practices—window shopping, street-walking (understood in a broad sense as urban perambulation), and crowd watching—as well as the shifting spaces in which these practices occur.

Sidewalks and Public Space

In 1961, at a time of great social and economic upheaval in urban America, the urbanist Jane Jacobs famously argued for the importance of public space to the development and renewal of cities. In *The Death and Life of Great American Cities*, she describes sidewalks as "the main public spaces of the city" and "its most vital organs."[4] The significance of this claim is twofold. First, it identifies sidewalks not as inconsequential appendages to the street in need of order and rationalization as they had frequently been treated in urban planning up to this point, but instead as complex, active sites of social expression, exchange, and experiment capable of creating and sustaining urban communities. More than that, Jacobs's claims for the social value of sidewalks generated new interest in forms of urban planning centered on the needs of city publics, while simultaneously expressing optimism in the potential of well-designed cities to improve the lives of their inhabitants. Whether or not such optimism is justified remains a topic of debate. What matters here, however, is the idea, advanced by Jacobs and picked up and refined by generations of later urban thinkers, that sidewalks are far from being trivial public spaces on the margins of the street.

Building on Jacobs's insights from the 1960s, Anastasia Loukaitou-Sideris and Renia Ehrenfeucht argue in *Sidewalks: Conflict and Negotiation over Public Space* that, as a historically "undervalued element of the urban form," the sidewalk is more productively understood today as a site of "conflict and negotiation over public space" revolving around competing concerns about "distinctiveness, publicness, diversity and contestation, and regulation."[5] Although Loukaitou-Sideris and Ehrenfeucht develop this view mainly in relation to case studies of American cities from the late twentieth century onward, their understanding of the sidewalk as a site of conflict and negotiation applies much more broadly, and as the following discussion seeks to demonstrate, it has particular relevance for New York City between 1890 and 1940.

Like the architectural form of the skyscraper, which migrated to Manhattan from another city entirely, New York sidewalks—or at least their form and function within the modern city—can be said to have their roots elsewhere. That is to say, the evolution of what we might call the "modern sidewalk" in New York, by which I simply mean the sidewalk as it existed and was used in New York during the city's modernist moment in art and urbanism, is partly indebted to urban developments and social practices that emerged from European cities like London, Berlin, Vienna, and especially Paris during the eighteenth and early nineteenth centuries.

As an urban form, sidewalks have been a feature of cities for significantly longer, of course, and, according to Spiro Kostof in *The City Assembled*, their existence can even be traced as far back as 2000 BC to the *karum* of Kültepe on the high plains of Anatolia in central Turkey.[6] It was not until the Renaissance, however, that the sidewalk as we think of it today—that is, as a freely accessible and clearly demarcated pedestrianized part of a street—began to appear in cities across Europe. It then took until the nineteenth century for this fledgling urban form to become a standard feature of Western cities and, more importantly, to be deliberately and systematically incorporated into planning, design, and public law.

Paris in particular was a site of innovation in the history of both sidewalks and sidewalk culture. As the progenitor of the boulevard, which, as Loukaitou-Sideris and Ehrenfeucht note, "developed as broad, tree-lined streets that segregated vehicles from pedestrians"[7] in the middle of the eighteenth century, Paris was among the first cities to integrate sidewalks into its street system. One result was the regulation and regularization of the use of sidewalks in the city. New laws protecting pedestrians from vehicles quickly passed, for instance, as did laws enforcing the separation of vehicular and foot traffic. Another effect was fostering the emergence of a new pedestrian culture, made possible and encouraged by the new, spacious walkways of the boulevard, which stood in sharp contrast to the narrow, haphazard spaces of the older Parisian *trottoirs*.

While certainly not new to eighteenth-century Europe, the performative practice of the promenade, or "ritualized leisure strolling,"[8] acquired heightened significance and visibility with the arrival of the boulevard. Street-walking—or more exactly, street-walking in public view—became a popular practice through which individuals, in unprecedented numbers, could both observe and participate in the spectacle of the city. While the arrival of the boulevard in Paris and other major European cities like Barcelona and Vienna opened up city streets to a larger pedestrian public, the practice of street-walking itself nonetheless remained predominantly the domain of the leisure class. After all, strolling through the city for the pleasure of the activity itself required both free time and freedom from work. It is not surprising, therefore, that the development of sidewalk culture in the late eighteenth and early nineteenth centuries took place alongside and frequently in conjunction with the emergence of a consumer society, including the retail institution of the department store, as elaborately explored by Emile Zola in his 1883 novel *Au Bonheur des dames* (*The Ladies' Paradise*).

In this naturalist novel about the interconnections between the rise of modern commerce and the rebuilding of Paris under Baron Haussmann in the 1860s, Zola repeatedly calls attention to the importance of human desire in keeping the circulatory systems of capital and city streets moving. Among his insights into the urban-retail nexus is the idea, innovative for its time, that the experience of modern shopping and the experience of modern sidewalks are partly sexual in nature. Both are driven by an essentially erotic desire produced by, and directed toward, a visually promiscuous commodity spectacle surging from the shops into the streets and back again:

> The shop windows stretched along the Rue de la Michodière and Rue Neuve-Saint-Augustin.... [T]he spectacle seemed to Denise to be endless.... Denise stood transfixed before the display at the main door. There, outside on the street, on the pavement itself, was a mountain of cheap goods, placed at the entrance as bait, bargains which stopped the women as they passed by.... It was a giant fairground of display, as if the shop were bursting and throwing its surplus stock into the street.[9]

In *The Ladies' Paradise*, the boundaries between the store and the sidewalk blur to the point where both spaces—one private and interior and the other public and exterior—become marked by the same eroticized consumer experience. As Zola elaborates throughout the novel's various street-walking and shopping scenes, it is an experience characterized by spectacle, seduction, manipulation, and capitulation, as well as by ecstasy, delirium, fantasy, hysteria, and release.[10]

Within this dynamic of desire and display, the shop window acquires heightened significance in Zola's writing as a mediating space that not only ties together the sidewalk and the store but also helps to construct and even reflect individual consumer and social identities. Beyond showing how the shop window plays a prominent role in the emerging sidewalk culture of capitalist urban modernity, *The Ladies' Paradise* also highlights the gendered dimensions of that culture, emphasizing the extent to which, in mid-nineteenth-century Paris, the *grands magasins* and the boulevards were both spaces that aggressively targeted the new female public of an emerging consumer society.

In identifying these sorts of links between sex and shopping, as well as between the street and the store, Zola points to one of the most significant social functions of the sidewalk—namely, its function as a staging space where individual identities, and their component parts such as gender, sexuality, race, class, and ethnicity, can be publicly expressed, tested, and explored. Paris was a key site of early experimentation and innovation in the sidewalk performance of identity, and so too was New York in equally important ways.

By the late nineteenth century, following decades of rapid urbanization and industrialization, thousands of miles of sidewalks had been built in American cities and, starting in the 1890s, most of these sidewalks were publicly funded and paved with cement, establishing a model of financing and building that continues today. The use of sidewalks in the United States, however, differed slightly from those of European cities, at least in official municipal thinking. In contrast to cities like Paris, where the emphasis of sidewalk use was first placed on leisure strolling as an evolution of earlier promenade practices, American cities like New York additionally viewed the sidewalk in far more utilitarian terms as a space of efficient public transportation, as Loukaitou-Sideris and Ehrenfeucht describe:

> People, goods, and vehicles crowded the American streets and sidewalks, and with growth came an increasingly professionalized municipal government, municipal improvements, and public-space controls. As municipalities began to provide sidewalks, they exerted increasing control over how they were used. And one use, walking for transportation, became the primary purpose for which the sidewalks were constructed. The pedestrian's unobstructed mobility became the justification that underlay other activity restrictions, and the pedestrian became the public for whom the sidewalks were being provided. The assumption that walking is the primary use for sidewalks has carried into the twenty-first century.[11]

American sidewalks enabled leisure strolling and provided a space for the public staging of identity, but they simultaneously fulfilled a practical need within increasingly crowded urban centers for facilitating the mobility of pedestrian traffic. Indeed, in the decades preceding the opening of the New York subway in 1904 and related efforts to expand the public transportation system, street-walking was an efficient and necessary way of moving around various parts of the city, particularly for many of New York's poorer residents and newly arrived immigrants, for whom public transportation in the form of horsecars, trolleys, and elevated railways, later supplemented by the underground transport of the subway, was not always an affordable option for everyday use. Thus, in contrast to Paris, New York's sidewalk culture placed a greater emphasis on speed, movement, and accessibility, effectively blending the performative aspects of sidewalk use with much more pragmatic ones concerned with the rapid circulation and control of a particular kind of urban traffic: the pedestrian (figure 27).

New York was not unique in adopting a mixed approach toward sidewalks, however. Other major U.S. cities such as Boston, Chicago, and Los Angeles similarly treated their sidewalks as hybrid spaces of sociality and mobility, and the multiple functions of the sidewalk have always been implicit and articulated to varying degrees in the urban form of the sidewalk itself. But there is a way in which the evolution of New York's modern sidewalks was distinctive. This distinctiveness is connected to the impact of New York's cultural and ethnic heterogeneity on the city's street life, and, even more importantly, to the prominence of that street life in cultural production concerned with addressing the lived experience of the modern metropolis. Not unlike the city's skyline, the sidewalks of New York, and the broader streetscape to which they belong, emerged during the late nineteenth century as an emblematic—even paradigmatic—site of social experiment and cultural expression.

FIGURE 27. *Heavy pedestrian traffic on Fifth Avenue, 1904. (Courtesy Library of Congress, Prints and Photographs Division)*

A Short History of the Grid

Manhattan's grid plan played a significant part in ensuring the emergence of the sidewalk as an iconic feature of urban modernity. The grid was the product of the Commissioners' Plan of 1811, an ambitious and forward-looking state legislative proposal for the orderly division, sale, and development of land in Manhattan between Fourteenth Street and Washington Heights at the northern tip of the island (figure 28). Although Central Park and a few other green spaces that exist today were not included in the original plan, the division of land outlined in the 1811 plan was followed very closely as the city grew rapidly northward in the early decades of the nineteenth century, and the current layout of Manhattan above Fourteenth Street, including the strictly gridded street system and its compass-point orientation, dates to this period.

The implementation of the grid in Manhattan, and slightly later in Brooklyn, Queens, and the Bronx, marked an approach to urban planning informed by Enlightenment principles of order and reason. It is possible, for instance, to trace a line of influence from the pioneering grid experiment of James Craig's 1767 plan for Edinburgh's New Town, which was heralded as a triumphant product of the Scottish Enlightenment, to New World developments ranging from Pierre L'Enfant's 1792 plan for Washington, DC, to the commissioners' vision for New York two decades later. A common feature in each of these

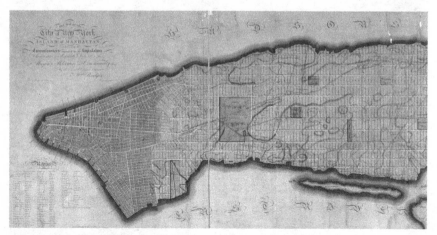

FIGURE 28. *Detail from map of the city of New York as laid out by the Commissioners' Plan, 1811. (Courtesy Library of Congress, Geography and Map Division)*

plans is the prioritizing of a precisely formulated geometric design over topographic and geographic realities existing on the ground, so that the abstract, predetermined layout of the city prevails regardless of how the existing space is shaped, used, or inhabited. Such an aggressive, uncompromising pursuit of realizing an ideal, rationalized image of spatial order did not disappear after the Enlightenment but, rather, gained momentum across the industrializing world, finding one of its most extreme articulations in the transatlantic currents of modernist art and urban planning of the 1920s and '30s, where, as discussed in part I in relation to Hugh Ferriss and Le Corbusier, the emphasis on order and reason sometimes bordered on obsession.

The art historian Rosalind Krauss goes as far as to argue in her seminal essay "Grids" (1979) that the abstract form of the grid is "an emblem of modernity" and that "it is what art looks like when it turns its back on nature."[12] Although Krauss is referring to the emergence of the grid as an aesthetic and conceptual concern in the work of modernist painters like Piet Mondrian, Kazimir Malevich, and the cubists, her insight nonetheless touches on a broader cultural development. "Flattened, geometricized, ordered," she writes, the grid is "antinatural, antimimetic, antireal," adding that "in the flatness that results from its coordinates, the grid is the means of crowding out the dimensions of the real and replacing them with the lateral spread of a single surface."[13] These comments may be directed at the geometric abstractions of modernist painting, but they also describe the thinking behind—and, to a certain extent, the desired effects of—the imposition of the Manhattan grid by the Commissioners' Plan. Such a resonance between painting and planning makes sense given that the grid emerged in both fields as a means of privileging abstraction.

Nonetheless, there are important differences between the grid experiments of painting and those of urban planning. Most notable among these is that, through implementation, city grids are not just representational forms but also material realities that directly affect the organization, development, and experience of cities in profound, lasting, and inescapable ways. Picking up on this distinction, the architectural theorist Teresa Stoppani stresses in *Paradigm Islands: Manhattan and Venice* that, through adaptation and use, the Manhattan grid has become more than the "unchallenged and inflexible geometry" or "neutral and indifferent mesh" of its original plan, but instead has evolved into a "matrix for a selective making of space that, while it is traced on the ground, evolves, designs transparencies and opacities, and hides or reveals certain elements."[14] As these comments suggest, the grid can be understood as being simultaneously rigid and flexible, abstract and material, planned and unpredictable.

Central to Stoppani's thinking are the concepts of "grid effect" and "grid operations" made possible, in her view, by Manhattan's artificiality as an enactment of the grid:

> As it builds itself in its own artificiality, the Manhattan grid intentionally confounds its relation with an origin. There is no "origin" in Manhattan, but rather the continuous repetition of foundational acts whenever the Grid is traced on the ground (confirmed or transgressed).... The fabricated origin of Manhattan consists of total (and yet incomplete) artificiality. Even this artificial origin, though, has to take into account a "pre-existing" that is not only historical (violently erased and brushed away) and topographic (intentionally and systematically ignored), but also geological (so difficult and powerful that it continues to resist and re-emerge— and needs to be constantly dressed as artificial).... Manhattan does not have a sacred foundational act, but is made and remade by the totalizing and equalizing violence of its Grid.[15]

Stoppani's claims are both provocative and unclear. For example, it is difficult to follow precisely why the grid provides the only foundational myth for Manhattan, especially given that the grid only applies to part of the island and that the city itself has a long, complex history of repeated foundation, formation, and renaming—complete with accompanying cultural mythologies—dating back to its Dutch colonial origins and its even earlier European "discovery." Alongside the indigenous settlement of the island, this, presumably, is the category of the "pre-existing" that Stoppani cites. Similarly, it is worth asking what makes the Manhattan grid so much more artificial, totalizing, or violent than other implementations of urban master plans, which always involve some degree of enacting or imposing of an abstract vision onto the history and geography of a place.

Even if exaggerated, Stoppani's emphasis on the tyranny and artificiality of the grid, as both concept and practice, is useful in the sense that it reinforces the idea that the Manhattan grid has had a formative—at times coercive—influence on the city in material, spatial, and cultural terms. Her insight, which she develops in relation to more contemporary architectural and design experiments such as

Zaha Hadid's 2006 "soft grid" proposal for Istanbul, is to link the enforcement of the grid to certain kinds of operations and effects. Stoppani understands grid operations as occurring when the grid functions "not as a form or as a device for representation, but as an agent in the making of place."[16] The grid effect, meanwhile, is explained in terms of "the complications of the 'operation' of the grid...when it is employed as an organizing system in the urban space and territory."[17] As Stoppani elaborates, "unlike the modern pictorial grid, the 'grid effect' does not produce a separation from the world but, inseparable from its implementation, it produces a dynamic and evolving space."[18]

The broader point to take from this articulation of the grid's multiple functions is that the implementation and evolution of the Manhattan grid can be understood as much more than the realization of a visionary urban master plan. The grid has also become an embedded and formative feature of the city's everyday identity and a catalyst for the flourishing of its street life, not only opening up new public spaces for movement and exchange but also providing new sights and scenes of interest for artists, writers, and filmmakers, as well as new design challenges for architects and planners.

These ideas were at the center of a major exhibition organized by the Museum of the City of New York in 2011 to commemorate the bicentennial of the Commissioners' Plan. Titled "The Greatest Grid," the exhibition and accompanying book drew on extensive archival material, new historical and theoretical analysis, and visual ethnography and documentation to understand the Manhattan grid in its social and cultural contexts. Among the many different views of the grid to emerge—which include seeing it variously as an emblem of American democracy, an ideal of Cartesian order, a monster of laissez-faire urbanism, an antiarchitectural quashing of urban creativity, and a celebratory paradigm of density and congestion—Hilary Ballon's contribution stands out for the connection it makes between the grid, the street, and the public realm:

> [T]he grid is typically seen as standing in opposition to public space because it blanketed the city with development lots, providing few parks and squares. However, as Jane Jacobs stressed in her tributes to New York's vibrant street life, the grid also constituted the streets and sidewalks as the city's public realm. Unlike the plazas of old European cities or of Washington, D.C., the 1811 plan endowed New York with a distinctive type of public space

enmeshed with the ordinary street system of the city. The establishment of the grid in the nineteenth century set in motion an expanded understanding of the public realm and the role of government in fostering it. Simply put, the idea of the public realm in New York is inseparable from its streets.[19]

Ballon's point that the implementation of the grid expanded the boundaries of what constituted the public realm in New York to include the city's new rectilinear network of public spaces is important to understanding the social and spatial conditions that supported the formation of a vibrant sidewalk culture. As Amanda M. Burden notes, "the Manhattan street grid, adopted in large parts of the other boroughs as well, is the city's armature for sustaining a pedestrian-focused, walkable city, infused with energy and vitality."[20] Together with the creation of the New York city block, the implementation of the grid produced the iconic urban form of New York's modern sidewalk.

Unlike city blocks, however, sidewalks were an unintended consequence of the Manhattan grid, even if they quickly became inseparable from it, as Carolyn Yerkes points out: "Sidewalks are the invisible third element of the Commissioners' plan of 1811. The plan itself does not show them, and the commissioners' remarks never mention them, but sidewalks are as much a part of the grid as the streets and blocks that they join."[21] Although this blind spot in the 1811 plan and the accompanying explanatory remarks indicates that the commissioners may not have been quite as visionary or progressive in their thinking as the results of their work would suggest,[22] there was nothing invisible about New York's sidewalks following the implementation of the grid.

Throughout the nineteenth century, and increasing once the spatial and planning constraints of the grid began to push construction rapidly northward in the 1880s and '90s, the interrelation of the grid and the sidewalk was a subject of wide public and artistic interest. Popular among pictorial representations of New York in the mid- to late nineteenth century, for example, were elevated and panoramic views of the city showing not only the scope and scale of new construction afforded by the implementation of the Commissioners' Plan but also the place of the sidewalk within the expanding and maturing system of the street grid (figure 29).

FIGURE 29. *The expanding grid: view from the roof of George Ehret's home at Park Avenue and 94th Street. Looking west. 1882–3. (Courtesy Museum of the City of New York)*

This interest in the relation of the grid to the city reaches an aesthetic and conceptual extreme in the New York paintings of Piet Mondrian. In *New York City, New York* (1940–2), completed after he moved to New York from Europe in 1940, Mondrian extends his long-standing artistic interest in the grid as an abstract compositional tool to an interpretation of the modern city. In this "top down and distanced view," as Douglas Tallack characterizes the painting,[23] the grid appears not just as an abstraction of intersecting, perpendicular lines but also as a decontextualized fragment of a larger maplike sprawl seen from above. Yet the carefully varied layout of lines and mix of colors—all operating within the larger structural logic of the grid—brings differentiation and variation to the image. Although some critics see Mondrian's grids as "pointedly flat artworks,"[24] many more agree that they deliberately and strategically explore the relation between surface and depth, fluctuating between visual effects of flatness and layering. In its representation of New York, the painting posits the city's grid system as a source of repetition and variation, capable of generating—but also shaping and constraining—movement and play.

Such an understanding of the grid's simultaneous effects of liberating and ordering lies at the heart of *Broadway Boogie Woogie* (1942–3), Mondrian's last completed painting and his best-known New York–themed work. Here, Mondrian uses the motif of the New York grid to combine his fascination with American jazz and his commitment to the philosophical and aesthetic principles of neoplasticism and the Dutch-centered De Stijl movement, which advocated total abstraction in the pursuit of order and balance. Mondrian had long been interested in the improvisational qualities of jazz, as well as its possibilities for transcending form. What makes *Broadway Boogie Woogie* particularly significant in the context of this discussion is that the New York grid becomes the scene for exploring "the spatial and architectural implications of neo-plastic painting and jazz," as David Brown argues in *Noise Orders: Jazz, Improvisation, and Architecture*: "Both employ open-form compositions focusing on extended relations rather than closure, and both (in Mondrian's estimation) indicate an open potential in architecture that leads to a transcendent utopian future unconstrained by form."[25] In such a reading of the painting, New York's grid becomes both the site and the vehicle for transcendence, offering an underlying structure capable of supporting free play and improvisation on it. Here, the modern city emerges not as an overbearing threat of geometric tyranny, as in the celluloid cityscapes of Fritz Lang's *Metropolis* (1927) or Charles Sheeler and Paul Strand's *Manhatta* (1921), but instead as a utopian space of openness and possibility, where energy, rhythm, and movement flow harmoniously from (and back into) the open, abstract form of the grid.

Such exuberance for the New York grid is questionable in terms of its lived realities, particularly considering how its implementation in certain areas of the city such as Harlem and the Bronx, exacerbated by geographic and economic marginalization, was a contributing factor in the emergence of high-rise ghettos in the twentieth century. Earlier still, and in relation to a different dynamic of urban development, the grid was also instrumental in financializing New York's land by standardizing the size and layout of building lots across Manhattan, setting in motion one of the world's most hyperbolic and rapacious real-estate markets, as Max Page outlines in *The Creative Destruction of Manhattan*.[26] Nevertheless, Mondrian's insight that the grid articulates an ideal of what he called "equilibrated relationships,"[27] however far removed from everyday experience and practice, connects to the broader appeal of the form in American urban planning and public life. Whatever its faults, the New York grid attempts to embrace in its conceptual framework—if not in practice—the quintessentially democratic values of equality and transparency by making the spatial organization of the city explicit and visible, and by treating the resulting city blocks as identically as possible in terms of size and layout.

Street-Walking

Despite enduring cultural interest in the New York grid as both a source and a site of urban invention, which continues well beyond Mondrian and modernism, it is the sidewalk—or, more exactly, the forms of street life, public exchange, and urban mobility enabled by the sidewalk—that attracts heightened attention and interest across the arts, including literature and film. For example, alongside the phenomenon of the skyscraper, the spectacle of everyday street life features as a recurring motif in the early, experimental actualities of New York's emergent film industry in the late 1890s, ranging from documentary shorts showing chaotic scenes of street vending to celebratory commemorations of community parades, to curbside ethnographic inquiries into homelessness, poverty, and overcrowding.

Among the many subgenres of what could be called the "sidewalk actuality," those explicitly featuring scenes of street-walking stand out not just for their popularity among New York's early viewing public but also for the ways in which they deliberately explore the meaning and function of the sidewalk as a public space within the modern city. *What Happened on 23rd Street*, a one-minute short filmed by the Thomas Edison Company in 1901, is significant in these regards. Shot in one take from a stationary position at street level, the film combines actuality footage of pedestrians strolling along Twenty-third Street with a moment of staged drama involving two actors planted among the public. The actors, a man and a woman, walk slowly together toward the camera. At this point in the film, there is nothing to distinguish the couple from the other people on the street. Just before they reach the camera, the woman walks above an air shaft, which suddenly lifts her dress, revealing her legs (figure 30). As she struggles to hold down the dress, the woman and her companion

FIGURE 30. *Frame enlargements,* What Happened on 23rd Street, *1901. (Courtesy Library of Congress, Motion Picture, Broadcasting and Recorded Sound Division)*

laugh lightheartedly at the "surprise" event, before moving on past the camera. The film ends as the pair exits the shot.

Although only a little over a minute in length, the film is far more complex and sophisticated than it initially appears to be. First, the film deliberately blurs the boundaries between documentary realism and narrative drama, only revealing its shift from reality to narrative when the woman's misadventure above the air shaft occurs directly in front of the camera—centered and framed too perfectly to be an accident. Even then, the film leaves it to the viewer to interpret the scene as a staged event and to identify the protagonists as actors who are following a carefully planned scenario. Second, the title itself, *What Happened on 23rd Street,* signals the film's narrativity, priming the viewer to look for a story from among the various moving bodies on the street. The story itself is not immediately evident and only comes gradually into focus as the couple walks closer and closer to the camera. Finally, and most importantly, the film takes the cultural life of the sidewalk as its subject. In this case, the film explores the erotic potential of street-walking. It also exploits the ability of this emerging medium to serve as a source of voyeurism.

In fact, the film's scopophilia is made explicit in the Edison Company's catalog, which was originally used to sell the title to nickelodeon operators. Throughout the catalog's description, the emphasis remains firmly on the erotic content and its pleasurable qualities:

> This is a winner and sure to please. The scene as suggested by the title is made on 23rd street, New York city. In front of one of the large newspaper offices on that thoroughfare is a hot air shaft through which immense volumes of air is [*sic*] forced by means of a blower. Ladies crossing these shafts often have their clothes slightly disarranged, (it may be said much to their discomfiture). As our picture was being made a young man escorting a young

lady, to whom he was talking very earnestly, comes into view and walks slowly along until they stand directly over the air shaft. The young lady's skirts are suddenly raised to, you might say an almost unreasonable height, greatly to her horror and much to the amusement of the newsboys, bootblacks and passersby.[28]

Although this text deliberately skews toward sensationalism in order to meet the commercial needs of the catalog, it nonetheless succeeds in capturing the film's attitude toward, and presentation of, women. In many ways, *What Happened on 23rd Street* illustrates Laura Mulvey's long-standing argument in "Visual Pleasure and Narrative Cinema" that women systematically figure on screen as objects of sexual desire for visual consumption by a male heterosexual gaze.[29] Mulvey's argument was originally developed in the 1970s in response to classical Hollywood cinema, but the pattern of objectification and sexualization she critiques takes form much earlier and is already evident in the Edison Company's 1901 screen experiment with narrative cinema. Indeed, the transformation of the film's female character from everyday pedestrian to object of desire—a scene that includes leering male onlookers, as the catalog unabashedly points out—is the full extent of the narrative.

The parallels between the sidewalk scene in *What Happened on 23rd Street* and Marilyn Monroe's equally contrived and gratuitous encounter with an air shaft in Billy Wilder's 1955 New York film *The Seven Year Itch* are hard to miss. It would be difficult to prove a direct line of influence from the 1901 nickelodeon short to the 1955 Hollywood spectacular, although many critics and commentators have pointed out the similarities between the two scenes, right down to the color of the dress, the position of the actress above the grate, and the framing of the shot. Accordingly, a more productive way to think through the uncanny coexistence of the two scenes—and one that bypasses tired questions of influence, authenticity, and fidelity—is to understand *What Happened on 23rd Street* as a variation on what David Simpson has described as a "prefigurative imaginative experience."[30] Although he is writing about 9/11 and the ways in which twenty-first-century media obsessively fantasize about urban disaster, Simpson's idea that cultural production, whether in the form of literature, film, or art, can provide prefigurative experiences that work to normalize the new, the strange, and the different is applicable here. *What Happened on 23rd Street* similarly rehearses a scene that becomes a recurring cultural fantasy—albeit one driven by desire rather than fear, and one responding to the newness of the modern street rather than the shock of urban disaster. As confirmed by Marilyn Monroe's remediation of the air shaft scene some fifty years later, as well as by countless adaptations and imitations since, it is a fantasy that revolves around the sidewalk's potential to provide voyeuristic pleasure.

Broadway Promenade

The libidinal energy and gendered eroticism of the sidewalk register in New York's urban imaginary in other ways too. In *Sister Carrie* (1900), Theodore Dreiser's naturalist novel about an ambitious and sexually assertive Chicago shopgirl who achieves stardom on the New York stage, the sidewalk figures as an almost carnivalesque space of conspicuous consumption and female objectification, re-calling the Parisian window-shopping scenes in Zola's *The Ladies' Paradise* discussed earlier. The following passage details Carrie's first walk along an affluent section of Broadway under the guidance of a more experienced and glamorous female companion:

> The walk down Broadway...was one of the remarkable features of the city. There gathered...not only all the pretty women who love a showy parade, but the men who love to gaze upon and admire them. It was a very imposing procession of pretty faces and fine clothes. Women appeared in their very best hats, shoes, and gloves, and walked arm in arm on their way to the fine shops or theatres strung along from Fourteenth to Thirty-fourth streets. Equally the men paraded with the very latest they could afford....In all her stay in the city, Carrie had never heard of this showy parade; had never even been on Broadway when it was taking place. On the other hand, it was a familiar thing to Mrs. Vance, who not only knew of it as an entity, but had often been in it, going purposely to see and be seen, to create a stir with her beauty and dispel any ten-dency to fall short in dressiness by contrasting herself with the beauty and fashion of the town.[31]

Newly arrived from Chicago, and still unaccustomed to wealth, Carrie is overwhelmed yet enthralled by her first encounter with Broadway's promenade culture. By presenting the street through the eyes of a newcomer in this way, Dreiser is able to call attention to the crowd's emphasis on materiality, sexuality, and display. Not only does Broadway's sidewalk scene encourage people to look at others as objects of consumer and sexual desire but it also encourages those same people to participate in and contribute to their own sexualized commodification by willfully parading both their fashion and their bodies in public view.

As Dreiser goes on to describe in some detail, the result is a street-walking spectacle that is not only highly performative but also highly competitive, and in which the objectifying power of the gaze plays an important role:

Carrie stepped along easily enough after they got out of the car at Thirty-fourth Street, but soon fixed her eyes upon the lovely company which swarmed by and with them as they proceeded. She noticed suddenly that Mrs. Vance's manner had rather stiffened under the gaze of handsome men and elegantly dressed ladies, whose glances were not modified by any rules of propriety. To stare seemed the proper and natural thing. Carrie found herself stared at and ogled. Men in flawless top-coats, high hats, and silver-headed walking sticks elbowed near and looked too often into conscious eyes. Ladies rustled by in dresses of stiff cloth, shedding affected smiles and perfume. Carrie noticed among them the sprinkling of goodness and the heavy percentage of vice. The rouged and powdered cheeks and lips, the scented hair, the large, misty, and languorous eye, were common enough. With a start she awoke to find that she was in fashion's crowd, on parade in a show place—and such a show place! Jewellers' windows gleamed along the path with remarkable frequency. Florist shops, furriers, haberdashers, confectioners—all followed in rapid succession. The street was full of coaches. Pompous doormen in immense coats, shiny brass belts and buttons, waited in front of expensive salesrooms. Coachmen in tan boots, white tights, and blue jackets waited obsequiously for the mistresses of carriages who were shopping inside. The whole street bore the flavour of riches and show, and Carrie felt that she was not of it. She could not, for the life of her, assume the attitude and smartness of Mrs. Vance, who, in her beauty, was all assurance. She could only imagine that it must be evident to many that she was the less handsomely dressed of the two. It cut her to the quick, and she resolved that she would not come here again until she looked better. At the same time she longed to feel the delight of parading here as an equal. Ah, then she would be happy![32]

This passage elucidates a number of theories about the rise of capitalist modernity and its effects on everyday urban practices, ranging from ideas developed by Thorstein Veblen in the late nineteenth century to more recent insights into cities and consumerism by cultural critics like Rachel Bowlby, Anne Friedberg, and Jean Baudrillard.

For instance, Dreiser's description of Broadway street-walkers wonderfully illustrates the phenomenon of conspicuous consumption identified by Veblen in his 1899 socioeconomic study of the American nouveau riche, *The Theory of the Leisure Class*. Seeking to understand and explain the emergence of a new social class dedicated to the ostentatious and gratuitous display of wealth, Veblen pinpoints two interrelated social practices designed to communicate elevated social status in an increasingly consumer-oriented world. The first practice is "conspicuous leisure," in which individuals flaunt their wealth by visibly pursuing leisure in public, thereby signaling that they are affluent enough not to be working.[33] The second practice, which extends from the first, is "conspicuous consumption," which involves publicly displaying objects and acts of luxury consumption as part of the social performance of wealth, with the same aim of communicating and elevating social prestige.[34] Vital to both conspicuous leisure and conspicuous consumption is that the practices are carried out in full public view, since their effectiveness hinges on their visibility. Also important is that both practices need to be seen by a public that not only recognizes the signals being given but also shares the same consumer values and embracement of materialism. Although certainly not new to nineteenth-century society, such performative displays of wealth and social status through consumer spectacle mark an intensification and expansion of earlier promenade practices, a trend that Veblen links to a steady rise in the level of material prosperity following the Industrial Revolution. Given the importance of visibility to these performative practices, it makes perfect sense that the sidewalk—as a public space that facilitates the staging of identity—should become a key locus of conspicuous leisure and consumption in modern New York alongside similarly visible spaces of social flow such as urban parks and squares.

Dreiser's description of Broadway street-walking in *Sister Carrie* not only makes explicit this connection between the sidewalk and the conspicuous consumer but also goes beyond Vebler's socioeconomic reflections to comment on the competitive and paranoid mental workings of what David Scobey has called the "bourgeois sociability" of the elite stroller.[35] Writing about the social history of the promenade in nineteenth-century New York, Scobey draws on Jürgen Habermas's concept of the "bourgeois public sphere"[36] as a formative discursive arena to argue that "seeing and being seen, in public and in motion [were] a core rite of sociability" in New York and a "test of inclusion within the metropolitan gentry."[37] Scobey also stresses "the twofold function of promenading as a drama of mutual recognition and a tableau of hierarchical display": "On the one hand, seeing and being seen affirmed genteel New Yorkers' sense of place within the shifting topography of urban life and affirmed their notions of class and sexual order. On the other hand, it cast the larger public as witness to the spectacle of elite authority."[38] The double function of the promenade registers prominently in Dreiser's text, where "to stare seemed the proper and natural thing," and where "Carrie found herself stared at and ogled." In addition to this explicit articulation of the see-and-be-seen mantra of the promenade, the psychological effects of simultaneously witnessing and participating in Broadway's fashion parade are explicitly explored by Dreiser. As she becomes swept up in the phantasmagoria of the sidewalk spectacle, Carrie experiences delirium and elation, as well as shame and envy when she compares herself to the more fashionable crowd around her. Perhaps the most telling effect, however, is Carrie's longing "to feel the delight of parading...as an equal" and her sense that such an experience would make her "happy." As the novel goes on to illustrate through the story of her quest for belonging among New York's elite, Carrie does not achieve any form of happiness by becoming an integrated and recognized participant of the Broadway promenade scene. Yet her initial enchantment proves powerful enough to interpolate her into the practices and values of conspicuous consumption, including its elitist class distinctions and materialistic embrace of surface and appearance.

This, of course, is the realm of capitalist ideology and Dreiser's insight into Carrie's state of delusion is effectively rehearsing the classical Marxist formula for commodity fetishism, whereby, as Karl Marx explains in *Capital*, the social relation between people "assumes, in their eyes, the fantastic form of a relation between things,"[39] leading to the objectification of people and the humanization of objects. Literature of the nineteenth and early twentieth centuries is replete with iterations of the commodity fetish, ranging in the American context from the dehumanizing Wall Street of Herman Melville's "Bartleby the Scrivener" (1853) to the exploited poor of Stephen Crane's *Maggie: A Girl of the Streets* (1893), to the profligate big spenders of F. Scott Fitzgerald's Roaring Twenties in *The Great Gatsby* (1925), to name just a few examples centered on New York. What makes Dreiser notable is his remarkably prescient understanding of how the act of looking helps to enable and sustain the consensual hallucination involved in the public performance of consumerism, whether articulated in the Marxist tradition as commodity fetishism or in Veblen's terms as conspicuous consumption.

In her landmark study of consumer culture, *Just Looking*, Rachel Bowlby attaches particular importance to the rise of the department store in the mid- to late nineteenth century, and the ways in which, as a prominent new retail institution in cities like New York, Chicago, Paris, and London, the department store's elaborate window displays helped to inaugurate a sidewalk culture fueled by the seemingly innocent activity of window shopping. For Bowlby, window shopping is never the innocuous pastime it affects to be. Rather, the ritual of "just looking" at merchandise on display plays an important psychological role in generating consumer desire and forming consumer identities.[40] In *Window Shopping: Cinema and the Postmodern*, Anne Friedberg elaborates on the department store's historical role in inaugurating a visual culture of consumption organized around "commodified forms of looking,"[41] stressing the importance of the "imbrication of images in the social relations of looking."[42]

Jean Baudrillard explores similar ideas in *The Consumer Society*, offering the following commentary on the significance of the shop window that aligns with Bowlby's argument about looking and desire, as well as Freidberg's point about images and social relations:

> The shop-window—all shop-windows—which are…the foci of our urban consumer practices, are also the site *par excellence* of that 'consensus operation', that communication and exchange of values through which an entire society is homogenized by incessant daily acculturation to the silent and spectacular logic of fashion.

That specific space which is the shop-window,... and which is already the street while maintaining, behind the transparency of its glass, the distance, the opaque status of the commodity— is also the site of a special social relation. Tracking along the shop-windows, with their *calculated riot of colour*, which is always at the same time a frustration, this hesitation-waltz of shopping is the Kanak dance in which goods are exalted before being exchanged. Objects and products are offered there in a glorious *mise-en-scène*, a sacralizing ostentation.... This symbolic giving, aped by the objects themselves on their stage-set, this symbolic, silent exchange between the proffered object and the gaze, is clearly an invitation to real, economic exchange inside the shop.[43]

Baudrillard may be writing about shop windows, but in terms of the dynamic of fantasy, desire, and scopic identification he identifies, he could just as easily be writing about Dreiser's sidewalk scene in *Sister Carrie*, where the tableau vivant of the parading, objectified crowd functions almost exactly like a shop-window display, providing an elaborate and animated spectacle of goods for visual consumption. In addition, to draw on Bowlby's formulation, "just looking" at the people on display along Broadway causes Carrie to identify with, and crave participation in, the consumer world being modeled before her, which is precisely the desired effect of the shop window on passersby.

This link between street-walking and window shopping in Dreiser's writing is no accident. Carrie begins her working life as a shop-girl in a Chicago department store, before moving on to an acting career on the New York stage. As Dreiser makes clear at various points in the novel, the two jobs, like the two spaces to which they belong, bear uncanny resemblances to each other in their performative, sexualized, and exploitative dimensions. For Dreiser, the sidewalk becomes the city's porous border between the theatrical worlds of the shop and the stage, a space where an emergent consumer society driven by desire, rather than need, can rehearse and refine its public expression. In this respect, Dreiser captures what becomes a defining feature of consumer society over the course of the twentieth century—namely, as Guy Debord so forcefully argued during the countercultural turn of the 1960s, the production and exploitation of desire through spectacle.[44]

Manhattan *Flâneuse*

The thematic and narrative focus on street-walking female characters in both *What Happened on 23rd Street* and *Sister Carrie* are far
from isolated incidents in cultural production at the turn of the
twentieth century. Rather, these examples reflect the changing role of
women in urban public life and, in particular, women's increasing
visibility and agency in spaces of public intersection within the
modern city. In this sense, the two texts—one cinematic and the
other literary—illustrate a growing cultural and aesthetic preoccupation with the figure of the *flâneuse*: the female counterpart to the
conventionally male figure of the meandering urban observer exalted in the city poetry of Charles Baudelaire and theorized in the
Parisian writings of Walter Benjamin.

Inspired by but also critiquing the work of Baudelaire, Benjamin's
concept of the flâneur as a fashionable and bourgeois urban figure has
been exhaustively discussed in critical theory, influencing numerous
generations of urban-social thinkers ranging from Benjamin's Marxist contemporaries at the Frankfurt School in the 1930s to more recent
reconceptualizations of the concept in light of feminist, queer, postcolonial, and globalization theory.[45] For Benjamin, the flâneur is both an
observer of and an active participant in the capitalist city of modernity,
exemplified in his own experience and writing by the commodity-
saturated spaces of the Parisian boulevards, alleyways, and arcades of
the early twentieth century. Although he never provides a clear definition of the flâneur, which partly accounts for the array of different
inflections the concept has received in the years and decades since,
Benjamin does identify certain general characteristics.

First, the flâneur is a product of the street: "The street becomes a
dwelling for the flâneur. He is as much at home among the facades of
houses as a citizen is in his four walls."[46] Second, the flâneur is a man
of the crowd: "someone abandoned in the crowd,"[47] seeking out but
also trying to come to terms with "the obliteration of the individual's
traces in the big-city crowd."[48] Third, the flâneur is mobile, able not
just to move around and navigate the city but also to pause within it
and absorb its experiences, "attracted by the magnet of the mass
which constantly has him in his range."[49] Fourth, and echoing Veblen,
the flâneur is a figure of idleness and indulgence: "a man of leisure
and…an anonymous consumer."[50]

While additional characteristics could be added to this list, the four listed above bring Benjamin's profile of the flâneur into sufficient focus to advance the following points of critique. To begin, Benjamin's relationship to the very concept he develops is somewhat conflicted, since, at one level, he critiques the flâneur for being so deeply implicated in the soul-sapping spectacle of the capitalist city, and at another level he posits the concept of the flâneur as a tool for urban analysis and as a loose model for his own method for conducting urban research, as illustrated in his sprawling posthumous collection *The Arcades Project*.[51] As David Frisby similarly argues in *Cityscapes of Modernity*,

> Benjamin creates not merely one of the first attempts at a history of the *flâneur*; he also provides us with an analytic of *flânerie* that reveals potential affinities between this activity and the sociologist's investigation of the social world. In part, this analytic emerges out of Benjamin's own reflections upon his methodology for the Arcades Project. It shifts the focus of the *flâneur* from the negative conception of the stroller and producer of harmless physiognomies to the notion of the more directed observer and investigator of the signifiers of the city.[52]

Frisby's comments are, in part, a response to the ambiguity and instability of the flâneur in Benjamin's thinking and the way in which the figure occupies a sliding scale of observational positions in Benjamin's own writing and practice, ranging from an unthinking urban witness cruising the city on consumer autopilot to a skilled and detached interpretive intellectual making new sense of the chaotic urban scene.

Another point to emphasize is that the flâneur embodies many of the thematic tensions of life under conditions of capitalist modernity, such as tensions between individuality and anonymity, belonging and estrangement, or private and public. In this respect, Benjamin's writings on the flâneur can be understood as addressing broader social and cultural developments than simply the anatomy of a particular urban type. This helps to explain why the flâneur has been pursued and reinterpreted across so many different fields of inquiry, ranging from sociology and ethnography to film and media studies, leading to a rich variety of new incarnations such as the *plâneur* (aerial flâneur),[53] the *driveur* (the flâneur driving a car),[54] and, in a more roundabout way, the *zonard* (disaffected youth of the Parisian *banlieues*).[55]

A more significant point in light of my discussion, however, is that Benjamin conceives the flâneur in almost exclusively male terms. This is more than a reflection of early twentieth-century gender politics or strict adherence to the gender conventions of French grammar, although both of these factors play a role. Rather, the overwhelming maleness of Benjamin's flâneur connects to a larger, historical pattern of underexamining the place and role of women in the life of the modern city, particularly in the early twentieth century when the field of urban studies, bringing together disciplines like philosophy, sociology, history, and economics, was starting to take form. Yet as feminist critics such as Janet Wolff, Judith Walkowitz, and Griselda Pollock have argued,[56] there is much to be missed by overlooking or underthinking the relationship between gender, cities, and modernity, not least in relation to the masculinized figure of the flâneur.

This insight is at the center of Deborah Parsons's reappraisal of Benjamin in *Streetwalking the Metropolis*, where she studies the implications of "the ambiguous gendering of *flânerie*" for "defining a *flâneuse*."[57] Parsons's interest in studying the female flâneur is connected to the contradictory, ambivalent position that this figure represents in urban culture around the turn of the twentieth century. The flâneuse is linked, on the one hand, to women's newfound social and spatial freedoms in the modern city and, on the other hand, to women's symbolic recuperation back into the system of power and meaning being challenged:

> By the late nineteenth century, women's access to the metropolis was expanding both in terms of leisure and employment.... Women's legitimate participation in city life was an extremely significant divergence from Victorian conventional belief.... Regarded as manifest in huge and growing numbers, the woman in the city was characterized, examined, and theorized into one or more male-authored stereotyped pathological states.... The convention of the woman in public as a possessable object continues in these images, which themselves become publicly available tropes.... However,...the ambiguities of these categories themselves allow for an alternative perception of women's presence in the city, one that suggests the woman as an increasingly autonomous and observing presence.[58]

Although Parsons is writing about London and Paris, her argument is just as relevant to New York City and is supported by the examples of *What Happened on 23rd Street* and *Sister Carrie*, where the female protagonists appear in both cases not only as "possessable objects" but also as "publicly available tropes." The difference between the two texts, however, is that Dreiser's is ultimately questioning of the objectifying process and is open to exploring what Parsons's describes as an "alternative perception of women's presence in the city." Indeed, the entire novel is about exploring the possibilities of constructing new social and sexual identities for women in the city.

As Parsons demonstrates in her analysis of the urban novels of European writers such as Doris Lessing, Dorothy Richardson, and Virginia Woolf, images of the flâneuse as an "autonomous and observing presence" in the city tend to be more pronounced and developed in women's writing, where "the city operates as not just a setting or image, but as a constituent of identity" through which women's "experience of urban space" is translated into "narrative form."[59] In the case of New York, the narrative exploration of women's experience of urban space—particularly in relation to the public setting of the street—is similarly at the heart of Nella Larsen's Harlem novels, which bring issues of race into consideration alongside those of gender and modernity.

Blending autobiography and fiction in the fragmented style associated with transatlantic modernism of the 1920s, while also sharing many of the central political concerns of the Harlem Renaissance, Larsen's writing addresses the indeterminate place of mixed-race women in American society and the challenges of negotiating the borderlands and contact zones between white and African-American communities. Her first novel, *Quicksand* (1928), which closely parallels the trajectory of her own life, follows the travels of Helga Crane, an independent young woman of Danish and West Indian descent, who moves restlessly around the country in search of a place that feels like home.

In the following passage, which leads up to Helga's departure for New York, Larsen describes the lure of the street as her character looks out the window of her Chicago apartment:

She stood intently looking down into the glimmering street, far below, swarming with people, merging into little eddies and disengaging themselves to pursue their own individual ways. A few minutes later she stood in the doorway, drawn by an uncontrollable desire to mingle with the crowd. The purple sky showed tremendous clouds piled up, drifting here and there with a sort of endless lack of purpose. Very like the myriad human beings pressing hurriedly on. Looking at these, Helga caught herself wondering who they were, what they did, and of what they thought. What was passing behind those dark molds of flesh. Did they really think at all? Yet, as she stepped out into the moving multi-colored crowd, there came to her a queer feeling of enthusiasm, as if she were tasting some agreeable, exotic food—sweetbreads, smothered with truffles and mushrooms—perhaps. And, oddly enough, she felt, too, that she had come home. She, Helga Crane, who had no home.[60]

The search for belonging is a recurring theme in Larsen's writing. Here, the street provides a momentary sense of home to someone experiencing feelings of loneliness and alienation. What attracts and comforts Helga is the crowd: its anonymity, its energy, its unthinking movements, actions, and flows. More specifically, the crowd provides an ephemeral, intoxicating experience to which she can temporarily surrender autonomy and control while maintaining the emotional distance and social disconnection to which she clings throughout the novel. Helga's immersion into this nocturnal street scene simultaneously alleviates and deepens her isolation in the city, thereby illustrating the peculiar paradox of urban living diagnosed by Benjamin and others in their readings of *flânerie* whereby the individual is both constituted and "obliterated" by the crowd.[61]

This early sidewalk scene in *Quicksand* is important to the novel because it prefigures Helga's later street experiences in Harlem, where the lure of the crowd intensifies but so too does an underlying feeling of disconnection. Leaving a dinner party late one night with friends, Helga finds herself reluctantly swept up in the group's pursuit of pleasure and fun as they move across the nocturnal city:

It was a sulky, humid night, a thick furry night, through which the electric torches shone like a silver fuzz.... After much consultation and chatter they decided upon a place and climbed into two patiently waiting taxis, rattling things which jerked, wiggled, and groaned, and threatened every minute to collide with others of their kind, or with inattentive pedestrians. Soon they pulled up before a tawdry doorway in a narrow crosstown street and stepped out. The night was far from quiet, the streets far from empty. Clanging trolley bells, quarelling cats, cackling phonographs, raucous laughter, complaining motor-horns, low singing, mingled in the familiar medley that is Harlem. Black figures, white figures, little forms, big forms, small groups, large groups, sauntered, or hurried by. It was gay, grotesque, and a little weird. Helga Crane felt singularly apart from it all.[62]

Setting aside the ways in which this depiction of Harlem perpetuates a clichéd image of the neighborhood as a space of interracial festivity, a view popular at the time of Larsen's writing when the jazz-age mania for underground nightclubs was at its height, the passage is interesting in its use of the carnivalesque to evoke the atmosphere and activity of the street. Filled with the chaos of moving people, shifting sights, and competing sounds—exacerbated by the crosstown movements of the taxi ride—Harlem emerges as a raucous and chaotic space geared toward the hedonistic pursuits of nighttime revelers. One key difference between this street scene and the earlier one in Chicago is that the novelty of being immersed in the crowd has now worn off, leaving Helga feeling weary and depleted by her participation in the spectacle of the city, one in which she has become inextricably immersed.

Larsen's attention to the psychological effects of New York street life, filtered in her writing through the experience of a female African-American character struggling to cope with an outsider identity, does more than regender and racialize the Benjaminian flâneur in terms that expand the affective possibilities of the figure beyond those of a passive observer or interpreter of the city. Her writing also captures the mental state of numbness and separation that various urban thinkers of the early twentieth century, such as Georg Simmel, came to associate with the everyday experience of the modern city. This is particularly evident in the above passage where Helga feels "singularly apart" from her environment and no longer able to summon the requisite energy and interest needed to cope with all the demands that Harlem's street life places on her attention. This state of mental fatigue and psychological retreat is what Simmel,

commenting on the effects of the "big city" on the individual, terms
the "blasé metropolitan attitude."[63]

Blasé Metropolitan Attitude

Writing at the turn of the twentieth century, the German sociologist
Georg Simmel suggests in his 1903 essay "The Metropolis and Mental
Life" that the inhabitants of cities tend to develop a blasé attitude in
order to cope with the anonymity, intensity, and velocity of urban
life.[64] For Simmel, the modern city is overwhelming and relentless in
its assault on the senses and the blasé attitude, which is characterized
by a posture of disinterest, serves as a form of protection against the
mental invasions of the city:

> Thus the metropolitan type...creates a protective organ for itself
> against the profound disruption with which the fluctuations and
> discontinuities of the external milieu threaten it. Instead of react-
> ing emotionally, the metropolitan type reacts primarily in a ra-
> tional manner.... Thus the reaction of the metropolitan person to
> those events is moved to a sphere of mental activity which is least
> sensitive and which is furthest removed from the depths of the
> personality.... There is perhaps no psychic phenomenon which is
> so unconditionally reserved to the city as the blasé outlook.... This
> incapacity to react to new stimulations with the required amount
> of energy constitutes in fact that blasé attitude which every child
> of a large city evinces.[65]

Simmel presents the blasé individual, not unlike Benjamin's figure of
the roving flâneur, as a kind of modern intellectual capable of abstraction and rationality, but also deeply implicated in the urban
spectacle. And like Benjamin's flâneur, Simmel's blasé individual is
specifically linked to the great cities of capitalist modernity (Paris,
Berlin, Vienna, London) and reflects their impersonal systems of
commodity exchange.

Such a view of the metropolitan individual as a blasé observer-par-
ticipant is evident, as illustrated above, in Helga Crane's nocturnal
urban wanderings in *Quicksand*, where the protagonist's psychological detachment from Harlem's chaotic street life coincides with a
growing disenchantment over what she perceives as the African-

American community's compromised and hypocritical approach to race relations in the city. Far from being rare occurrences, blasé figures feature prominently in creative responses to the modern city. In John Dos Passos's *Manhattan Transfer* (1925),[66] for example, the disjointed and fragmented narrative, inspired by James Joyce's expressionistic writing and Sergei Eisenstein's cinematic collages, reflects the characters' own disconnected and emotionally deadening experiences of a hostile urban environment. And in Gilded Age novels like William Dean Howells's *A Hazard of New Fortunes* (1889),[67] the prevailing attitude among New Yorkers is one of emotional hardness, which is deliberately and repeatedly contrasted against the naïve effusiveness of the newlywed protagonists who, newly arrived in town, need to be slowly desensitized to all of the city's stimuli in order to function effectively in the bustling metropolis.

Looking beyond literature to the visual arts, blasé figures can similarly be identified in works as diverse as John Sloan's *Sixth Avenue and Thirtieth Street, New York City* (1907) and Berenice Abbott's photo-documentary project *Changing New York* (1935–8), where scenes of everyday street life yield to portraits of isolation and detachment. In Sloan's painting (figure 31), which exhibits the Ashcan School's characteristic sympathy for the poor and neglected inhabitants of the city, an impoverished woman, who appears disoriented and drunk, lurches as she crosses the street. On the right, two fashionably dressed female pedestrians look on dismissively as they pass by. Idling in the background, a group of men are gathered on the corner outside a bar, surveying the scene with indifference. From the inebriated woman drinking herself into solitary oblivion to the haughty fashionistas, to the male loiterers, the painting depicts three levels, or layers, of disengaged behavior. Given the broader movement of social realism to which Sloan's work belongs, it is likely that the depiction of such blasé attitudes is meant not only to critique a breakdown of social relations within the public spaces of New York's urban community but also to provoke the very feeling of social concern for others that the figures in the painting appear to lack.

The theme of isolation and detachment also pervades Berenice Abbott's depiction of New York's sidewalk culture in *The Tempo of the City 1* (figure 32), albeit in a different way than Sloan's painting. Shot in 1938 as part of her Depression-era WPA project *Changing New York*,[68] the photograph is part of a larger series of images aimed

FIGURE 31. *John Sloan,* Sixth Avenue and Thirtieth Street, New York City, *1907.*
(Courtesy Philadelphia Museum of Art/Artist Rights Society, New York,
c/o Pictoright Amsterdam)

at both documenting and aestheticizing the city's rapid architectural
transformation in the mid- to late 1930s. Although many of the project's photographs depict either modern skyscrapers or largely depopulated urban vistas contrasting old and new New York, *The
Tempo of the City 1* is more concerned with people than buildings.
Taken from a slightly elevated position, the photograph shows pedestrians walking past a tall metal street clock on a crowded sidewalk at the corner of Fifth Avenue and Forty-fourth Street in the
early afternoon. Mirroring the heavy traffic visible along Fifth
Avenue in the background, the pedestrians look rushed, purposeful,
and nearly identical in appearance and movement. The dominance
of the clock—both in terms of its towering size and its central position in the foreground of the image—conveys the importance of
regulated time to this synchronized, mechanized street-walking
scene in the fast-moving heart of the metropolis. "The neat collective
geography of bodies," writes G. F. Mitrano in her evocative reading
of the image, "betrays the silent push and shove of a world in agony,

caught in the obsession of a punishing sameness."[69] The photograph's visualization of this punishing sameness shows how humanity's subordination to the clock generates anonymous, accelerated bodies unable to give each other time or attention as they move along the street.

Such a portrayal of the city's rhythms in the blasé terms of anonymity and sameness, what Simmel describes as "indifference towards the distinctions between things,"[70] recalls some of the scenes of architectural gigantism and human dwarfing in *Manhatta*, the 1921 experimental film in which Charles Sheeler and Paul Strand chronicle a working day in the life of New York in order to emphasize the modern city's aesthetic transformation and dehumanizing

FIGURE 32. *Berenice Abbott,* Tempo of the City 1, *1938. (Courtesy Museum of the City of New York)*

effects. In particular, the film's often-cited shot of Wall Street, which carefully replicates a photograph taken from the same position by Strand six years earlier in 1915 (figure 33), shows pedestrians reduced to impersonal silhouettes as they walk beneath the austere, monumental architecture of the J. P. Morgan Trust Building. The severe geometry and extreme facelessness of the building reflect not only the impersonality of the economic system it embodies but also the insignificance of the human individual within that system. Here, the disconnection and fatigue associated with the blasé metropolitan attitude register in the radical depersonalization and crushing anonymity involved in the pedestrian experience of Wall Street. The resulting image is one of inscrutability: the architecture, people, and street all defy—even discourage—interpretation beyond their uninviting surfaces.

The impenetrability of the city's surfaces (both human and architectural) can be understood in Simmel's terms as an expression, a well as a consequence, of a broader, more systemic process of objectification:

FIGURE 33. *Paul Strand,* Wall Street, New York, *1915. (Courtesy Aperture Foundation)*

Perhaps less conscious than in practical activity and in the obscure complex of feeling which flow from him, [the individual] is reduced to a negligible quantity. He becomes a single cog as over against the vast overwhelming organization of things and forces which gradually take out of his hands everything connected with progress, spirituality and value. The operation of these forces results in the transformation of the latter from a subjective form into one of purely objective existence. It need only be pointed out that the metropolis is the proper arena for this type of culture which has outgrown every personal element. Here in buildings and in educational institutes, in the wonders and comforts of space-conquering technique, in the formations of social life and in the concrete institutions of the State is to be found such a tremendous richness of crystallizing, de-personalized cultural accomplishments that the personality can, so to speak, scarcely maintain itself in the face of it.[71]

Building on Marx's critique of capital, but also prefiguring aspects of Georg Lukács's 1923 *History and Class Consciousness* and Henri Lefebvre's 1974 *The Production of Space*,[72] Simmel links the city's obliteration of the individual to the inescapability of capitalism's reifying effects, which extend in his thinking to the spatial organization and built environment of the city, as well as to the ideological conditioning of its inhabitants. As America's symbolic, geographic, and architectural center of finance, Wall Street therefore represents an ideal site for Sheeler and Strand to seek out the numbing, hardening, and atomizing forces that capitalist modernity exerts on the metropolitan individual. What their wider body of New York work reveals, both in paintings like Sheeler's *Church Street El* (1920) and photographs like Strand's *City Hall Park* (1915; figure 34), is that those same forces operate throughout the spaces and scenes of the modern city, much as Simmel suggests in his writing.

Whether in the form of Sheeler and Strand's solitary and diminished human figures, Larsen's fatigued and jaded urban migrants, Sloan's melancholy street corners, or Abbott's homogenous midtown drones, cultural production in modern New York pursues many of the same concerns animating early twentieth-century critical thinking about street life. To cite examples discussed above, this extends from representations of conspicuous consumption in Broadway promenades through gendered iterations of sidewalk flânerie

FIGURE 34. *Paul Strand,* City Hall Park, *1915. (Courtesy Aperture Foundation)*

to chilling panoramas of blasé indifference and anonymity. What connects these practices, identified in different but interrelating ways by thinkers like Veblen, Benjamin, and Simmel, is the impact of capitalism on the form, space, and lived experience of the modern city.

This impact was often at its most visible in and around the public space of the street, particularly in relation to the eye-catching practices of street-walking, window shopping, and crowd watching. Because of this relationship, much critical thinking and creative practice in the late nineteenth and early twentieth centuries is geared toward the more affluent, spectacular dimensions of street life, where flânerie, conspicuous consumption, blasé attitudes, and related behaviors all flourished. Yet as certain contemporary urban observers also find ways to emphasize in the material of their work, poverty was also integral to New York's street life, producing another form of spectacle altogether: the spectacle of the slum.

City of Slums

In *Planet of Slums*, Mike Davis redirects a long-standing interest in the unequal distributions and articulations of power toward the phenomenon of the twenty-first-century megacity and its proliferation of slums. Surveying locations from Lagos, Manila, and Mumbai to Cairo, Johannesburg, and São Paulo, Davis argues that the neoliberal mode of globalization is not only widening the gap between urban rich and urban poor but has also become dependent on producing poverty on a previously unprecedented scale in order to maintain the level of wealth enjoyed by the world's urban elite. The explosion in the number and size of slums over the last half century, writes Davis, reveals how, "instead of being a focus of growth and prosperity," cities have become "a dumping ground for a surplus population working in unskilled, unprotected, and low-wage informal service industries and trade."[73]

As Davis takes care to note, the expanding "slumification" of twenty-first-century cities, particularly in the Global South, "both recapitulate[s] and confound[s] the precedents of nineteenth- and early-twentieth-century Europe and North America,"[74] and has significant roots in the Industrial Revolution and the process of rapid urbanization that it set in motion. The rise of neoliberalism in the twenty-first century may have done much to grow and globalize poverty, as the geographer David Harvey has argued,[75] but the spatial ordering and socioeconomic exclusions producing twenty-first-century slums belong to an older, deeper dynamic of urban poverty that, as Friedrich Engels had already observed in 1844 in *The Condition of the Working Class in England*,[76] has been integral to the development and functioning of cities under industrial capitalism.

Alongside other Western metropolises such as Berlin, Chicago, London, and Paris, New York has long been part of this dynamic. The city's explosive growth in the nineteenth century led not just to new spaces of affluence and leisure being opened up across the city, such as the upmarket neighborhoods of the Upper East and West Sides or the civic expanse of Central Park, but also to the increased ghettoization of historically poor neighborhoods like the Bowery, the Lower East Side, and Hell's Kitchen, as described in great and colorful detail by Luc Sante in his popular history of New York's underbelly, *Low Life: Lures and Snares of Old New York*.[77] Behind much of New York's growth, in both labor and population, was a steady influx of immigrants, who accounted for upward of 40 percent of the city's inhabitants in 1890.[78] Although nothing new, of course, since New York has been an epicenter of transnational migration since its founding, the presence of these outsider populations was essential for building, servicing, inhabiting, and vitalizing the everyday spaces of the modern city.

Contrary to the prevailing pattern of twenty-first-century slums, which have tended to develop around the edges of cities in peri-urban zones of deprivation and exclusion, such as the banlieues surrounding Paris or Soweto outside Johannesburg, nineteenth- and early twentieth-century slums tended to be located within the heart of the city. One reason is that the spatial reordering of the city under globalization, which has resulted in the increased spatial marginalization of poverty, did not gather momentum until the late 1940s and 1950s. In the case of Manhattan, the combination of the island's space limitations and the extreme overdeterminism of the Commissioners' Plan further restricted possibilities for slums to develop far from the geographic center of the borough. Instead, the trend in modern Manhattan was an entrenchment of inner-city poverty, rather than a displacement of that poverty to (and beyond) the geographic margins of the city, although later reform efforts, particularly in the 1960s and '70s, would lead to experiments in that direction. Just as importantly, as Thomas Kessner observes, it was essential for New York's poor and newly arrived immigrant populations to have ready access to the sources of job supply, which were concentrated in "the industrial-commercial-core of the city," and thus made commuting from the outskirts impractical and expensive.[79]

These conditions meant that, throughout the nineteenth and early twentieth centuries, poverty coexisted cheek by jowl with wealth throughout much of New York City, although especially in the densely populated space of Manhattan. The presence of poverty, as well as the extreme contrasts it created with the wealthier features of the city, was a subject of concern and fascination, just as it had been in the industrial novels of Elizabeth Gaskell and the social realism of Charles Dickens in Victorian England several decades earlier. In response, architects and planners, such as Hugh Ferriss, Raymond Hood, and George E. Waring, dreamed up sanitized urban futures designed to tackle New York's poverty through innovations in engineering and design. To take one extreme example, Waring's 1897 treatise *Street-Cleaning and the Disposal of a City's Waste*, which is written from the perspective of a newly appointed street commissioner with a background in sanitary engineering, proposes improving public health and reducing urban squalor through aggressive waste management.[80] In their own ways, artistic movements like the Ashcan School sought to raise public awareness of poverty by making it a dominant theme in their New York paintings, etchings, and drawings, such as in Everett Shinn's *Eviction* (1904), which depicts the helplessness of a destitute family being thrown out of their tenement home in the Lower East Side (figure 35). Similarly, many writers and filmmakers took up poverty as explicit concerns in their work, ranging from Jewish ghetto narratives like Abraham Cahan's *Yekl* (1896) to urban squalor films like Raoul Walsh's *Regeneration* (1915), which follows the life of an abandoned street urchin who grows up to become a notorious mobster.

Throughout this body of work, the street figures as key site through which to engage and represent urban poverty. This is particularly evident in the fiction of Stephen Crane and the photojournalism of Jacob Riis, whose cotemporaneous work in the early to mid-1890s was not only instrumental in raising public awareness about the city's spaces and cycles of poverty but also pioneering in its efforts to develop new aesthetic and narrative techniques for representing the city's outcast populations.

FIGURE 35. *Everett Shinn,* Eviction, *1904. (Courtesy Smithsonian American Art Museum, bequest of Henry Ward Ranger through the National Academy of Design)*

In his study of Riis, Crane, and the ethnography of the slum, *The Virtues of the Vicious*, Keith Gandal tracks these representational innovations, linking them to "the decline of Protestant morality and the rise of an alternative ethics" centered on individuality and self-determinism.[81] For Gandal, this shift is both expressed by and caught up in the spectacle of the poor created within an emergent mass culture:

> In the course of the 1890s, the slum emerged as a spectacle in the popular arts of representation: the urban poor were discovered as a fresh topic by police reporters, novelists, photographers, true-crime writers, muckrakers, and social reformers, some of whom were expressly challenging traditional moral descriptions as well as moralistic analyses that attributed poverty to individual vice.[82]

In Gandal's account of turn-of-the-century New York, the literature of the poor functions as a "discursive field," to use Michel Foucault's phrase,[83] for an American middle class negotiating its transition into an emergent consumer society. Just as importantly, as Gandal also argues,[84] the spectacle of the slum further functions as a source of urban exoticism, providing a way for readers to explore, yet remain safely distanced from, a world of deprivation and suffering. This double function of the slum in the American cultural imagination informs both Crane's *Maggie: A Girl of the Streets* (1893) and Riis's *How the Other Half Lives: Studies Among the Tenements of New York* (1890), where the motif of the sidewalk continues to yield portraits of a street culture dominated by speed, movement, and dislocation—except that now those conditions are produced by poverty rather than the forms of wealth that drive conspicuous consumption or flânerie.

Reflecting Crane's background in freelance journalism and short-story writing, *Maggie* consists of a series of fragmented episodes written in an impressionistic style that most critics view as both an exemplar of Gilded Age realism and a precursor to American naturalism. The novel is set in and around the Bowery, a rough neighborhood in 1890s New York that was well known for its seedy mix of flophouses, bars, and brothels. The narrative revolves around the violence and degradation of the city's impoverished underbelly and, in particular, tracks the eponymous Maggie's slide into prostitution.

Much of the novel's action takes place in the street, such as in the following passage containing one of the story's most significant yet elusive episodes. Following several chapters detailing Maggie's slow, painful transformation from sweatshop worker to sex worker, Crane cuts away from the main narrative to offer an extended description of an unnamed woman walking at night from the bright lights of Broadway and the Tenderloin district to the dark backstreets of the Lower East Side:

> A girl of the painted cohorts of the city went along the street. She threw changing glances at men who passed her, giving smiling invitations to men of rural or untaught pattern and usually seeming sedately unconscious of the men with a metropolitan seal upon their faces.
>
> Crossing glittering avenues, she went into the throng emerging from the places of forgetfulness. She hurried forward through the crowd as if intent upon reaching a distant home.... The girl walked on out of the realm of restaurants and saloons. She passed more glittering avenues and went into darker blocks than those where the crowd travelled.... The girl went into the gloomy districts near the river, where the tall black factories shut in the street and only occasional broad beams of light fell across the pavements from saloons.... Further on in the darkness she met a ragged being with shifting, blood-shot eyes and grimey hands.... She went into the

blackness of the final block. The shutters of the tall buildings were closed like grim lips. The structures seemed to have eyes that looked over her, beyond her, at other things. Afar off the lights of the avenues glittered as if from an impossible distance. Street car bells jingled with a sound of merriment.[85]

Although the woman in this passage remains unnamed, most readers from Crane's time to ours have interpreted her as being Maggie.[86] Yet by rendering the woman anonymous, Crane is able to shift the focus away from the individual story of one woman's misfortunes and toward broader, more systematic patterns of disenfranchisement in the city. In this respect, as Howard Horwitz argues, Crane adopts a quasi-sociological approach to identifying problems and dangers in the city.[87] The lone streetwalker may be Maggie, but she also represents any unfortunate woman forced by the extremes of poverty and desperation to seek livelihood in prostitution, an occupation that is repeatedly referenced in loosely coded terms in the passage.

More to the point, Crane's nocturnal street-walking passage begins in the bright, crowded realm of the flâneur—the sort of nocturnal leisure scene captured by John Sloan in his 1907 Tenderloin painting *The Haymarket, Sixth Avenue* (figure 36)—and ends in the underlit, desolate space of the slum. This transition from a space of movement, illumination, and inhabitation to one of stillness, darkness, and abandonment allows Crane to highlight the proximity and coexistence of these two extremes of the city. The first, embodied by Broadway, is centered on pleasure, consumption, and visibility. The second, signaled by the shuttered warehouses and darkened tenements, revolves around work, production, and obscurity. As the lone woman's pathway through the city indicates, the two worlds—though vastly different in terms of appearance and conditions—are nonetheless closely connected and easily traversed. Their juxtaposition suggests not only a relationship of mutual dependence but also that the boundaries between the two remain fluid and movable.

Significantly, it is the form of urban mobility associated with the flâneur—street-walking—that Crane employs to move his anonymous female pedestrian from the space of the spectacle to the space of the slum. Here, however, that mobility is motivated not by desire or leisure, as in the case of flânerie, but instead by necessity and work. The lone woman appears to be cruising the streets in search of

FIGURE 36. *John Sloan, The Haymarket, Sixth Avenue, 1907. Oil on canvas, 26 1/8 x 34 13/16 in. (66.3 x 88.5 cm). (Courtesy Brooklyn Museum, gift of Mrs. Harry Payne Whitney, 23.60)*

clients, smiling enticingly at those male onlookers who appear less blasé and, thus, more receptive to her presence and invitations. The gaze of the male onlookers becomes more attentive and menacing, however, as the woman moves further and further from the lights and crowds, culminating in an uncomfortable encounter with a predatory male figure:

> When almost to the river the girl saw a great figure. On going forward she perceived it to be a huge fat man in torn and greasy garments.... His small, bleared eyes, sparkling from amidst great rolls of red fat, swept eagerly over the girl's upturned face. He laughed, his brown disordered teeth gleaming under a grey, grizzled moustache from which beer-drops dripped. His whole body gently quivered and shook like that of a dead jelly fish. Chuckling and leering, he followed the girl of the crimson legions.
>
> At their feet the river appeared a deathly black hue. Some hidden factory sent up a yellow glare, that lit for a moment the waters lapping

oilily, against timbers. The varied sounds of life, made joyous by distance and seeming unapproachableness, came faintly and died away to a silence.[88]

The indeterminacy running through this chapter of *Maggie* is heightened in this closing passage, culminating in the image of the "huge fat man" following the lone woman as she disappears into the darkness of the city night. It is unclear what happens to the woman, although the language used to describe the riverside setting contains multiple references to death and silencing. This has prompted many to read the scene as an indirect depiction of a prostitute's murder. Such a reading is reinforced by the opening of the next chapter, in which Maggie's death is announced but left unexplained, inviting readers to identify the unnamed streetwalker as Maggie and to interpret the riverside episode as the moment of her death, most likely at the hands of the leering male stalker.

Even so, some critics, such as Robert M. Dowling and Donald Pizer, dispute such a reading of Maggie's death, arguing through a literal cartographic analysis of the streetwalker's route from Broadway to the East River, as well as through a comparative analysis of textual variants in different editions of the novel, that the geography of Manhattan and the historical popularity of the East River as a site for prostitutes to commit suicide in the late nineteenth century mean that the two women are not meant to be related and, even if they are, suicide is more likely than murder.[89] Whatever the case, the ambiguity surrounding both the streetwalker's fate and Maggie's death does not detract from the more substantive point Crane makes about poverty and city life. Crane is entirely unambiguous in the link he identifies between violence and the slum, whether in the form of a prostitute's premature death or in one of the novel's many other expressions of brutalism, pain, or force.

Sidewalks and Fear

It is worth noting, therefore, that *Maggie* begins with a street brawl between rival gangs in the Bowery, and is punctuated throughout by various eruptions of public violence that take both physical and verbal forms. In the novel's opening, the fighting between the youths begins somewhat playfully, but quickly becomes more sinister:

> A very little boy stood upon a heap of gravel for the honor of Rum Alley. He was throwing stones at howling urchins from Devil's Row who were circling madly about the heap and pelting at him....
>
> On their small, convulsed faces there shone the grins of true assassins. As they charged, they threw stones and cursed in shrill chorus.
>
> The little champion of Rum Alley stumbled precipitately down the other side. His coat had been torn to shreds in a scuffle, and his hat was gone. He had bruises on twenty parts of his body, and blood was dripping from a cut in his head. His wan features wore a look of a tiny, insane demon....
>
> In the yells of the whirling mob of Devil's Row children there were notes of joy like songs of triumphant savagery. The little boys seemed to leer gloatingly at the blood upon the other child's face....
>
> Down the avenue came boastfully sauntering a lad of sixteen years, although the chronic sneer of an ideal manhood already sat upon his lips. His hat was tipped with an air of challenge over his eye. Between his teeth, a cigar stump was tilted at the angle of defiance. He walked with a certain swing of the shoulders which appalled the timid. He glanced over into the vacant lot in which the little raving boys from Devil's Row seethed about the shrieking and tearful child from Rum Alley.[90]

The pleasure that the fighting boys take in inflicting pain, as well as the rage accompanying their violence, foreshadows the cruelty and bravado of the street life they are destined to lead as they grow older, aspects of which are already suggested by the comportment of the swaggering teenage thug who wades into the brawl to take charge. The more important point to note, however, is that the brawl occurs in a public space adjoining the street.

In Crane's writing, the sidewalk remains a space of sociality and encounter, but one that produces conflict and violence rather than dialogue and resolution. The reason is its location in the slum—a space where, in his writing, social values and practices begin to break down. In this respect, Crane explores one of the central issues that comes to dominate Jane Jacobs's critique of American urbanism more than half a century later: the relationship between sidewalks, safety, and urban fear. In *The Death and Life of Great American Cities*,

Jacobs argues that the ways in which people experience a city's side-walks largely determine how they perceive and feel about the city itself. Safe cities, she suggests, have safe sidewalks: "if a city's streets are safe from barbarism and fear, the city is tolerably safe from bar-barism and fear. When people say that a city, or a part of it, is dan-gerous or a jungle, what they mean primarily is that they do not feel safe on the sidewalks.... To keep the city safe is a fundamental task of a city's streets and its sidewalks."[91] Among the factors that help to make a sidewalk safe in Jacobs's thinking are "a clear demarcation between what is public space and what is private space," the watchful presence of "eyes upon the street," and the continuous presence of "users."[92]

Although she goes on to qualify and refine how these factors inter-relate to reduce urban fear and produce safe streets, Jacobs's principal idea is that a sidewalk functions best when it is able to accommodate and thrive in the presence of strangers:

> By definition...the streets of a city must do most of the job of handling strangers, for this is where strangers come and go. The streets must not only defend the city against the predatory strang-ers, they must protect the many, many peaceable and well-meaning strangers who use them, ensuring their safety too as they pass through. Moreover, no normal person can spend his life in some artificial haven, and this includes children. Everyone must use the streets.[93]

The idea that the street is both a ubiquitous and inescapable part of everyday urban life is similarly at the heart of *Maggie* and its depic-tion of slum living, where every character's life is centered on, and largely determined by, the experience of the street. Yet rather than protecting their users and reconciling strangers, Crane's sidewalks emerge from the narrative as sites of menace and fear—spaces of vi-olence that estrange and exploit their users.

Viewed in Jacobs's terms, which remain compelling even if "laced with nostalgia,"[94] as Max Page puts it in *Reconsidering Jane Jacobs*, the slum sidewalks in *Maggie* are malfunctioning as public spaces. In the case of the street-fighting episode, the sidewalk not only breeds but also tolerates group violence and antisocial behavior. The sense of communal ownership over public space that Jacobs sees as crucial to the smooth, safe functioning of the city is distorted through gang rivalries into extreme territorial claims over neighborhoods and group identities. In the case of the lone, street-walking prostitute who disappears with the "huge fat man" into the urban night, the sidewalk fails at a far more fundamental level. The woman's safety is compromised by the absence of protective "eyes on the street" once she wanders from the crowded avenues of New York's main thoroughfares, leaving her to be followed, to use Jacobs's words, by one of the city's "predatory strangers." In both cases, the sidewalk fails to mediate the presence of different users, enabling street practices, such as fighting and stalking, that do not occur—at least not as frequently or visibly—on the more crowded, affluent, and surveilled sidewalks of consumer-oriented leisure streets like Broadway and Fifth Avenue.

While an argument could be made that Crane is sensationalizing the slum by portraying its sidewalks as sites of fear and danger, the fuller and more accurate explanation, as Keith Gandal has argued, is that Crane is attempting "to reinvent the tenement novel," which was highly popular throughout the 1890s, by refusing "to judge slum life according to middle-class standards."[95] To do this, Crane needed to depict the slum as a space of violence, misery, exploitation, and fear in keeping with the conventions set by his more sensationalist contemporaries, like Edgar Fawcett and Edward Townsend, so that he could then challenge readers by refraining from delivering any of the moralistic judgments or rehabilitory parables they had come to expect from the genre of the tenement novel. The goal was to achieve a heightened level of directness and honesty in the representation of the urban poor that would enable a new ethics of writing about poverty centered on revealing patterns and sources of inequality rather than moralizing or condemning them.

Tales of the Tenement

Alongside Stephen Crane, Jacob Riis was similarly involved in such a project, albeit with the more explicit goal of effecting immediate social change. The Danish-American photographer, journalist, and social reformer is best known for his hard-hitting exposé of slum living, *How the Other Half Lives: Studies among the Tenements of New York*. First published in 1890, the project uses the emerging genre of photojournalism, adapted from newspaper to book form, to document the poverty and squalor of New York's slums in the 1880s, focusing on the living and working conditions of their inhabitants. The idea was not only to complete one of the first ethnographic studies of a marginalized urban population that had been largely ignored in American society but at the same time to make middle-class New Yorkers more aware of the existence of that population and the inhuman conditions involved in slum living. The lack of awareness on the part of New York's middle class was due to a number of factors, but included what Thomas Bender describes in his discussion of nineteenth-century transformations of American domestic life as the "privatization of family life" and a narrowing of "social experience inherent in everyday life," which created "the spatial arrangement that enabled and required the message delivered to the middle classes by Jacob Riis in his classic book, *How the Other Half Lives*."[96]

For Riis, the publication of *How the Other Half Lives* was therefore intended to generate sympathy for the city's downtrodden underclass and to spark outrage at their treatment and exploitation by greedy landlords, sweatshop owners, corrupt police, and failing schools, as well as by the city and state governments and American society and politics more generally. The book went far in reaching these goals, in the sense that it became an instant bestseller, endorsed by the *New York Times* and influential local politicians like future U.S. president Theodore Roosevelt, then working for the U.S. Civil Service Commission.[97] This helped to build up the public pressure needed to galvanize the city into demolishing some of the worst tenement housing, taking the first steps toward improving sweatshop working conditions, fighting police corruption, widening access to health care, and strengthening education and protection for children in the poorest neighborhoods of the city.[98] Although such reform initiatives did not solve the underlying problem of poverty, or even diminish the size and density of the city's slums, they nonetheless initiated change, raised public awareness, and began shifting public attitudes toward urban poverty and social exclusion.

Of course, the effort to eradicate the slum—including the poverty that produces and perpetuates it—has been ongoing in cities worldwide long before and after Riis's work, but turn-of-the-century New York functioned as a particularly high-profile setting in which emerging notions of social justice and equality, as well as modern approaches to sanitation and planning, could be developed, tested, and refined. *How the Other Half Lives* marks only one intervention in the cultural politics of the slum, but it feeds into a larger discussion, inherited from earlier commentators like Engels and Dickens and fueled in the American context by the growing popularity of social reform movements, about the place of poverty in modern society.

Although Riis's prose descriptions and social commentary throughout *How the Other Half Lives* are evocative and elaborate, the book's accompanying images are what truly grabbed the public imagination. The photographs have endured since, acquiring a mixed status somewhere between historical document, art object, and cultural icon. Riis's photographic techniques, as well as the urban aesthetic he develops, derive from the gritty realism of photojournalism and, in particular, the gruesome intimacy of crime-scene photography, in which Riis previously specialized during his years as a police reporter. Alongside other photojournalists of the late nineteenth century, Riis pioneered the use of flash-powder photography, which was often needed to illuminate the cramped, underlit spaces in which he worked, both inside the tenements and out on the streets. This is one of the reasons why his images of urban squalor are often distinguished by strong contrasts between light and dark, which are further accentuated by the monochromatic technochemical constraints of nineteenth-century photography. Even Riis's naturally lit images frequently share the look of flash-illuminated shots, partly due to the enclosed architecture of the slum and the pervasiveness of shadows. The result in both thematic and aesthetic terms are overexposed scenes of underrepresented realities.

In one of the book's first photographs, *Bottle Alley, Mulberry Bend*, Riis strays from the public space of one of the city's most notorious crime-ridden streets, Baxter Street in Five Points, to the semiprivate enclosure of an adjacent alley widely known for being a gang hangout (figure 37). As it happens, the photograph depicts the scene of a gangland shooting and, in addition to being published in Riis's book, was also part of a series of photographs of the scene entered into evidence in a murder case.[99] In the left foreground, a wooden outhouse protrudes into the alley, a white cross on the side indicating the location of the shooting. In the right foreground is a wooden staircase, on the side of which another white cross is visible, marking in turn the location of the shooter. Although no corpse or other evidence of the crime is visible, the presence of the two crosses, as residue of the criminal investigation process, marks the alley as a site of danger and violence. The alley itself is narrow and cluttered, hugging the back of a row of tenement houses, from which rickety staircases descend. The cobblestone surface of the alleyway is littered with garbage and building debris, while the buildings themselves sag under the weight of age and neglect. Three solitary human figures are visible in the photograph. One stands, half concealed, in a doorway. Another sits on a staircase. A third leans on a balcony. All three figures are male and all three are staring directly at the camera. The look on their faces is difficult to read, but suggests a mix of awareness of and indifference toward the presence of the photographer. Although it is impossible to say how the men feel about being included in the photograph, as well as about the presence of the photographer, it is clear in their appearance that they belong to this space—are perhaps even produced by it—in the sense that they share the look of poverty, hardship, and abandonment overshadowing the scene as a whole.

Bottle Alley, Mulberry Bend is characteristic of Riis's photographic representation of the slum. The scene is enclosed, almost claustrophobic, with few to no geographic reference points and little sense of scale within the larger cityscape of New York. The space is dirty. The

FIGURE 37. *Jacob Riis,* Bottle Alley, Mulberry Bend. X shows where the victim stood when shot, *c. 1885. (Courtesy Museum of the City of New York)*

buildings are decrepit. The people are isolated. The living conditions are harsh. By depicting the slum in this way, Riis caters to—and even stimulates—a vicarious, middle-class fascination with the city's underbelly by coding the slum as a site of excitement (crime, violence, danger) and, simultaneously, a site of abjection (poverty, suffering, squalor). In such terms, his photographs prefigure the more sensationalist and morally ambiguous depictions of the modern city that come to dominate American hard-boiled fiction in the 1930s and, slightly later, Hollywood film noir in the late 1940s and early 1950s. They also align with and contribute to a growing transatlantic current in slum writing that includes Jack London's autobiographical foray into London's East End in *People of the Abyss* (1903) and George Orwell's slum-dwelling memoir *Down and Out in London and Paris* (1933).[100]

One of the most interesting aesthetic and thematic concerns running through Riis's photography is a tension between interior and exterior, domestic and public. Many of his outdoor photographs depict spaces so hemmed in by surrounding structures and so littered with traces and objects of domestic life that their status as public, exterior spaces becomes confused. This is visible in *Gotham Court*, for example, which shows a large group of children standing together in a narrow passageway. Their collective stance claims ownership over the space, while simultaneously forming an obstacle to outside intrusions, as if delineating the boundary of their home. The passageway itself is literally overhung by the overflow of domestic life in the form of laundry hung out to dry above the children. This sense of the domestic overflowing into public, exterior spaces is heightened in *Tenement-House Yard*, where the back alley is almost entirely obscured by piles of laundry heaped on the ground and pinned to washing lines. Here, again, there is a strong sense of the domestic spilling beyond the walls of the home, which is reinforced by the presence of women working on household chores while their children play alongside.

Reversing this dynamic, Riis's interior shots often show domestic spaces so barren and hostile to human living that they have more in common with the exterior roughness of the street than the interior retreat of the home. This is particularly pronounced in his series of police-station lodger photographs, which depict overnight dormitories charitably provided by the police in a precursor to the development of the homeless shelter (figure 38). The spaces are anything but homely. There is a basic lack of furniture, with hardwood planks serving as beds and buckets doubling as chairs. Groups of strangers seeking temporary shelter huddle around solitary stoves. Many of the lodgers are wrapped in rags and torn blankets that obscure their faces. Most of the defining elements of the home are missing. There is no sense of belonging, comfort, stability, familiarity, or safety. There is no decoration, personalization, or even genuine inhabitation of the space. Rather, the police-station dormitories in *How the Other Half Lives* are distinguished by anonymity and alienation. To adapt a phrase developed by Sudeep Dasgupta in relation to Mumbai's postcolonial slums, the spaces are marked by their "permanent transiency,"[101] which registers not only in their inhospitable material conditions but also, and quite literally, in their unhomely appearance. The same dynamic is repeated to varying degrees throughout Riis's interior photographs, ranging from portraits of tenement living rooms and lodgings-house bedrooms to snapshots of opium dens, two-cent taverns, and sweatshops.

FIGURE 38. *Jacob Riis,* Police Station Lodging Room 7: Women's Lodging Room in West 47th Street Station, *c. 1890. (Courtesy Museum of the City of New York)*

In part I, I use Anthony Vidler's concept of the architectural un-canny to help explain the defamiliarizing effects that New York's massive surge of skyscraper construction had on the urban imagi-nary in the late nineteenth and early twentieth centuries. The uncan-niness of the modern skyline, I argued via Vidler, arose from the newly scaled spaces and rapid transformation of the modern city. Riis's slum photography presents another articulation of the archi-tectural uncanny, one related not so much to the strangeness of urban change and the disorientation of spatial reordering, but rather to an unease produced by a disfiguration of the home.

Writing about unhomely houses and Edgar Allan Poe's short story "The Fall of The House of Usher" (1839), Vidler stresses that, in nine-teenth-century gothic writing, "the house provided an especially favored site for uncanny disturbances" because "its apparent domesticity, its residue of family history and nostalgia, its role as the last and most intimate shelter of private comfort sharpened by contrast the terror of invasion" and other forms of sudden distortion, threat, and change to this ultimate site of familiarity.[102] Vidler has in mind the haunted houses of the Romantic sublime, but the defamiliarization he associ-ates with spectral invasions of the home, as well as the inherent vul-nerability of the home itself to uncanny distortions, applies to Riis's slum photography, where the transformative effects of poverty not only distort the appearance and functioning of the home to the point of otherworldliness but also render the inhabitants themselves at times ghostly—haunting, liminal, anonymous figures neither fully present in nor entirely absent from the space.

Together, the New York tenement tales of Riis, Crane, and their contemporaries helped the slum to emerge in the 1890s as a popular cultural spectacle. Although some of this work, as Gandal argues, was "expressly challenging traditional moral descriptions as well as moralistic analyses that attributed poverty to individual vice," it nonetheless participated in the spectacle of the slum by rendering it in terms of a sensational, surveilled other.[103] Thus the question of whether reform projects like Riis's *How the Other Half Lives* or morality experiments like Crane's *Maggie, A Girl of the Streets* ultimately cri-tique or feed into an emerging society of the spectacle remains open for debate. On the one hand, the shock tactics of the slum spectacle were needed in the 1890s to awaken an apathetic middle-class public. On the other hand, the dominance of spectacle in social life played a part in producing precisely the conditions of neglect and invisibility, as well as exploitation and discrimination, that many tenement writers and artists sought to challenge in their representations of urban poverty. Regardless of this ambivalent relationship to spectacle, the work of Riis and Crane in particular provided a conspicuous, deliberate counterpoint to the more established public image of New York street life as a scene of consumer indulgence, flagrant fashion, and leisure practices.

The resulting tension between these two versions of the modern city—one predicated on deprivation and suffering and the other on plenitude and pleasure—has only been exacerbated in the period since. Particularly in the era of globalization, when the gap between the urban rich and the urban poor has been systematically widening in cities worldwide, the Janus-faced city of privilege and poverty has endured not only as a concern of urban representation but also as a reality of urban existence in New York and elsewhere. Riis's *How the Other Half Lives* and Crane's *Maggie, A Girl of the Streets* may have morphed into the global cinematic slum spectacles of films like Danny Boyle's rags-to-riches Mumbai fable *Slumdog Millionaire* (2008) and Katia Lund's and Fernando Meirelles's Brazilian favela epic *City of God* (2002), but both the underlying urban dynamic and its popular representation in the form of spectacle continue.

New York Underground

In contrast to the slum, which marked the endurance of long-established patterns of exclusion and deprivation in the heart of the modern metropolis, the New York subway opened up a new kind of urban space and experience, where cultures and practices of the street, as well as related cultures of mobility and transit, were adapted beneath the surface of the city. Opened in 1904, the subway quickly became what Mario Maffi describes in *New York: An Outsider's Inside View* as "a contradictory and dramatic compendium of urban experiences"[104] and a metaphor for the city itself:

> [It is] a mythical place of the unconscious and prehistory...the choice place of supreme urban alienation. It is an endless source of urban folklore....It has formed the backdrop to notorious acts of violence whose social and emotional impact was considerable....

The subway is the very *underneath* of New York, then, but also that *underneath* that each of us experiences on a more personal basis: the feverish sense of fatigue on emerging from subway steps and along chaotic streets after the frantic rush from the airport, the sense of disorientation when confronted with scenes so different from those we have left, the diabolical, and at times unbearable noise, the sense of turmoil as trains approach the unpleasant vibrating of the long platforms, the muggy heat and the chill of air-conditioning, the headlong rush along certain stretches of track, the rainbow variety of faces and behavior, the idiosyncrasies of individual passengers, the all-enshrouding graffiti, the Chinaman playing Bach and the a capella choir singing *Carmina Burana*, the broken-bottle quarrel in a rapidly emptying carriage, the interminable hanging around and the never-ending journey to Coney Island or the Northern-most tip of Manhattan.[105]

Maffi is writing about the twenty-first-century subway and the rich variety of sights, scenes, moments, and encounters it offers, from the strange, frightening, and grotesque to the familiar, comforting, and comic. The description romanticizes, even mythologizes, the subway as a contradictory space of community and connection as well as disorientation and estrangement. Most significant is that Maffi sees the subway as somehow metonymic for the experience of the city as a whole, perhaps even constitutive of New York's identity.

In both tone and content, Maffi's comments reflect a vision of the subway that has circulated in various forms and across different media from the moment New York's underground transit system opened in 1904. It is a vision captured by James W. Kerr's 1931 depiction of the interior of a subway car in *7th Avenue Subway* (figure 39). Showing a group of passengers riding an Interborough Rapid Transit train, the painting offers a portrait of subway riders that stresses the diversity and heterogeneity of the crowd. Each passenger is individualized, with his or her own distinct appearance and identity. Differences of age, occupation, ethnicity, and class are all carefully depicted, as Jan Seidler Ramirez and Barbara Ball Buff note in their reading of the painting:

The fur collar and cuffs and well-fitted gloves worn by the woman seated third from the right contrast sharply with the battered felt hat of the tieless African American man two seats to her left. The small girl with the dangling feet holds fast to the woman at her

side. Except for the men absorbed in their newspapers and the be-
spectacled woman who has just glanced up from her book, Kerr's
characters stare vacantly ahead, adhering to the urban etiquette
of eluding eye contact with fellow passengers and retreating into
private thoughts in order to block out the drab, noisy subway
system.[106]

These comments touch on three important aspects of the painting.
First, Kerr sees the subway as a space that simultaneously brings
people together and keeps them apart. A diverse mix of passengers is
pressed together into the cramped space of the subway car and they
share the same experience of underground travel. Yet the total lack
of interaction between passengers also points to their enduring
status as strangers to each other. Here, the shared subway experience
does nothing to break down the social barriers that the passengers
bring with them underground. Nor does the experience open up
new lines of communication or other forms of interpersonal exchange. As Ramirez and Buff rightly point out, the tension between
intimacy and anonymity in Kerr's painting marks a subterranean
continuation of everyday sidewalk behavior, where the crush and
swirl of the crowd, as well as the diversity of its composition, actually
reinforce feelings of isolation and loneliness despite the presence of

FIGURE 39. *James W. Kerr, 7th Avenue Subway, 1931. (Courtesy Museum
of the City of New York)*

so many people, but also, paradoxically, because of the presence of so many people.

The second point to stress about Kerr's painting is that it contains both a scene of urban mobility and a portrait of urban stillness. The subway car itself, which frames and contains the scene, signals mass transit, rapid movement, urban circulation. Yet the interior view of the car presents an image of immobility. The passengers may be hurtling through dark tunnels in a train beneath the city but they are frozen in immobile, statuesque positions (standing, leaning) and passive, quasi-domestic postures (sitting, reclining). Moreover, they look bored and fatigued by the sheer ordinariness of the durational experience. The effect is an additional tension no longer just between togetherness and seclusion but also between motion and stasis, traveling and waiting, direction and drifting.

Finally, it is worth stressing that the painting registers the egalitarian potential of the subway as a space designed around openness and accessibility, and where the city's population is both able and required to mix across ethnic, class, and gender boundaries. In this respect, Kerr's painting gestures toward the ideals of cosmopolitanism and democratic inclusion that frequently surrounded the subway in the early decades of the twentieth century, and which eventually give way to a more cynical view of the underground experience as a progenitor of urban decay and social exclusion in the second half of the twentieth century, especially during New York's grime and garbage years of the 1970s.[107] The following discussion traces the roots of this dynamic and the representational strategies involved, paying particular attention to interrelations between the subway and the street. First, however, it addresses the rise, demise, and repurposing of the elevated railroad, before returning to the underground.

Elevated City

Although scholarship on the cultural history of rapid transit in New York City, especially around the turn of the twentieth century, tends to focus on the subway as a radical shift in urban mobility, it is important to remember that, like the locomotive technology itself, most of the cultural practices and social attitudes evinced in the subway were inherited from, and for a long time coexisted with, the city's elevated railroad (figure 40). Constructed in the late 1860s using cable cars, but shifting over to steam engines in the 1870s, New York's elevated railroad system marked the first citywide effort to bring mass, rapid transit to New York in a widely accessible form.[108] And while the elevated railroad in turn has its technological and topographical roots in the city's older network of streetcars dating back to the horse-drawn carriages and omnibuses of the 1820s, it nonetheless marks a departure from life and travel at the level of the street. By raising the train off the ground, the El not only releases urban transit from the restrictions of traffic and the chaos of the street but in the process produces an entirely new visual perspective on the city, now seen and experienced from above, even if only marginally so. In many ways, the El combined the mobility and sociality associated with the sidewalk with the aerial liberation and technoindustrial fetishism associated with the skyscraper, effectively jumbling together the horizontal and vertical planes of the city.

FIGURE 40. *The Bowery, near Grand Street, c. 1900. (Courtesy Library of Congress, Prints and Photographs Division)*

As Douglas Tallack discusses at length in his study of urban visuality, *New York Sights*, the city's elevated railroad asserted a "dominance over the darkened sidewalks and the roadway below" and inaugurated its own distinctive "visual discourse of rapid transit" revolving around speed and flow.[109] Photography and painting quickly took up the challenge of representing not only the new high-speed transport experiences and views afforded by the El but also the El itself as a leitmotif of the rapidly modernizing city. Tallack provides a rich array of examples, the most striking of which include modernist critiques of the facelessness of geometric urbanism, such as Charles Sheeler's evacuated cityscape in *Church Street El* (1920), touristic commemorations of engineering wonder in popular guidebooks like *King's Handbook of New York City* (1892), and urban actualities such as the American Mutoscope and Biograph Company's *Elevated Railroad, New York* (1903), a one-minute film showing a train rounding the bend at 110th Street. Throughout these works, argues Tallack, the El is repeatedly "depicted as, at once, physically transcending the confusion of the city yet integral to it."[110]

The idea that the elevated railroad marks both a departure from the entanglements of the street and a continuation of its trajectories, practices, and cultures recurs just as forcefully in literature. In the following passage from William Dean Howells's *A Hazard of New Fortunes* (1890), a quintessential New York novel preoccupied with the difficulties of moving to Manhattan and finding a decent apartment on a budget, the protagonists (Basil and Isabel March) eulogize their experience of riding the El in terms that reference its connections with both the street and the home:

> At Third Avenue they took the elevated, for which she confessed an infatuation. She declared it the most ideal way of getting about in the world. . . . She now said that the night transit was even more interesting than the day, and that the fleeting intimacy you formed with people in the second and third floor interiors, while all the usual street life went on underneath, had a domestic intensity mixed with a perfect repose that was the last effect of good society with all its security and exclusiveness. He said it was better than theatre, of which it reminded him, to see those people through their windows: a family party of work-folk at a late tea, some of the men in their shirt-sleeves; a woman sewing by a lamp; a mother laying her child

in its cradle; a man with his head fallen on his hands upon a table; a girl and her lover leaning over the window-sill together. What suggestion! What drama! What infinite interest![111]

Partly because of the novelty of the experience, and partly in response to the aesthetic encounter with mobility and domesticity offered by the train, the El figures in this account as a source of excitement and inspiration, leaping "past convenience and wonder and into romance," as Mark Caldwell comments in his discussion of the city's nocturnal mystique in *New York Night*.[112] The elevated railroad serves as both a release from the street and, through the coziness of its interior and the glimpses afforded into people's homes, a retreat into the domestic sphere of the home, while maintaining a connection—albeit from a safe distance—to the street life below. The feeling of social harmony on the train, expressed in terms of "fleeting intimacy," "security," and "exclusiveness," permeates the scene, even if the emotional and social rapprochement is transient, even illusory. After all, Howells's elevated passengers do not interact with each other beyond being jointly present on the train, and the urban theater they enjoy through the window is only glimpsed momentarily in passing and without any genuine insight into the lives, stories, and domestic conditions of the unsuspecting actors involved.

Later in the same passage, Howells elaborates further on the aesthetic pleasures of riding the El at night, commenting in some detail on the play of lights, architectural forms, and ethereal spaces involved:

> At the Forty-second Street station they stopped a minute on the bridge that crosses the track to the branch road for the Central Depot, and looked up and down the long stretch of the elevated to north and south. The track that found and lost itself a thousand times in the flare and tremor of the innumerable lights; the moony sheen of the electrics mixing with the reddish points and blots of gas far and near; the architectural shapes of houses and churches and towers, rescued by the obscurity from all that was ignoble in them, and the coming and going of the trains marking the stations with vivider or fainter plumes of flame-shot steam—formed an incomparable perspective. They often talked afterward of the superb spectacle... but for the present they were mostly inarticulate before it.[113]

Howells invokes the aesthetic regime of the sublime to describe the gliding, mobile panorama offered by the elevated railroad's journey across the city. The passengers are left speechless before the spectacle, overwhelmed and mesmerized by their visual encounter with the scale, sweep, and shimmering beauty of the illuminated city at night. What is more, the language in the passage is positively painterly in its attention to color, texture, form, perspective, distance, and depth. The view from the El appears here—just as it frequently does in the visual imaginary—as a cityscape view, complete with the excess of presence that philosopher Jean-François Lyotard, writing about artists such as Rembrandt and sites such as New York's Times Square, links to the visual experience of landscape and pictorial treatments of the sublime.[114]

The word "spectacle" in Howells's description of the view from the El is also significant in another way, in that it registers a continuation of the urban scopophilia associated with the sidewalk. For new, middle-class transplants to New York, such as Howells's Mr. and Mrs. March, riding the elevated railroad becomes an opportunity to engage in the street practice of flânerie, only now in a new, technologically enhanced way. The passengers—at least in Howells's account—enjoy what might be described as a form of inert mobility, adopting stationary positions inside the carriage from which to observe the crowd, the street, and even the home, all the while speeding effortlessly across the city. Despite romanticizing the experience, Howells nonetheless signals in subtle ways some of the strange, new contradictions posed by riding the elevated railroad, which include traveling the city without moving, as well as belonging to, but being apart from, the street.

What celebratory accounts such as Howells's *Hazard of New Fortunes* gloss over, however, are the effects of New York's elevated railroad on the lived experience of the city. At street level, the construction and spread of the elevated railroad system across the city created new problems of noise pollution, infrastructural congestion, and blocking of natural light. One of the reasons was that the route tracks were mostly superimposed directly above existing streets, thus requiring that the massive supporting structure of the El be squeezed into the existing width of the street. Trains therefore frequently passed very close to neighboring buildings and rumbled above pedestrians and street traffic, while the massive elevated structure itself overshadowed the space below (figure 41).

What is more, the visual impact of the El on the appearance of the city was controversial, with many complaining about the ugliness of the elevated structure, its disproportionate size relative to its surroundings, and its obscuring of businesses and shop windows along the sidewalk. So although much of the initial engineering and design thinking behind the elevated railroad aimed at "simply a doubling of the street," as Michael Brooks notes in *Subway City*, in practice the El frequently threatened to replace or overpower the street.[115]

Within the space of a few decades between the 1870s and 1900, the El matured into an urban transit system that not only extended the possibilities and speed of mobility around the city more than ever before, but also hooked the city and its commuters on the conveniences of rapid transit. At the same time, the intrusion of the El into (and above) the space of the street, together with the effects of its size, noise, and overbearing physical presence, helped to create the public ambivalence needed to explore an underground alternative in the form of the subway.

FIGURE 41. *Fulton Street and Flatbush Avenue, Brooklyn, 1907. (Courtesy Brooklyn Public Library, Brooklyn Collection)*

High Line, Lowline

New York's experiment with the elevated railroad was relatively short-lived. Despite the enormous expense of building the various lines, as well as the extensive work and disruption involved in the projects, most of the system was closed down by 1940. Competition from the subway and, after the 1920s, the automobile and the city's growing public bus network, combined with rising operating costs and falterings in the economy, made the El increasingly unviable. Most of the tracks were torn down, especially in Manhattan, erasing all but a few traces of the network. Yet a few fragments survive, such as a 1.4-mile stretch of track on Manhattan's West Side, dating back to 1934 and extending from the meat packing district at Fourteenth Street through Chelsea up to the rail yards at Thirtieth Street. Eventually abandoned in the 1980s, the tracks were once part of the West Side Line of the New York Central Railroad, which ran from Penn Station in Midtown to Spring Street in Lower Manhattan (figure 42). In 2006, after extensive campaigning by local community groups, the city approved a building project to repurpose the segment of track into an elevated park called the High Line.

The design of the High Line was inspired by the Promenade Plantée in Paris, where a disused rail viaduct in the city center was transformed into an extensive, lavishly planted, green walkway. Sharing the Promenade Plantée's concern with bringing nature back into the city, the High Line similarly gives new life to a dead space and blends traditional park elements—such as formal plantings, manicured lawns, and delineated paths—into the surviving transport infrastructure. As discussed briefly in part I in relation to the Fresh Kills park project on Staten Island, the High Line belongs to a broader, international trend in twenty-first-century landscape urbanism, in which abandoned, postindustrial wastelands are creatively reoccupied and remade into ecofriendly public spaces.

What makes the High Line remarkable is its staggering popularity. From its opening in 2009 onward, the park has exceeded expectations in terms of the volume of visitors and quickly established itself as one of New York's must-see destinations and an alternative green space to the more traditional, nineteenth-century landscape design experience of Central Park. Within only a few years, the High Line's draw for both residents and tourists alike helped to regenerate the surrounding neighborhood, attracting property developers, businesses,

FIGURE 42. *Future site of the High Line: building the West Side Line, c. 1933.*
(Courtesy Friends of the High Line and New York Department of Parks
and Recreation)

and even major cultural institutions like the Whitney Museum of
American Art, which strategically placed its new building at the
southern entrance to the park. The story of the High Line's success
is much more complex, of course, and connects not only to the
design of the park and the vantage points, scenery, and activities it
contains but also to the high level of support and involvement it
has received from the local community.

In particular, the nonprofit organization Friends of the High Line,
which led the initial campaign to build the park, has since assumed
both operational responsibility and cultural stewardship over the
space in partnership with the New York City Department of Parks
and Recreation; as the organization's website describes its role:

> We seek to preserve the entire historic structure, transforming
> an essential piece of New York's industrial past. We provide
> over 90 percent of the High Line's annual operating budget
> and are responsible for maintenance of the park.... Through
> stewardship, innovative design and programming, and excel-
> lence in operations, we cultivate a vibrant community around
> the High Line.[116]

As this mission statement touches on, the park's design and operations consciously seek to activate cultural memory and draw on the city's industrial heritage, but in doing so to recast that memory and heritage into an elaborate, forward-looking experiment with community activism, public art, urban design, and cultural programming. All of this, I would argue, hinges on the High Line's former identity as an elevated railroad and, in particular, on the way in which that identity shapes and frames the perambulatory experience of the park's linear pathway.

This idea was made visible in the outdoor exhibition of a photograph commissioned by Friends of the High Line and displayed in a large-scale format on a billboard adjacent to the park in 2011. The work, titled *A Railroad Artifact*, comes from a series of photographs by New York–based artist Joel Sternfeld, who spent a year photographing the High Line in 2000–1. Taken long before the park construction began, the image shows the tracks of the abandoned elevated railroad, overgrown with grass and wild flowers, receding into the distance and eventually disappearing into the urban canyon formed by the adjoining brick buildings (figure 43). The absence of people, the material neglect, and the resurgence of nature all contribute to giving the deserted railroad a look of wilderness. The scene is reminiscent of an Ansel Adams landscape, only here the landscape is resituated in the postindustrial, urban environment of New York's West Side. Looking at Sternfeld's photograph, it does not require a large leap of the imagination to envisage a park springing from this space. Indeed, much of the finished design of the High Line looks like a cleaner, more ordered and controlled version of what was already there.

The placement of the photograph on a billboard next to the High Line and directly above a parking lot is significant too (figure 44). The relationship between the photograph's image of emptiness and stillness resonates strangely with the congested stasis of the unoccupied vehicles in the parking lot. The more powerful resonance, however, occurs between the billboard and the park located beside it. This juxtaposition of the site's postindustrial history of abandonment with its present-day condition of revival and reoccupation delivers a poignant, visual reminder of the park's status as a transformed and revivified urban ruin. In other words, the positioning of Sternfeld's photograph in the direct view of park visitors helps to reinforce the desired public image of the High Line, which

FIGURE 43. *Joel Sternfeld, A Railroad Artifact, 30th Street, May 2000, original in color. (© 2000, Joel Sternfeld; courtesy of the artist and Luhring Augustine, New York)*

James Corner, the park's lead designer, once described as "a post-industrial artifact maintaining a sense of melancholy and other-worldliness in a city context that, by contrast, [is] ever-evolving and modernizing."[117]

The sense of melancholy and otherworldliness to which Corner refers is integral to the popularity of the park, which partly functions as a nostalgic memory walk for a bygone era of industrial urbanism, and is enhanced by the spatial configuration of the experience. The elevated walkway lifts visitors up from the level of the street just enough to provide a different perspective on the city. Yet unlike the original railroad, which moved rapidly and inexorably across the city, the park offers a slow encounter with the surrounding urban landscape. Pause, interruption, delay, and detour are all possible on the High Line, and are encouraged by the meandering design of the central walkway and the various stopping places spread along the way, such as the Sunken Overlook, which provides amphitheater-style seating suspended above Tenth Avenue and facing a glass window that frames the street below. In these sorts of ways, the High Line keeps visitors close to the street, immersed in the city, yet released from the everyday.

As a reinvention of the urban promenade, the High Line speaks to the depth of our cultural investment in street-walking as an urban practice tied to leisure and pleasure. It is therefore somewhat ironic that Paris's Promenade Plantée, although popular, has not attracted anything like the public attention of the High Line, since this earlier experiment with repurposing an elevated railroad cuts across the very city where the modern boulevard and its attendant promenade practices were invented. Most likely, the High Line's greater public visibility as a landscape architecture project is connected to the cityscape it inhabits as much as to the design itself, in the sense that the extreme iconicity of the New York skyline and the opportunity provided by the park to encounter that skyline—even inhabit it—in a different, more intimate, and decelerated way is at the core of the High Line experience. Whatever the reasons for its success as both

FIGURE 44. *Billboard next to the High Line: Joel Sternfeld,* Landscape with Path: A Railroad Artifact, 2011. *Commissioned by High Line Art, presented by Friends of the High Line and the New York City Department of Parks and Recreation. On view June 2–30, 2011, on the High Line, New York. Photo by Bill Orcutt. (Courtesy of the artist and Friends of the High Line)*

an urban park and an engine of urban renewal, the High Line has directly inspired similar projects to repurpose disused elevated railroads in cities such as Bangkok, Detroit, London, Hong Kong, Rotterdam, Sydney, and Toronto.

Many of these projects have not been realized, but the trend in seeking to build elevated green walkways has been rapidly gathering momentum since the High Line. In New York City, for example, a campaign was launched in Queens in 2011, led by the community coalition Friends of the QueensWay, to "transform the blighted structure that housed the LIRR Rockaway Beach Branch and was abandoned over 50 years ago into a public greenway."[118] Both the QueensWay proposal itself and the grass-roots organizational approach behind it consciously seek to replicate the High Line model.

Back in Manhattan, another High Line–inspired project was also announced in 2011. Called the Lowline, it takes the design concept behind the elevated railroad park in a new direction: underground. The Lowline is a proposal by designers James Ramsey and Dan Barasch to build an underground park at the site of the abandoned Williamsburg trolley terminal, located under Delancey Street on Manhattan's Lower East Side. The bold, imaginative design envisages an expansive subterranean space with walkways, trees, plants, and abundant natural light made possible by "remote skylights" using fiber optics (figure 45). Unlike the High Line, the Lowline specifically places technology at the center of the park's design, and experiments with how that technology can help to solve urban design problems, such as the lack of available space for public parks in dense urban environments. So although it shares the High Line's concern with repurposing abandoned railroad tracks for ecofriendly public use, the Lowline goes one step further by seeking to conjoin smart city and sustainable city design.

Yet if we strip away all the high-tech solar technologies of the Lowline, what remains is remarkably similar to the High Line and, indeed, Paris's original Promenade Plantée: a green walkway shaped by the linear spatiality of a rapid transit railroad and made possible by the abandonment of that transport infrastructure in a time of postindustrial urban decay. More than that, all these projects hinge on producing what Sunny Stalter, writing about 1950s artists concerned with the obsolescence of the El, has called a "nostalgic urban visuality."[119] The key difference is that the Lowline seeks to achieve its

FIGURE 45. *Rendering of the Lowline at Delancey Street, 2012. (Courtesy Raad Studio)*

nostalgia and otherworldly transformation by submerging visitors beneath the street, whereas the High Line and Promenade Plantée achieve these effects by gently elevating visitors above the street. Yet in both the elevated and underground versions of the railroad park, the aim remains to disrupt the street by relocating its sidewalk practices to a decelerated space of urban mobility where those practices do not conventionally belong, but where, through defamiliarizing transformations of the space, they can be newly enacted.

At the time of this book's publication, construction on the Lowline has yet to begin. Even so, the project has already met with enormous public interest and support, as evidenced by the eleven thousand visitors who, over a two-week period in 2012, attended an exhibition of the project's concept in the form of "a full-scale model of the solar technology and the green park in an abandoned warehouse directly above the actual site."[120] In combination with the intense media interest surrounding the project, the exhibition points toward the powerful draw of the Lowline's inversion of the elevated park concept.

Together, landscape architecture projects like the Promenade Plantée, the High Line, QueensWay, and the Lowline demonstrate the intricate spatial, historical, and cultural relationships that exist between transport spaces and sidewalk practices in cities, both above and below the ground. Although those relationships have shifted and evolved over time, they have animated and informed the development of many cities' street cultures and transport systems from industrialization onward. As the discussion demonstrates next, this is particularly the case with the underground space of the New York City subway, which has been central to New York's cultural imagination precisely because of its intimate connections to, and simultaneous departures from, the street.

Subway City

Proposals to build a subway in New York predate the construction of the elevated railroad. As early as 1864, the city was actively debating whether to elevate or submerge the city's planned transit railroads. Various imaginative proposals for both elevated and underground train systems were floated by engineers, planners, and city officials in popular newspapers and magazines in the hope of drumming up public support for the competing visions. Many of these proposals were far-fetched, technologically untested, and financially improbable, such as Rufus H. Gilbert's 1871 proposal for a covered atmospheric railway (figure 46).

Driving this imaginative public discussion about future transit in New York was the need to address two problems facing the city in the mid-nineteenth century, both of which were steadily worsening. The first problem was that the growth of the city, both northward in Manhattan and outward in Brooklyn and Queens, was making everyday travel distances increasingly difficult to manage. The second problem was that urban density, particularly in Midtown and Lower Manhattan, was creating street congestion, not only because of an excess of vehicles but also because of an excess of pedestrians. A new rapid transit system seemed like a solution to both sets of problems in that it could move people quickly around the city while also absorbing a high volume of passengers, thereby reducing traffic on roads and sidewalks and making distances in the city manageable again.

This moment of possibility and imagination in New York's transport history is the starting place of Michael W. Brooks's *Subway City: Riding the Trains, Reading New York*, in which he suggests that the city's transport debate was not just technical but social and cultural as well:

> New Yorkers used their discussions of alternate plans for subways
> and els to visualize a city that they hoped to create. They started by

FIGURE 46. *"Improved Project of a Covered Atmospheric Elevated Railway for City Transit," by Dr. Rufus H. Gilbert, 1871. (Courtesy Library of Congress, Prints and Photographs Division)*

asking what routes the tracks should follow and quickly extended their discussions into such areas as the cost of political corruption, the relations of men and women in public spaces, and the ability of the poor to escape their crowded tenements. Seemingly dry questions of engineering led to utopian visions of a reborn city.[121]

The utopian railroad visions circulating in New York in the mid- to late nineteenth century thus belonged to a broader discussion about the future shape and functioning of the city, one in which mobility itself and access to mobility were recognized as determining factors.

Although the El triumphed in the first phase of New York's transition from "a walking city to a riding City,"[122] it soon became evident that, while helping to compensate for the spatial elongations of urban sprawl, it nonetheless made many streets and sidewalks more congested, had deleterious effects on the appearance of the city, and increased noise pollution. Meanwhile, European cities were busy building the first underground railroads, with London opening the underground Metropolitan Railway in 1863 and expanding new lines rapidly thereafter. By comparison, New York was beginning to look anachronistic in its choice of rapid transport technology, and this was a sore point for a city that had always thought of itself in futuristic terms.

These factors all contributed to generating support for building a subway in New York. Despite a few false starts, such as Alfred Ely Beach's pneumatic tube railroad comprising a 312-foot demonstration tunnel that briefly opened in 1870,[123] the city finally broke ground on an interborough underground transportation system in 1900, opening the first line to the public in 1904 (figure 47). From the beginning, the subway functioned as a conflicted symbol within and for New York, as Brooks delineates:

> The subway was the city's preeminent symbol of unity and hope.... Like any symbol, however, it contained uncertainties and tensions. Urban theorists proclaimed that the subway resolved a contradiction in urban form—it reconciled the economic need for concentration and the human need for dispersal. But while New Yorkers agreed that the subway would make possible the future city, they did not agree on the kind of city they expected to create. While some used the subway to support a dignified vision of the City Beautiful, others employed it to make possible the Skyscraper City of triumphant commerce.[124]

Despite the tensions surrounding the significance of the subway as an urban symbol, one common thread remained: the subway was seen as a progenitor of the city's future, however contested and uncertain that future might be. The city also projected its utopian aspirations onto the subway, which the jolting, jostling, and overcrowded experience involved in actually riding the trains often challenged, especially in the early years when capacity was limited and the train technology was more rudimentary. This clash of ideals, symbolism, and everyday experience is one of the reasons why the subway emerged—and has endured—as an iconic space within the city, enabling it to possess a variable, shifting identity as engine of hope, despair, equality, change, alienation, and more.

Another, related reason is because the subway system connected the city geographically by linking its many neighborhoods and boroughs, and in the process became an indispensable part of New Yorkers' daily routine. More than any other icon of urban mobility and connection of this era, such as the El or the Brooklyn Bridge, the subway became a common factor and shared experience for a

FIGURE 47. *City Hall subway station, c. 1906. (Courtesy Library of Congress, Prints and Photographs Division)*

majority of the population, even if its subterranean setting made it distinctly less conspicuous. As Thomas Bender argues in his comparison of the subway and the Brooklyn Bridge as arteries of urban flow:

> The social geography of the modern metropolis derives from a less visible, but equally remarkable technological feat: the subway system. The city we know was defined topographically by the subways; the vast pattern of subway stations gives us an orientation to the metropolis independent of its natural geography.... The city was unified perceptually and practically on a metropolitan scale for the first time.[125]

To say that the subway succeeded in uniting the city at geographic and cognitive levels may be overstating its impact and effects. After all, many areas of New York, especially during the first few decades of the system's expansion, had to wait for the system to reach them and alternative modes of transport have always operated alongside the subway. Meanwhile, certain neighborhoods have remained controversially cut off from subway access from the beginning, such as parts of Manhattan's Lower East Side, reflecting the uneven geographic development of the system. Nonetheless, Bender's broader point that the subway served as an influential space of connection within the city is important. So too is his insight that, in the process, the subway defied natural geography while reshaping social geography.

The subway's ambivalent relationship with the street in both spatial and cultural terms played a role in producing these dynamics. For example, one of the challenges facing the initial planning of the subway was deciding where and how to intersect with the city's street system. The placement of stations, the construction and location of lines, and the entry and exit points all needed to integrate with the city's street life, traffic flows, and infrastructural design. The solution was to superimpose the spatial logic of the grid on the subway, as Bender goes on to note: "The triumph of the street-level grid over the underground technology in defining horizontal movement in New York is embodied in the names given the subway stations. The subway lines do not follow a grid pattern, but the system surfaces only at streets on the grid."[126] These comments capture a key aspect of the subway's relation to the grid. Below ground and out of sight, the subway moves independently of the grid (although it is worth noting as an aside that most of the subway lines in Manhattan nonetheless trace the north-south axis of the avenues). Yet the points where the subway resurfaces—the entrances and exits where the system regains visibility at the everyday level of the street—correspond to coordinates on the grid.

Thus, in its invisible underground mobility the subway departs from the street, but in its connection points into and out of the city, it is recuperated by the street. Bender interprets this outcome as a triumph of the grid over the subway, and it certainly can be read in this way. It is also possible, however, to recalibrate this view slightly to see the subway not as a separation from—or an appendage to—the street, but instead as an extension or rearticulation of the street, including its mobilities, users, practices, and spatiality. From this perspective, the modern sidewalk does not end at the entrance to the subway but continues underground, eventually reemerging elsewhere in the city.

The insight that the subway occupies a ghostly visibility (present throughout the city yet beyond view), and that in the process it incorporates yet problematizes defining aspects of the street, is at the heart of cultural responses to New York's rapid transit system. Some of this thinking surfaces already in representations of the El in literature, art, and early cinema, where the elevated railroad is seen as a force of simultaneous connection and separation.[127] But this view becomes more pronounced and explicit in cultural production concerned with the subway. One of the contributing factors was that, unlike the El, the underground subway offers no views from its windows, except for the momentary bursts of light and people that occur at station platforms. Not only does this redirect the gaze back into the interior space of the train, but it leaves nothing to see when travelling underground except the subway system itself. The absence of external coordinates further contributes to a sense of spatial disorientation when immersed in the subway system, which again differs from the El. It is therefore not surprising that, in contrast to visual treatments of the El which tend to focus on either the panoramas and streetscapes visible from the train or the setting of the train within the larger urban landscape, representations of the subway focus almost entirely on the rapid transit experience—the stations, passengers, and cars—of the underground system.

Underground Fantasies

Various art critics and cultural historians have noted that it took until the 1920s for the subway to truly take hold of the visual imagination of New York. This is not to say that artists and other visual practitioners were not concerned with representing the subway in its early years. Far from it, since the novelty of the technology, as well as the scale of the construction projects involved, attracted intense public interest and generated new urban scenes, perspectives, and aesthetic possibilities that visual artists were quick to recognize and incorporate into their work. In popular cultural production, urban actualities of subway trains stopping at underground stations, as well as films showing passengers riding the train, were common in the 1910s. So too were tourist and other commercial images—postcards, advertisements, magazine illustrations—that catered to a growing public fascination with the subway both within and beyond New York. But it took until the mid-1920s for the subway to gather what Brooks describes as the "semantic weight and emotional complexity" needed "before finally making its appearance in novels and paintings."[128]

For example, in John Dos Passos's *Manhattan Transfer* (1925), which draws its title from the name of a New Jersey train station that used to serve as an entry point into New York's rapid transit system, the subway features prominently throughout. It moves characters and their stories into (and out of) the heart of New York from their lives in the margins and peripheral sprawl of the city. The subway precipitates and frequently forces encounters between strangers. And it serves as a microcosm of the depleted, empty spectacle animating the novel's "vision of New York's capitalist-cultural periphery inhabited by the chewed up and wasted remains of the consumerist day."[129] In Dos Passos's writing, the subway loses all the utopian veneer accompanying the hype of its initial construction and opening. The subway figures instead as a decaying space of filth, loneliness, and disconnection where the rush and anonymity of life at street level are intensified: "Faces, hats, hands, newspapers jiggled in the fetid roaring subway car like a corn in a popper. The downtown express passed clattering in a yellow light, window telescoping window till they overlapped like scales."[130] Here, the subway's occupants are reduced to isolated body parts and lonely objects pressed together in a forced and uncomfortable intimacy as they hurtle through the city's underground tunnels in a mechanical pressure cooker.

The theme of compression—both emotional and physical—recurs several times in *Manhattan Transfer*'s subway scenes. In the following passage, a Western Union messenger boy, en route to the Upper West Side to deliver a telegram, finds himself pressed against an attractive woman and begins indulging fantasies of sexual contact on the train:

> In the crammed subway car the messenger boy was pressed up against the back of a tall blond woman. . . . Elbows, packages, shoulders, buttocks, jiggled closer with every lurch of the screeching express. His sweaty Western Union cap was knocked onto the side of his head. If I could have a dame like dat, a dame like dat'd be wort havin de train stalled, de lights go out, de train wrecked. I could have her if I had de noive an de jack. As the train slowed up she fell against him, he closed his eyes, didnt breathe, his nose was mashed against her neck. The train stopped. He was carried in a rush of people out the door.[131]

The threat of sexual harassment has long been part of the stress of riding subways, especially for women who are the most frequent targets of such behavior. The combination of overcrowding and anonymity, as well as the general sense of distance from the reach and control of the law, creates conditions that facilitate harassing behavior and other forms of inappropriate physical contact and exhibitionism.[132]

In the subway vignette above, Dos Passos draws on this anxiety by taking the reader inside the erotic thought process of a young man who fantasizes about assaulting a female passenger if the lights go out or the train crashes. The fantasy is then interrupted by the jolting of the train, which pushes the two bodies closer together, and the young man allows his face to remain pressed against the woman until the flow of disembarking passengers carries him away. There is a distinct lack of agency on the part of these subway riders. They are not in control of the sudden movements of their bodies, and the messenger boy is swept off the train by the swell of exiting passengers. It is even questionable whether the messenger boy is in control of his own thinking, as his erotic daydreaming seems to be triggered automatically and uncontrollably by his physical proximity to the woman. Meanwhile, the female passenger has no voice or presence beyond her status as an object of sexual desire. Dos Passos does not narrate the scene from the woman's perspective and the reader learns nothing about how the physical encounter affects her. In this version of the subway, underground New York is a place of encounter between strangers, but one where the moments of contact or exchange remain largely involuntary, fleeting, frenetic, ambiguous, and ultimately isolating, reflecting precisely the novel's overall vision of everyday life in modern New York as well as its modernist sensibility toward the fragmentation of the subject.

Another version of the subway in which the isolation of the subject dominates can be found in the work of the abstract-expressionist painter Mark Rothko. In the mid- to late 1930s, Rothko completed a series of paintings of the New York subway that prefigure his move toward abstraction and in which the geometry of the city's rapid transit infrastructure and the architectural space of the subway station—more than trains and travel experiences—preoccupy his compositions. As James Breslin comments in his reading of Rothko's subway paintings and their relationship to the artist's commuting experience between Manhattan and Brooklyn, "Rothko's interest is not in the trains, but in the platforms: modern, urban public spaces where strangers come and go—or wait. His stations are not grimy, dark, hellish underground spaces; nor are they filled with quick-moving, shoving, noisy, rush-hour crowds. Rather, they are bare, compressed areas which contain a slow, quiet, and solitary mobility."[133] By avoiding the predominant image of the subway as a space of extreme crowding, incessant motion, and subterranean disorder, such as in Dos Passos's *Manhattan Transfer* or chaotic transit paintings like Beys Afroyim's multileveled *Metropolis Movement* (1939; figure 48), Rothko is able to present another, calmer side of underground New York. In the process, he foregrounds the individual's relationship to the surrounding space in terms that strongly recall practices and conditions of the street.

In *Underground Fantasy* (1940), one of the last paintings in the subway series, Rothko depicts a group of scattered passengers waiting for a train on an underground platform (figure 49). The scene is distinctly tranquil, introspective, even meditative: an ephemeral moment of repose in the midst of urban rush and flow. As in the subway series as a whole, the Giacomettiesque human figures are unnaturally, almost grotesquely elongated. Their thin, stretched bodies parallel the narrow, steel columns holding up the low and oppressive ceiling. A few of the figures lean heavily against the columns, almost merging their bodies into the station's supporting architecture and effacing

FIGURE 48. *Beys Afroyim*, Metropolis Movement, 1939. *(Courtesy Museum of the City of New York)*

their own presence. At the center of the painting stands a solitary man engrossed in reading a newspaper. A small distance next to him stands a solitary woman staring at the ground. Nobody in the painting appears to be looking at—or seeing—anyone else. In this, Rothko captures a frequent tendency or reflex in subway travel: tuning out the presence of others. The space itself is bare, heavily geometrical, flattened, and monochromatic. Most of all, it is confined. Interestingly, the image shows no trains, tracks, ticket booths, entrances, or exits, and there are few details available to identify the setting as a subway platform beyond the blue B on the wall referencing Bleecker Street Station. Yet the architectural enclosure of the space, combined with the passengers' time-killing postures of inattention and indifference, makes the painting immediately recognizable as a subway scene.

The space and postures also recall the modern sidewalk, to the extent, even, that Rothko's underground fantasy looks like a conscious relocation of an urban sidewalk below ground. A blasé metropolitan attitude can be discerned in the mutual disinterest of the waiting passengers. The spatial isolation of the human figures suggests a corresponding state of social and psychological disconnection. Meanwhile, the passengers' styled appearance (fashionable hats, dresses, suits) combined with the prominent presence of the newspaper in the center foreground gloss the metropolitan sensibility and cosmopolitan orientation of the modern streetwalker, while also evoking that figure's emphasis on appearance and consumption. It is not just that Rothko's subway passengers are waiting for the train. They are also performing urbanity. Finally, the platform setting itself echoes the pedestrian topos of the sidewalk, and shares its linear spatial configuration. The difference, however, is that Rothko's subway platform is stripped of ornamentation, spectacle, movement, and distraction. What emerges from this radically pared-down refiguring of the sidewalk is a vision of everyday life in the modern city consisting of lonely people in constrained spaces.

In *Art and the Subway*, an extensive study of visual culture and underground New York from the 1800s onward, Tracy Fitzpatrick identifies Rothko's subway paintings as being among "the best examples of the rider subsumed by the subway in art," adding that "riders appear consumed by their surroundings," trapped in a state

FIGURE 49. *Mark Rothko,* Underground Fantasy, *1940. (Courtesy National Gallery of Art)*

of "spatial limbo, or encapsulation."[134] Fitzpatrick's double notion of spatial limbo and encapsulation corresponds closely to my interpretation of *Underground Fantasy* above, but it captures even more precisely the status that the subway occupies not only in Rothko's work but more widely in New York's urban imaginary. Variously seen, at one extreme, as an emblem of inclusiveness and social harmony and, at another extreme, as an underground war zone, the subway has always been a source of ambivalence in the public and artistic imaginations.

Rothko, however, takes this ambivalence a step further by specifically identifying the subway as a liminal space. Neither fully present nor entirely absent from the city—and neither a destination in itself nor an operative space of mobility and flow—Rothko's subway offers a ghostly, interstitial counterpart to the street. It becomes a precursor to what Marc Augé, writing about the proliferation of underdefined spaces of transcience in the late-capitalist era of "supermodernity," calls "non-places": spaces of mobility, consumption, and communication (like airports, malls, and supermarkets) where "people coexist or cohabit without living together."[135] Rothko's subway may not yet possess the extreme, debilitating "experiences and ordeals of solitude"[136] that Augé links to life in non-places, but the underlying sense of transience and placelessness accompanying the generic urbanism of globalization that Augé critiques is already palpable in aesthetic responses to the modern city such as *Underground Fantasy*.

Slow Street

Focusing on the sidewalk as both an urban-spatial form and a site of creative cultural practice, part II has argued that New York's street life has been integral to the city's public identity and cultural imagination from the beginning, but especially under the transformative industrial, capitalist conditions of urban modernity. As illustrated through analysis of New York's urban development and planning, as well as through analysis of work by Berenice Abbott, Stephen Crane, William Dean Howells, Nella Larsen, Jacob Riis, Mark Rothko, Paul Strand, and many others, those conditions not only generated new spaces or reshaped existing ones within modern New York, such as the sidewalk, the slum, the grid, the El, and the subway, but also produced new or reworked archetypes of urban life, such as the flâneur *and* flâneuse or the blasé metropolitan individual. The discussion further argued that a key factor in the shaping of New York's street culture was an emphasis on speed, movement, and dislocation, discernible in the dominant sidewalk practices of window shopping, street-walking, and crowd watching, as well as in the refiguring of those practices in marginal or liminal spaces like the slum and the subway.

   In closing, I want to consider how these concerns converge in a photofilmic installation that was exhibited at the New York Metropolitan Museum of Art in 2013. Made in 2011 by British artist James Nares, *Street* is a sixty-one-minute digital film shot in super high definition from a moving car cruising around Manhattan at thirty miles per hour. Scored with original music by Thurston Moore, the guitarist from Sonic Youth, the edited footage is shown in extreme slow motion. The sixty-one minutes of the finished film consist of three minutes of real-time footage. The result is an unbroken flow of radically decelerated, gliding, sliding streetscapes in which intimacies of movement, embodiment, and encounter become strangely, newly observable.

Street can be placed within two intersecting visual traditions. One is animal locomotion photography, extending from Eadweard Muybridge's images of galloping horses in the late 1870s (figure 50) to Harold Edgerton's scientific films of hovering hummingbirds in the 1940s, and in which the stop-motion and slow-motion possibilities of visual media are used to understand and analyze physical movement. The other tradition is the actuality film, which emerged at the turn of the twentieth century and took a special interest in everyday scenes of the city. Nares combines the aesthetics, concerns, and techniques of both of these traditions. He pushes the technical capabilities of the medium of film. He slows motion to the radical extent that it reveals new or hidden realities. And he documents scenes and spaces of everyday life at the level of the street. The overall effect of this decelerated New York, aided by Moore's hypnotic, looping melodies on the acoustic guitar, is to engineer a contemplative experience of a space that normally defies pause, meditation, and scrutiny of everyday minutiae.

What the film helps to make newly visible are the asynchronous temporalities and mobilities of the sidewalk: each person is on a different track, moving at a different speed, completing a different gesture or movement (figure 51). In this, the film is an excellent example of what, writing about globalization and street photography, Miriam Meissner and I have called "slow art": "aesthetic interventions that emerge from, but also strategically counter, the conditions of speed, mobility, and invisibility (anonymity) that have become so ubiquitous in rapidly globalizing cities."[137] This slowness also succeeds in interrupting the fast flows of the global city and our accelerated experience of those flows.

Yet as an interruption of the sidewalk's conditions of speed and movement, the film is open to critique in a number of ways. First, its gallery viewing conditions in the formal, institutional setting of the Metropolitan Museum of Art place the film—as art installation—in a highly controlled space far removed from the everyday space and feel of the street. The effect is to place much greater emphasis on form and technique over content, so that the film's deceleration of the sidewalk becomes the focus rather than what that deceleration reveals about the sidewalk. This is reflected, for example, in reviews

FIGURE 50. *Eadweard Muybridge,* The Horse in Motion, *1878. (Courtesy Library of Congress, Prints and Photographs Division)*

of the installation, where the technique and visual effects of slow motion form the overwhelming focus of discussion.[138] Second, *Street* is filmed entirely in Manhattan, mostly in Midtown and other congested areas of commerce and tourism, giving the film aesthetic continuity but also a certain monospatiality. The sidewalk changes very little over the course of the sixty-one minutes and the same curbside sights and scenes recur with minor variations: yellow taxis, crosswalks, traffic lights, hot-dog stands, and so on. Third, and in light of the above, it could be argued that *Street* reveals the mundane and the banal for the act of revelation itself, rather than offering insight into, or understanding beyond, the surface of the city. In this, *Street* constitutes an example of what Shirley Jordan, writing about contemporary photographic practices in global cities, has called "urban skimming": a deliberate and strategically superficial engagement with the city resulting in fleeting, glancing encounters.[139]

Thus I would argue that *Street* interrupts the image and experience of the New York sidewalk at the level of aesthetics and perception. In doing so, the film not only draws on the visual traditions of animal locomotion photography and urban actualities developed in the late nineteenth and early twentieth centuries but returns to their technical and aesthetic concerns with, respectively, slowing movement and figuring the everyday city. As in the cultural representation of the modern sidewalk and its associated spaces discussed throughout part II, New York's street life continues to be dominated by what have become deeply engrained practices of street-walking,

FIGURE 51. *Stills from James Nares,* Street, *2011, music by Thurston Moore, sixty-one minutes. (Courtesy of the artist and Paul Kasmin Gallery)*

crowd watching, and window shopping. Even more to the point, *Street* reveals the ways in which the sidewalk—as a space of public intersection and everyday encounter—persists as a source of cultural fascination in the twenty-first century, shaping both cultural production and spatial practice in the contemporary global city just as it did in the modern metropolis.

{ AFTERWORD }

This book is organized according to two dominant spatial perspectives on modern New York. Part I, "Skylines," addresses the vertical city. Part II, "Sidewalks," refocuses on the horizontal city. This splitting of the city along vertical and horizontal lines is, of course, necessarily constructed, in the sense that the lived experience of the metropolis always, already mixes, confuses, and sometimes even outright defies such divisions. Yet within the urban imaginary of New York, skylines and sidewalks (as articulations of the city's vertical and horizontal orientations) do occupy a privileged place. As we have seen, they figure across a rich variety of material in literature, urbanism, and the visual arts as sites of creative expression where the conditions and possibilities of the modern city are explored and rehearsed in response to new forms of (and new encounters with) urban space.

In this afterword, I want to consider one last image in which concerns articulated earlier in this book in relation to the vertical and horizontal axes of the city converge. Obviously, no single image can encapsulate the entirety of a city or the full sweep of a book's discussion. Yet in the vast visual archive of the city, one painting stands out for the way it both figures and critiques modern New York in terms that resonate with my thinking about skylines and sidewalks. The painting in question is George Bellows's *New York* (1911). In the Ashcan tradition of portraying scenes of everyday urban life, Bellows depicts the daytime melee of Madison Square in midtown Manhattan (figure 52). The foreground is crowded with pedestrians, delivery carriages, motor vehicles, and street vendors all jostling for space. The background shows the flat wall of skyscrapers encircling the square and the narrow canyon of Broadway rapidly vanishing into the distance. The tall buildings not only overhang the space, contributing to a sense of enclosure and density, but also present a barrage of spectacular facades in the form of giant advertising signs. The vertical architecture, clogged arteries, lurid advertising, pressed crowds, jammed traffic, and aggressive consumerism all contribute to giving the scene the look and feel that have long been associated with public

space in New York and that are strongly linked in the popular imagination to similar sites of spectacle and congestion like Times Square,
from its corporate branding in 1904 through its decline into red-light
commerce and entertainment to its more recent renewal as a Dis-
neyfied tourist playground.[1]

Many art historians have commented on Bellows's *New York*, re-
marking on its uncharacteristic fixation with the commercial face of
the city, as well as on its commitment to the roughshod realism of
Ashcan painting at a time when more abstract representational concerns and aesthetics were emerging in the modernism of European-
influenced art.[2] Douglas Tallack in particular contrasts Bellows's *New
York* with the "cubist-futurist amalgams" of Max Weber's *New York*
(1913), suggesting that "the overlapping titles confirm a shared ambition to capture the city as a whole," even if "the modernists' attempt
tends to be from the outside," whereas "Bellows operates more from
the inside out."[3] I would contest the notion that Bellows operates
from the inside out in this particular painting, especially given that
the viewer is positioned slightly above street level and looks pano-
ramically across the space and, from a slightly panoptic and distanced
perspective, gently down over the heads of the crowd. Further, the
flattening effect of the wall of skyscrapers in the background gives a

FIGURE 52. *George Bellows,* New York, *1911. (Courtesy National Gallery of Art)*

feeling of impenetrability, as if suggesting that the city denies access beyond its surfaces. Nonetheless, I do take Tallack's broader point that Bellows renders the city in substantially different terms than modernists like Weber, even if the two artists share a concern with the chaotic totality of the metropolis. Specifically, Bellows's *New York* stresses urban legibility even as it confronts the viewer with urban chaos, whereas Weber's exploding cubist composition of the city is deliberately fragmented and inscrutable.

In Bellows's painting, the legibility of the city is most explicitly figured through advertising signs, some of which specify product names like "Zeno" while others simply gesture impressionistically at them. These signs can be understood as articulating the commercial-consumer orientation of the modern city, including its public spaces. The capitalist appropriation of public space through spectacle, which Guy Debord describes in far stronger (and more alarmist) terms in *The Society of the Spectacle* as part of the commodity's "colonization of social life,"[4] is a phenomenon with a long, intricate history in Western culture dating back to the rise of mass printing and the advertising industry in the nineteenth century, as demonstrated by David Henkin in *City Reading: Written Words and Public Spaces in Antebellum New York* and Thomas Richards in *The Commodity Culture of Victorian England: Advertising and Spectacle, 1851–1914.*[5] Bellows captures this phenomenon at a pivotal phase in its development when urban surfaces in the commercial heart of Manhattan were being permanently ceded to advertising—a process that reaches an apotheosis in Times Square's aggressive visual spectacle of illuminated, animated advertising. The capitalist orientation of modern New York, registered and expressed in its architecture, planning, and spatial ordering as much as in its literary, visual, and material cultures, has been a major concern of this book, just as it is in Bellows's painting. And like Bellows's painting, this book both critiques that orientation for its excesses and distortions while also recognizing its energizing, formative impact on the city.

Looking beyond advertising signs and the spectacle of public space, Bellows's *New York* is also significant in the way that it stages an encounter between the two dominant spatial perspectives on the city that have structured this book. The bottom half of the painting presents the horizontal drama of modern street life, while the top half presents the vertical excesses of the skyscraper city. Certainly, there are aesthetic and thematic tensions between the two halves of the painting. The street is populated, active, chaotic, and near. The skyline is depopulated, immobile, ordered, and distanced. The street defies control. The skyline exerts control. The street is at human scale, the skyline beyond human scale. These sorts of contrasts could be enumerated at some length, but it is also important to stress the interrelations between the two halves of the painting. First, they share the same compositional frame, and in this most basic sense are placed in the same space together. The work's title, *New York*, similarly has a unifying effect: it refers to one city, one view, one experience. Within the painting itself, the same color palette and brush techniques are used to render both the vertical and horizontal spaces of the city, suggesting aesthetic if not spatial congruity. Further, the placement of advertising signs throughout the painting—both on the side of tall buildings and on the side of carts, stalls, and storefronts at ground level—crosses lines between street and skyline. The overall effect is that the horizontal foreground and vertical background become mutually constitutive, interdependent, coexistent.

It is precisely this idea that I wish to stress in closing. Part I of this book argues that the modern skyline of New York is distinguished in the urban imaginary by a dynamic, unresolved tension between the sublime (as aesthetic encounter grounded in wonder) and the uncanny (as the familiar rendered newly strange). Part II argues that the modern sidewalk—and its rearticulation in spaces like the slum, the El, and the subway—gave rise to a street culture dominated by speed, movement, and dislocation. Yet as many of my examples have shown, ranging from the Stieglitz circle's Flatiron photography to the retro-futuristic promenade of the High Line, both the hovering otherworldliness of the skyline and the mobile, performative practices of the sidewalk belong to a broad set of interrelating spatial and cultural dynamics that, together, generated modern New York as both a place and an idea, and that continue even now to shape this endlessly mutable city.

{ NOTES }

Introduction

1. Le Corbusier, *When the Cathedrals Were White*, trans. Francis E. Hyslop (New York: McGraw-Hill, 1964), 90.

2. Rem Koolhaas, *Delirious New York* (New York: Monacelli Press, 1994), 293.

3. Henry James, *The American Scene* (New York: Penguin, 1994).

4. Ralph Ellison, *Invisible Man* (New York: Vintage, 1995); Piri Thomas, *Down These Mean Streets* (New York: Random House, 1997).

5. Stanley Corkin, *Starring New York: Filming the Grime and the Glamour of the Long 1970s* (New York: Oxford University Press, 2011).

6. Koolhaas, *Delirious New York*, 293, 29–31.

7. Koolhaas, *Delirious New York*, 9.

8. Andreas Huyssen, *Present Pasts: Urban Palimpsests and the Politics of Memory* (Stanford, CA: Stanford University Press, 2003), 7.

9. William B. Scott and Peter M. Rutkoff, *New York Modern: The Arts and the City* (Baltimore: Johns Hopkins University Press, 1999), xvii.

10. Samuel Zipp, *Manhattan Projects: The Rise and Fall of Urban Renewal in Cold War New York* (New York: Oxford University Press, 2010); William Chapman Sharpe, *New York Nocturne: The City after Dark in Literature, Painting, and Photography, 1850–1950* (Princeton, NJ: Princeton University Press, 2008); Max Page, *The City's End: Two Centuries of Fantasies, Fears, and Premonitions of New York's Destruction* (New Haven, CT: Yale University Press, 2008).

11. Henri Lefebvre, *The Production of Space*, trans. Donald Nicholson-Smith (Oxford: Blackwell, 1991); Kevin Lynch, *The Image of the City* (Cambridge, MA: MIT Press, 1960).

12. Edward W. Soja, *Postmetropolis: Critical Studies of Cities and Regions* (Oxford: Blackwell, 2000), 324.

13. Andreas Huyssen, "Introduction: World Cultures, World Cities," in *Other Cities, Other Worlds: Urban Imaginaries in a Globalizing World*, ed. Andreas Huyssen (Durham, NC: Duke University Press, 2008), 3.

14. Soja, *Postmetropolis*, 324.

15. This articulation of the urban imaginary is adapted from Christoph Lindner, "Amsterdam–New York: Transnational Photographic Exchange in the Era of Globalization," *International Journal of Cultural Studies* 16.2 (2012): 151–68.

16. Thomas Bender, *The Unfinished City: New York and the Metropolitan Idea* (New York: New Press, 2002), 24.

17. Douglas Tallack, *New York Sights: Visualizing Old and New New York* (New York: Berg, 2005); Maria Balshaw, *Looking for Harlem: Urban Aesthetics in African-American Literature* (London: Pluto Press, 2000); Angela Blake, *How New York Became American, 1890–1924* (Baltimore: Johns Hopkins University Press, 2009).

18. Michel Foucault, "Of Other Spaces," in *The Visual Culture Reader*, ed. Nicholas Mirzoeff (London: Routledge, 1998), 229–36.

19. Lefebvre, *Production of Space*, 22–9.

20. Peter Brooker, *Modernity and Metropolis: Writing, Film, and Urban Formations* (London: Palgrave, 2002), 186.

21. Brooker, *Modernity and Metropolis*, 186.

22. Brooker, *Modernity and Metropolis*, 187.

23. David Harvey, *Spaces of Hope* (Edinburgh: Edinburgh University Press, 2000); Rob Shields, ed., *Cultures of the Internet: Virtual Spaces, Real Histories, and Living Bodies* (London: Sage, 1996); Edward W. Soja, "Six Discourses on the Metropolis," in *Imagining Cities: Scripts, Signs, Memories*, ed. Sallie Westwood and John Williams (London: Routledge, 1994), 19–30.

24. Ricky Burdett and Deyan Sudjic, eds., *The Endless City* (London: Phaidon, 2007); Ricky Burdett and Deyan Sudjic, eds., *Living in the Endless City* (London: Phaidon, 2011).

25. Christoph Lindner, "The Postmetropolis and Mental Life: Wong Kar-Wai's Cinematic Hong Kong," in *The New Blackwell Companion to the City*, ed. Gary Bridge and Sophie Watson (Oxford: Blackwell, 2011), 327–36; Pedram Dibazar, Christoph Lindner, Miriam Meissner, and Judith Naeff, "Questioning Urban Modernity," *European Journal of Cultural Studies* 16.6 (2013): 643–58.

26. Rem Koolhaas, "The Generic City" in *S,M,L,XL*, by Rem Koolhaas and Bruce Mau (New York: Monacelli Press, 1995), 1238–64; Soja, *Postmetropolis*; Paul Virilio, "The Overexposed City," in *Rethinking Architecture: A Reader in Cultural Theory*, ed. Neil Leach (London: Routledge, 1997), 381–9.

27. Neil Brenner, *New State Spaces: Urban Governance and the Rescaling of Statehood* (New York: Oxford University Press, 2004); Neil Brenner and Nik Theodore, eds., *Spaces of Neoliberalism: Urban Restructuring in North America and Western Europe* (Oxford: Blackwell, 2003).

28. Edward W. Soja, "Urbanizing the Globe, Globalizing the Urban" (lecture, Amsterdam Centre for Globalisation Studies, University of Amsterdam, October 30, 2013).

29. Neill Brenner and Chistian Schmid, "Planetary Urbanization," in *Urban Constellations*, ed. Matthew Gandy (Berlin: Jovis, 2012), 10–3.

Part I

1. Albert Camus, "The Rains of New York," in *Lyrical and Critical Essays*, ed. Philip Thody, trans. Ellen Conroy Kennedy (New York: Vintage, 1970), 185.

2. Ezra Pound, *Patria Mia* (Chicago: Ralph Fletcher Seymour, 1950), 32–3.

3. Horst Hamann, *New York Vertical* (New York: teNeues, 2001).

4. Berenice Abbott, *Changing New York: The Complete WPA Project*, ed. Bonnie Yochelson (New York: New Press, 1999).

5. Thomas Bender, *The Unfinished City: New York and the Metropolitan Idea* (New York: New Press, 2002), 53.

6. James Sanders, *Celluloid Skyline: New York and the Movies* (London: Bloomsbury, 2002); Jan Seidler Ramirez, ed., *Painting the Town: Cityscapes of New York* (New York: Museum of the City of New York, 2000).

7. Douglas Tallack, *New York Sights: Visualizing Old and New New York* (New York: Berg, 2005); also see Tallack, "City Sights: Mapping and Representing New York City," in *Urban Space and Representation*, ed. Maria Balshaw and Liam Kennedy (London: Pluto, 2000), 24–38.

8. Michel de Certeau, *The Practice of Everyday Life*, trans. Steven Rendell (Berkeley: University of California Press, 1988), 92.

9. De Certeau, *Practice of Everyday Life*, 92.

10. De Certeau, *Practice of Everyday Life*, 92.

11. De Certeau, *Practice of Everyday Life*, 91.

12. Jean Baudrillard, "Requiem for the Twin Towers," in *The Spirit of Terrorism*, trans. Chris Turner (London: Verso, 2002), 46–7.

13. Baudrillard, "Requiem," 42–4.

14. Baudrillard, "Requiem," 43.

15. Mark Wigley, "Insecurity by Design," in *After the World Trade Center: Rethinking New York City*, ed. Michael Sorkin and Sharon Zukin (New York: Routledge, 2002), 74.

16. Baudrillard, "Requiem," 45.

17. Stephen Graham, "Introduction: Cities, Warfare, and States of Emergency," in *Cities, War, and Terrorism: Towards an Urban Geopolitics*, ed. Stephen Graham (Oxford: Blackwell, 2004), 9.

18. Max Page, *The Creative Destruction of New York, 1900–1940* (Chicago: University of Chicago Press, 1999), 7.

19. Sarah Bradford Landau and Carl W. Condit, *Rise of the New York Skyscraper, 1865–1913* (New Haven, CT: Yale University Press, 1996), 280.

20. Carol Willis, *Form Follows Finance: Skyscrapers and Skylines in New York and Chicago* (New York: Princeton Architectural Press, 1995), 180.

21. David Ward and Olivier Zunz, "Between Rationalism and Pluralism: Creating the Modern City," in *The Landscape of Modernity: New York City, 1900–1940*, ed. David Ward and Olivier Zunz (Baltimore: Johns Hopkins University Press, 1992), 4.

22. Robert Hughes, *The Shock of the New: Art and the Century of Change* (London: Thames and Hudson, 1991).

23. David Nye, *American Technological Sublime* (Cambridge, MA: MIT Press, 1994), 89.

24. Marco d'Eramo, *The Pig and the Skyscraper*, trans. Graeme Thomson (London: Verso, 2002), 53.

25. See Gerald R. Larson and Roula Mouroudellis Gerantiotis, "Towards a Better Understanding of the Evolution of the Iron Skeleton Frame in Chicago," *Journal of the Society of Architectural Historians* 46.1 (1987): 39–48.

26. Quoted in "Early Skeleton Construction," *Engineering Record* 40 (1899): 238.

27. Landau and Condit, *Rise of the New York Skyscraper*, 166.

28. Landau and Condit, *Rise of the New York Skyscraper*, 168.

29. Willis, *Form Follows Finance*, 145.

30. Willis, *Form Follows Finance*, 67.

31. See Willis, *Form Follows Finance*, 160–87.

32. George E. Kidder Smith, *Looking at Architecture* (New York: Abrams, 1990), 152.

33. Lewis Mumford, *Sidewalk Critic: Lewis Mumford's Writings on New York*, ed. Robert Wojtowicz (New York: Princeton Architectural Press, 2000), 100.

34. Mumford, *Sidewalk Critic*, 150.

35. Mumford, *Sidewalk Critic*, 81.

36. Mumford, *Sidewalk Critic*, 85.

37. Mumford, *Sidewalk Critic*, 69.

38. Thomas Bender and William R. Taylor, "Architecture and Culture: Some Aesthetic Tensions in the Shaping of Modern New York City," in *Visions of the Modern City: Essays in*

History, Art, and Literature, ed. William Sharpe and Leonard Wallock (Baltimore: Johns Hopkins University Press, 1987), 216.

39. Roland Barthes, *The Eiffel Tower and Other Mythologies*, trans. Richard Howard (Berkeley: University of California Press, 1997), 149.

40. Giovanni da Verrazano, *The Voyage of John de Verrazano, along the Coast of North America, from Carolina to Newfoundland, A.D. 1525*, trans. Joseph G. Cogswell (New York: New-York Historical Society, 1841), 45–6.

41. Verrazano, *The Voyage*, 45–6.

42. Frances Trollope, *Domestic Manners of the Americans* (London: Penguin, 1997), 260.

43. See John Aldrich Christie, *Thoreau as World Traveler* (New York: Columbia University Pres, 1965), 8–19.

44. Henry David Thoreau, *The Correspondence of Henry David Thoreau*, ed. Walter Harding and Carl Bode (New York: New York University Press, 1958), 110–1.

45. Edgar Allan Poe, "The Man of the Crowd," in *Selected Writings of Edgar Allan Poe*, ed. David Galloway (London: Penguin, 1967), 179–88.

46. Walter Benjamin, *Charles Baudelaire: A Lyric Poet in the Era of High Capitalism*, trans. Harry Zohn (London: Verso, 1997), 43.

47. Benjamin, *Charles Baudelaire*, 34.

48. Walt Whitman, "Manhattan from the Bay," in *Walt Whitman: Complete Poetry and Collected Prose* (New York: Library of America, 1982), 823.

49. Peter Brooker, *New York Fictions: Modernity, Postmodernism, the New Modern* (New York: Longman, 1996), 29.

50. Henry James, *The American Scene* (New York: Penguin, 1994), 61.

51. James, *The American Scene*, 60.

52. Morton White and Lucia White, *The Intellectual versus the City: From Thomas Jefferson to Frank Lloyd Wright* (Cambridge, MA: Harvard University Press and MIT Press, 1962), 75.

53. Thoreau, *Correspondence*, 110.

54. Sigmund Freud, "The Uncanny," in *The Penguin Freud Library*, vol. 14, *Art and Literature*, ed. and trans. James Strachey (London: Penguin, 1985), 363–4.

55. Anthony Vidler, *The Architectural Uncanny: Essays in the Modern Unhomely* (Cambridge, MA: MIT Press, 1999), 6.

56. Vidler, *Architectural Uncanny*, 4.

57. Vidler, *Architectural Uncanny*, 6–7.

58. Henry Adams, *The Education of Henry Adams* (London: Penguin, 1995), 471.

59. De Certeau, *Practice of Everyday Life*, 91.

60. De Certeau, *Practice of Everyday Life*, 92.

61. Willa Cather, "Behind the Singer Tower," in *Willa Cather's Collected Short Fiction, 1892–1912*, ed. Virginia Faulkner (Lincoln: University of Nebraska Press, 1970), 44.

62. Robert K. Miller, "'Behind the Singer Tower': A Transatlantic Tale," in *Willa Cather's New York: New Essays on Cather and the City*, ed. Merrill Maguire Skaggs (London: Associated University Presses, 2000), 75.

63. For an excellent in-depth analysis of the architectural and cultural significance of the Singer Tower, which places the skyscraper in the broader context of the site's redevelopment in the 1960s, see Eric J. Sandeen, "Looking After the Singer Tower: The Death and Life of Block 62," *Prospects: An Annual of American Culture Studies* 30 (2005): 597–621.

64. Cather, "Behind the Singer Tower," 46.

65. Cather, "Behind the Singer Tower," 44.

66. Cather, "Behind the Singer Tower," 44.

67. Richard Drew, "The Horror of 9/11 That's All Too Familiar," *Los Angeles Times*, September 10, 2003.

68. Cather, "Behind the Singer Tower," 45.

69. Slavoj Žižek, *Welcome to the Desert of the Real* (London: Verso, 2002), 16.

70. Daniel Libeskind, "Memory Foundations," *Studio Daniel Libeskind: World Trade Center Design Study*, accessed August 19, 2004, http://www.daniel-libeskind.com/press/index.html.

71. Baudrillard, "Requiem," 42.

72. Thomas Adams, *Regional Plan of New York*, vol. 2 (New York: Committee on the Regional Plan of New York and Its Environs, 1931), 576.

73. Shaun O'Connell, *Remarkable, Unspeakable New York: A Literary History* (Boston: Beacon, 1995), 98.

74. Abraham Cahan, *The Rise of David Levinsky* (New York: Penguin, 1993), 86–8.

75. Abraham Cahan, "The Imported Bridegroom," in *"Yekl" and "The Imported Bridegroom" and Other Stories of Yiddish New York* (New York: Dover, 1970), 119.

76. Cahan, *Rise of David Levinsky*, 89.

77. Cahan, *Rise of David Levinsky*, 90.

78. Cahan, "Imported Bridegroom," 120.

79. Cahan, "Imported Bridegroom," 120.

80. James Weldon Johnson, *The Autobiography of an Ex-Coloured Man* (New York: Vintage, 1989), 90.

81. Johnson, *Autobiography*, 89.

82. James Weldon Johnson, *Black Manhattan* (New York: Da Capo Press, 1991), 4.

83. Maria Balshaw, *Looking For Harlem: Urban Aesthetics in African-American Literature* (London: Pluto Press, 2000), 1.

84. Balshaw, *Looking for Harlem*, 1.

85. Balshaw, *Looking for Harlem*, 2.

86. Theodore Dreiser, *The Color of a Great City* (Syracuse, NY: Syracuse University Press, 1996), 1.

87. Dreiser, *Color of a Great City*, 284–5.

88. Merrill Schleier, *The Skyscraper in American Art, 1890–1931* (Ann Arbor, MI: UMI Research Press, 1986), 1–2, 16–17.

89. Jonathan Crary, *Techniques of the Observer: On Vision and Modernity in the Nineteenth Century* (Cambridge, MA: MIT Press, 1992); James Donald, *Imagining the Modern City* (London: Athlone, 1999).

90. Joan Ramon Resina, "The Concept of After-Image and the Scopic Apprehension of the City," in *After-Images of the City*, ed. Joan Ramon Resina and Dieter Ingenschay (Ithaca, NY: Cornell University Press, 2003), 1.

91. Resina, "After-Image," 1.

92. Resina, "After-Image," 1.

93. Resina, "After-Image," 1–2.

94. Resina, "After-Image," 2.

95. Mary N. Woods, "After-Images of the 'New' New York and the Alfred Stieglitz Circle," in Resina and Ingenschay, *After-Images of the City*, 183.

96. Woods, "After-Images," 183.

97. Woods, "After-Images," 187–8.

98. Katherine Hoffman, *Stieglitz: A Beginning Light* (New Haven, CT: Yale University Press, 2004), 212.

99. Woods, "After-Images," 190.

100. Woods, "After-Images," 189.

101. Alfred Stieglitz, "Six Happening I: Photographing the Flat-Iron Building, 1902–3," *Twice a Year* 14–15 (1946–7): 188.

102. Stephen Kern, *The Culture of Time and Space: 1880–1918* (Cambridge, MA: Harvard University Press, 1983).

103. Hoffman, *Stieglitz*, 246.

104. Woods, "After-Images," 207.

105. Sarah Hermandson Meister, *Michael Wesely: Open Shutter* (New York: Museum of Modern Art, 2004), 9.

106. Meister, *Michael Wesely*, 14.

107. Schleier, *Skyscraper*, 49.

108. Alvin Langdon Coburn, *Alvin Langdon Coburn, Photographer: An Autobiography*, ed. Helmut Gernscheim and Alison Gernsheim (New York: Courier Dover, 1978), 8.

109. Tamara L. Follini, "Habitations of Modernism: Henry James's New York, 1907," *Cambridge Quarterly* 37.1 (2008): 37.

110. Nicholas Royle, *The Uncanny* (Manchester: Manchester University Press, 2003), 1.

111. Vidler, *Architectural Uncanny*, 18.

112. Coburn, *Alvin Langdon Coburn*, 78.

113. Nancy Mowll Mathews, *Moving Pictures: American Art and Early Film, 1880–1910* (Manchester, VT: Hudson Hills Press, 2005).

114. This film, as well as many other early films about New York City, is available to view online as part of the Library of Congress's digital collection "Early Films of New York, 1898–1906."

115. Murray Pomerance, "Prelude: To Wake Up in the City That Never Sleeps," in *City That Never Sleeps: New York and the Filmic Imagination*, ed. Murray Pomerance (New Brunswick, NJ: Rutgers University Press, 2007), 5–6.

116. Jean Baudrillard, *America*, trans. Chris Turner (London: Verso, 1998), 56.

117. Juan A. Suárez, *Pop Modernism: Noise and the Reinvention of the Everyday* (Urbana: University of Illinois Press, 2007), 51.

118. Kamilla Elliott, *Rethinking the Novel/Film Debate* (Cambridge: Cambridge University Press, 2003), 157.

119. Walt Whitman, *Leaves of Grass and Selected Prose*, ed. Lawrence Buell (New York: Modern Library College Edition, 1981), 234.

120. T. S. Eliot, *The Waste Land* (New York: Norton, 2013), 35.

121. Suárez, *Pop Modernism*, 55.

122. Bender, *Unfinished City*, 108.

123. Bender, *Unfinished City*, 105.

124. Hugh Ferriss, *The Metropolis of Tomorrow* (New York: Princeton Architectural Press, 1986).

125. Schleier, *Skyscraper*, 86.

126. Mardges Bacon, *Le Corbusier in America: Travels in the Land of the Timid* (Cambridge, MA: MIT Press, 2001), 129.

127. Le Corbusier, *When the Cathedrals Were White*, trans. Francis E. Hyslop, Jr. (New York: McGraw Hill, 1964), 51–2.

128. Le Corbusier, *When the Cathedrals Were White*, 55.

129. Le Corbusier, *When the Cathedrals Were White*, 56.

130. Ferriss, *Metropolis*, 16.

131. Ferriss, *Metropolis*, 15.

132. Ferriss, *Metropolis*, 46.

133. Ferriss, *Metropolis*, 54.

134. Ferriss, *Metropolis*, 59.

135. Ferriss, *Metropolis*, 59.

136. Ferriss, *Metropolis*, 59.

137. Carol Willis, "Drawing towards Metropolis," in Ferriss, *Metropolis*, 171.

138. Ferriss, *Metropolis*, 111.

139. Willis, "Drawing towards Metropolis," 171.

140. Ferriss, *Metropolis*, 110.

141. Kevin R. McNamara, *Urban Verbs: Arts and Discourses in American Cities* (Palo Alto, CA: Stanford University Press, 1996), 129.

142. Willis, "Drawing towards Metropolis," 174.

143. Quoted in Thomas Elsaesser, *Metropolis* (London: BFI, 2000), 9.

144. For a fuller discussion of the motif of the empty city in film, see Christoph Lindner, "London Undead: Screening/Branding the Empty City," in *Branding Cities: Cosmopolitanism, Parochialism, and Social Change*, ed. Stephanie Hemelryk Donald, Eleonore Kofman, and Catherine Kevin (New York: Routledge, 2009), 91–104.

145. De Certeau, *Practice of Everyday Life*, 91.

146. De Certeau, *Practice of Everyday Life*, 92.

147. There is no evidence to suggest that Ferriss had seen Lang's *Metropolis* before completing *The Metropolis of Tomorrow*.

148. Brian J. Miller, "The Struggle over the Redevelopment at Cabrini-Green, 1989–2004," *Journal of Urban History* 34.6 (2008): 944–60.

149. For more on these aspects of contemporary urbanism, see Christoph Lindner, ed., *Globalization, Violence, and the Visual Culture of Cities* (London: Routledge, 2010).

150. Jane M. Jacobs, Stephen Cairns, and Ignaz Strebel, "Materialising Vision: Performing a High-Rise View," in *Visuality/Materiality: Images, Objects, and Practices*, ed. Gillian Rose and Divya Tolia-Kelly (Farnham, UK: Ashgate, 2012), 133–53.

151. Anthony DePalma, "Landfill, Park…Final Resting Place? Plans for Fresh Kills Trouble 9/11 Families Who Sense Loved Ones in the Dust," *New York Times*, June 14, 2004.

152. William L. Hamilton, "A Fence with More Beauty, Fewer Barbs," *New York Times*, June 18, 2006.

153. Thomas Hayden, "Fields of Dreams: Turning 'Brownfields' and Dumps into Prime Real Estate," *U.S. News & World Report* 132.2 (2002): 62.

154. Harold Crooks, *Giants of Garbage: The Rise of the Global Waste Industry and the Politics of Pollution* (Toronto: Lorimer, 1993); Mike Davis, *Planet of Slums* (New York: Verso, 2006).

155. Peter Marcuse and Ronald van Kempen, introduction, in *Globalizing Cities: A New Spatial Order?*, ed. Peter Marcuse and Ronald van Kempen (Oxford: Blackwell, 2000), 1–21.

156. New York City Department of City Planning, *Fresh Kills Park: Draft Master Plan* (New York: City of New York, 2006), 2.

157. New York City Department of City Planning, *Fresh Kills Park*, 2.

158. New York City Department of City Planning, *Fresh Kills Park*, 3.

159. New York City Department of City Planning, *Fresh Kills Park*, 3.

160. New York City Department of City Planning, *Fresh Kills Park*, 60.

161. Friends of the High Line, "High Line: Team Statement," May 5, 2006, accessed July 15, 2010, http://www.thehighline.org/design/fieldop.html.

162. Friends of the High Line, "High Line: Team Statement."

163. James Corner, "Lifescape – Fresh Kills Parkland," *Topos: The International Review of Landscape Architecture and Urban Design* 51 (2005): 15.

164. Corner, "Lifescape," 20.

165. Jean-François Lyotard, "Scapeland," *Revue des Sciences Humaines* 209 (1988): 39.

166. Wigley, "Insecurity by Design," 82.

Part II

1. Jane Jacobs, *The Death and Life of Great American Cities* (New York: Modern Library, 1993), 37.

2. Paul Auster, *City of Glass* (London: Faber, 1987), 3–4.

3. Thomas Bender, *The Unfinished City: New York and the Metropolitan Idea* (New York: New Press, 2002), 35.

4. Jacobs, *Death and Life*, 37.

5. Anastasia Loukaitou-Sideris and Renia Ehrenfeucht, *Sidewalks: Conflict and Negotiation over Public Space* (Cambridge, MA: MIT Press, 2009), 3–4.

6. Spiro Kostof, *The City Assembled: The Elements of Urban Form through History* (New York: Brown, 1992), 191.

7. Loukaitou-Sideris and Ehrenfeucht, *Sidewalks*, 15.

8. Loukaitou-Sideris and Ehrenfeucht, *Sidewalks*, 39.

9. Emile Zola, *The Ladies' Paradise*, trans. Brian Nelson (Oxford: Oxford University Press, 1998), 4–5.

10. For a fuller discussion of literature, shopping, and consumer society in the nineteenth century, see Christoph Lindner, *Fictions of Commodity Culture: From the Victorian to the Postmodern* (Aldershot, UK: Ashgate, 2003).

11. Loukaitou-Sideris and Ehrenfeucht, *Sidewalks*, 17.

12. Rosalind Krauss, "Grids," *October* 9 (1979): 50.

13. Krauss, "Grids," 50.

14. Teresa Stoppani, *Paradigm Islands: Manhattan and Venice: Discourses on Architecture and the City* (London: Routledge, 2011), 66.

15. Stoppani, *Paradigm Islands*, 66–77.

16. Stoppani, *Paradigm Islands*, 70.

17. Stoppani, *Paradigm Islands*, 70.

18. Stoppani, *Paradigm Islands*, 70–1.

19. Hilary Ballon, "Introduction," in *The Greatest Grid: The Master Plan of Manhattan, 1811–2011*, ed. Hilary Ballon (New York: Columbia University Press, 2012), 14.

20. Amanda M. Burden, "Reflection," in Ballon, *The Greatest Grid*, 193.

21. Carolyn Yerkes, "Reflection," in Ballon, *The Greatest Grid*, 203.

22. "Remarks of the Commissioners, March 22, 1811," reprinted in Ballon, *The Greatest Grid*, 40–2.

23. Douglas Tallack, *New York Sights: Visualizing Old and New New York* (Oxford: Berg, 2005), 83.

24. Robert Grafton Small, "Dead Men Walking: From Baudelaire to Bauhaus and Beyond," *Consumption, Markets, and Culture* 5.1 (2002): 14.

25. David P. Brown, *Noise Orders: Jazz, Improvisation, and Architecture* (Minneapolis: University of Minnesota Press, 2006), xxvvii.

26. Max Page, *The Creative Destruction of Manhattan, 1900–1940* (Chicago: University of Chicago Press, 1999).

27. Quoted in Brown, *Noise Orders*, 20.

28. *Edison Film Company Catalog*, from Library of Congress American Memory Collection, digital ID: lcmp002 m2a36374.

29. Laura Mulvey, "Visual Pleasure and Narrative Cinema," *Screen* 16.3 (1975): 6–18.

30. David Simpson, *9/11: The Culture of Commemoration* (Chicago: University of Chicago Press, 2006), 127.

31. Theodore Dreiser, *Sister Carrie* (Oxford: Oxford World's Classics, 1998), 285.

32. Dreiser, *Sister Carrie*, 285–6.

33. Thorstein Veblen, *The Theory of the Leisure Class*, ed. Martha Banta (Oxford: Oxford University Press, 2009), 28–32.

34. Veblen, *Theory of the Leisure Class*, 49–54.

35. David Scobey, "Anatomy of the Promenade: The Politics of Bourgeois Sociability in Nineteenth-Century New York," *Social History* 17.2 (1992): 203.

36. Jürgen Habermas, *The Structural Transformation of the Public Sphere: An Inquiry into a Category of Bourgeois Society*, trans. Thomas Burger (Cambridge, MA: MIT Press, 1989), xv.

37. Scobey, "Anatomy of the Promenade," 203.

38. Scobey, "Anatomy of the Promenade," 206.

39. Karl Marx, *Capital: A Critique of Political Economy*, vol 1, trans. Ben Fowkes (New York: Penguin, 1990), 165.

40. Rachel Bowlby, *Just Looking: Consumer Culture in Dreiser, Gissing, and Zola* (London: Methuen, 1985), 2–6.

41. Anne Friedberg, *Window Shopping: Cinema and the Postmodern* (Berkeley: University of California Press, 1993), 7.

42. Friedberg, *Window Shopping*, 16.

43. Jean Baudrillard, *The Consumer Society: Myths and Structures*, trans. Chris Turner (London: Sage, 1998), 166.

44. Guy Debord, *Society of the Spectacle*, trans. Donald Nicholson-Smith (New York: Zone Books, 1995).

45. See, for example, Pedram Dibazar, Christoph Lindner, Miriam Meissner, and Judith Naeff, "Questioning Urban Modernity," *European Journal of Cultural Studies* 16.6 (2013): 643–58.

46. Walter Benjamin, *Charles Baudelaire: A Lyric Poet in the Era of High Capitalism*, trans. Harry Zohm (London: Verso, 1997), 37.

47. Benjamin, *Charles Baudelaire*, 55.

48. Benjamin, *Charles Baudelaire*, 48.

49. Benjamin, *Charles Baudelaire*, 49.

50. Benjamin, *Charles Baudelaire*, 49.

51. Walter Benjamin, *The Arcades Project*, ed. Rolf Tiederman, trans. Howard Eiland (Cambridge, MA: Harvard University Press, 2002).

52. David Frisby, *Cityscapes of Modernity* (Cambridge: Polity Press, 2001), 35.

53. Davide Deriu, "The Ascent of the Modern *Plâneur*: Aerial Images and Urban Imaginary in the 1920," in *Imagining the City: The Art of Urban Living*, ed. Christian Emden, Catherine Keen, and David Midgley (Oxford: Lang, 2006), 189–212.

54. Oskar Juhlin, "The Automobile Flâneur," in *Social Media on the Road: The Future of Car Based Computing*, ed. Oskar Juhlin (London: Springer, 2010), 113–25; also see Steven Jacobs, "From Flaneur to Chauffeur: Driving through Cinematic Cities," in Emden, Keen, and Midgley, *Imagining the City*, 213–29.

55. Mustafa Dikeç, *Badlands of the Republic: Space, Politics and Urban Policy* (Oxford: Blackwell, 2007).

56. See Janet Wolff, "The Invisible *Flâneuse*: Women and the Literature of Modernity," *Theory, Culture and Society* 2.3 (1985): 37–46; Judith Walkowitz, *City of Dreadful Delight: Narratives of Sexual Danger in London* (London: Virago, 1992); Griselda Pollock, *Vision and Difference: Femininity, Feminism and the Histories of Art* (London: Routledge, 1988), 50–90.

57. Deborah L. Parsons, *Streetwalking the Metropolis: Women, the City and Modernity* (Oxford: Oxford University Press, 2000), 18.

58. Parsons, *Streetwalking the Metropolis*, 43.

59. Parsons, *Streetwalking the Metropolis*, 67.

60. Nella Larsen, *Quicksand*, ed. Deborah E. McDowell (New Brunswick, NJ: Rutgers University Press, 1986), 30.

61. Benjamin, *Charles Baudelaire*, 43.

62. Larsen, *Quicksand*, 58.

63. Georg Simmel, "The Metropolis and Mental Life," in *The Blackwell City Reader*, ed. Gary Bridge and Sophie Watson (Oxford: Blackwell, 2002), 14.

64. The elaboration of Simmel in this section is adapted from my essay "The Postmetropolis and Mental Life: Wong Kar-Wai's Cinematic Hong Kong," in *The New Blackwell Companion to the City*, ed. Gary Bridge and Sophie Watson (Oxford: Blackwell, 2011), 327–36.

65. Simmel, "Metropolis," 12–14.

66. John Dos Passos, *Manhattan Transfer* (New York: Mariner Books, 2000).

67. William Dean Howells, *A Hazard of New Fortunes* (New York: Modern Library, 2002).

68. Berenice Abbott, *Changing New York: The Complete WPA Project*, ed. Bonnie Yochelson (New York: New Press, 1999).

69. G. F. Mitrano, "Sontag and the Europeans," *Women's Studies* 37.8 (2011): 912.

70. Simmel, "Metropolis," 14.

71. Simmel, "Metropolis," 18–9.

72. Georg Lukács, *History and Class Consciousness*, trans. Rodney Livingstone (London: Merlin Press, 1971); Henri Lefebvre, *The Production of Space*, trans. Donald Nicholson-Smith (Oxford: Blackwell, 1991).

73. Mike Davis, *Planet of Slums* (London: Verso, 2006), 175.

74. Davis, *Planet of Slums*, 11.

75. David Harvey, *A Brief History of Neoliberalism* (Oxford: Oxford University Press, 2005).

76. Friedrich Engels, *The Condition of the Working Class in England*, ed. David McLellan (Oxford: Oxford University Press, 2009).

77. Luc Sante, *Low Life: Lures and Snares of Old New York* (New York: Farrar, Straus and Giroux, 2003).

78. Kenneth T. Jackson, ed., *The Encyclopedia of New York City* (New Haven, CT: Yale University Press, 1995), 582–3.

79. Thomas Kessner, *The Golden Door: Italian and Jewish Immigrant Mobility in New York City, 1880–1915* (Oxford: Oxford University Press, 1977), 136.

80. George E. Waring, *Street-Cleaning and the Disposal of a City's Waste* (New York: Doubleday and McLure, 1897).

81. Keith Gandal, *The Virtues of the Vicious: Jacob Riis, Stephen Crane, and the Spectacle of the Slum* (New York: Oxford University Press, 1997), 7.

82. Gandal, *Virtues of the Vicious*, 8.

83. Michel Foucault, *Archaeology of Knowledge* (London: Routledge, 2002), 172.

84. Gandal, *Virtues of the Vicious*, 9.

85. Stephen Crane, *Maggie: A Girl of the Streets, and Other Tales of New York*, ed. Larzer Ziff (New York: Penguin, 2000), 76–8.

86. See George Monteiro, ed., *Stephen Crane: The Contemporary Reviews* (Cambridge: Cambridge University Press, 2009).

87. Howard Horwitz, "*Maggie* and the Sociological Paradigm," *American Literary History* 10.4 (1998): 606–38.

88. Crane, *Maggie*, 77–8.

89. Robert M. Dowling and Donald Pizer, "A Cold Case File Reopened: Was Crane's *Maggie* Murdered or a Suicide?," *American Literary Realism* 42.1 (2009): 36–53.

90. Crane, *Maggie*, 3–4.

91. Jacobs, *Death and Life*, 29–30.

92. Jacobs, *Death and Life*, 35.

93. Jacobs, *Death and Life*, 35–6.

94. Max Page, "Introduction: More than Meets the Eye," in *Reconsidering Jane Jacobs*, ed. Timothy Mennel and Max Page (Washington, DC: APA Planners Press, 2011), 12.

95. Gandal, *Virtues of the Vicious*, 39.

96. Bender, *Unfinished City*, 9.

97. Janet B. Pascal, *Jacob Riis: Reporter and Reformer* (New York: Oxford University Press, 2005), 125.

98. Pascal, *Jacob Riis*, 98–110; see also Roy Lubove, *The Progressives and the Slums: Tenement House Reform in New York City, 1890–1917* (Pittsburgh: University of Pittsburgh Press, 1962).

99. Jacob Riis, *The Battle of the Slum* (New York: Cosima, 2008), 307.

100. Jack London, *People of the Abyss* (London: Pluto Press, 1993); George Orwell, *Down and Out in Paris and London* (New York: Mariner Books, 1972).

101. Sudeep Dasgupta, "Permanent Transiency, Tele-visual Spectacle, and the Slum as Postcolonial Monument," *South Asian Studies* 29.1 (2013): 148.

102. Anthony Vidler, *The Architectural Uncanny: Essays in the Modern Unhomely* (Cambridge, MA: MIT Press, 1999), 17.

103. Gandal, *Virtues of the Vicious*, 17.

104. Mario Maffi, *New York City: An Outsider's Inside View* (Columbus: Ohio State University Press, 2004), 31.

105. Maffi, *New York City*, 31.

106. Jan Seidler Ramirez and Barbara Ball Buff, "Catalogue," in *Painting the Town: Cityscapes of New York*, ed. Jan Seidler Ramirez (New York: Museum of the City of New York, 2000), 228.

107. See Stanley Corkin, *Starring New York: Filming the Grime and the Glamour of the Long 1970s* (New York: Oxford University Press, 2011).

108. Roger P. Roess and Gene Sansone, *The Wheels That Drove New York: A History of the New York City Transit System* (Heidelberg: Springer, 2013), 105–9.

109. Tallack, *New York Sights*, 57, 73.

110. Tallack, *New York Sights*, 60.

111. Howells, *Hazard of New Fortunes*, 76.

112. Mark Caldwell, *New York Night: The Mystique and the History* (New York: Scribner, 2005), 152.

113. Howells, *Hazard of New Fortunes*, 76–7.

114. Jean-François Lyotard, "Scapeland," *Revue des Sciences Humaines* 209 (1988): 39–48.

115. Michael W. Brooks, *Subway City: Riding the Trains, Reading New York* (New Brunswick, NJ: Rutgers University Press, 1997), 11.

116. Friends of the Highline, "About Friends of the High Line," accessed October 4, 2013, http://www.thehighline.org/about/friends-of-the-high-line.

117. Corner quoted in Jill Fehrenbacher, "Interview: Architect James Corner on NYC's High Line Park," in *Inhabitat*, accessed October 4, 2013, http://inhabitat.com/interview-architect-james-corner-on-the-design-of-high-line.

118. Friends of the QueensWay, "About Us," accessed October 6, 2013, http://www.thequeensway.org/about-us.

119. Sunny Stalter, "Farewell to the El: Nostalgic Urban Visuality on the Third Avenue Elevated Train," *American Quarterly* 58.3 (2006): 871.

120. Lowline, "Timeline," *TheLowline.org*, accessed October 6, 2013, http://www.thelowline.org/about/project.

121. Brooks, *Subway City*, 7.

122. Brooks, *Subway City*, 7.

123. Roess and Sansone, *The Wheels That Drove New York*, 144–9.

124. Brooks, *Subway City*, 53–4.

125. Bender, *Unfinished City*, 23.

126. Bender, *Unfinished City*, 40.

127. Stalter, "Farewell to the El," 871.

128. Brooks, *Subway City*, 4.

129. Carey James Mickalites, "Manhattan Transfer, Spectacular Time, and the Outmoded," *Arizona Quarterly* 67.4 (2011): 64.

130. Passos, *Manhattan Transfer*, 256.

131. Dos Passos, *Manhattan Transfer*, 148.

132. Carolyn Whitzman, Crystal Legacy, Carline Andrew, Fran Klodwasky, Margaret Shaw, and Kalpana Viswanath, eds., *Building Inclusive Cities: Women's Safety and the Right to the City* (Abingdon: Routledge, 2013).

133. James E. B. Breslin, *Mark Rothko: A Biography* (Chicago: University of Chicago Press, 1993), 128.

134. Tracy Fitzpatrick, *Art and the Subway: New York Underground* (New Brunswick, NJ: Rutgers University Press, 2009), 91.

135. Marc Augé, *Non-Place: An Introduction to an Anthropology of Supermodernity* (London: Verso, 1995), 94.

136. Augé, *Non-Place*, 93.

137. Christoph Lindner and Miriam Meissner, "Slow Art in the Creative City: Globalization, Street Photography, and Urban Renewal," *Space and Culture* (2014). doi: 10.1177/1206331213509914.

138. See, for example, Ken Johnson, "Walking the Walk, in a Rhapsodic New York Ballet: 'Street' at the Metropolitan Musuem," *New York Times*, March 14, 2013, accessed October 20, 2013, http://www.nytimes.com/2013/03/15/arts/design/street-at-the-metropolitan-museum.html.

139. Shirley Jordan, "The Poetics of Scale in Urban Photography," in *Globalization, Violence, and the Visual Culture of Cities*, ed. Christoph Lindner (London: Routledge, 2010), 149.

Afterword

1. William R. Taylor, ed., *Inventing Times Square: Commerce and Culture at the Crossroads of the World* (Baltimore: Johns Hopkins University Press, 1998); Bart Eeckhout, "The 'Disneyfication' of Times Square: Back to the Future?," *Research in Urban Sociology* 6 (2001): 379–428.

2. John Fagg, *On the Cusp: Stephen Crane, George Bellows, and Modernism* (Tuscaloosa: University of Alabama Press, 2009).

3. Douglas Tallack, *New York Sights: Visualizing Old and New New York* (Oxford: Berg, 2005), 83–4.

4. Guy Debord, *Society of the Spectacle*, trans. Donald Nicholson-Smith (New York: Zone Books, 1995), 24.

5. David Henkin, *City Reading: Written Words and Public Spaces in Antebellum New York* (New York: Columbia University Press, 1998); Thomas Richards, *The Commodity Culture of Victorian England: Advertising and Spectacle, 1851–1914* (Stanford, CA: Stanford University Press, 1991).

{ BIBLIOGRAPHY }

Abbott, Berenice. *Changing New York: The Complete WPA Project*. Edited by Bonnie Yochelson. New York: New Press, 1999.

Adams, Henry. *The Education of Henry Adams*. London: Penguin, 1995.

Adams, Thomas. *Regional Plan of New York*. Vol. 2. New York: Committee on the Regional Plan of New York and Its Environs, 1931.

Augé, Marc. *Non-Place: An Introduction to an Anthropology of Supermodernity*. London: Verso, 1995.

Auster, Paul. *City of Glass*. London: Faber, 1987.

Bacon, Mardges. *Le Corbusier in America: Travels in the Land of the Timid*. Cambridge, MA: MIT Press, 2001.

Ballon, Hilary. "Introduction." In *The Greatest Grid: The Master Plan of Manhattan, 1811–2011*, edited by Hilary Ballon, 13–5. New York: Columbia University Press, 2012.

Balshaw, Maria. *Looking for Harlem: Urban Aesthetics in African-American Literature*. London: Pluto Press, 2000.

Barthes, Roland. *The Eiffel Tower and Other Mythologies*. Translated by Richard Howard. Berkeley: University of California Press, 1997.

Baudrillard, Jean. *America*. Translated by Chris Turner. London: Verso, 1998.

Baudrillard, Jean. *The Consumer Society: Myths and Structures*. Translated by Chris Turner. London: Sage, 1998.

Baudrillard, Jean. "Requiem for the Twin Towers." In *The Spirit of Terrorism*, translated by Chris Turner, 41–52. London: Verso, 2002.

Bender, Thomas. *The Unfinished City: New York and the Metropolitan Idea*. New York: New Press, 2002.

Bender, Thomas, and William R. Taylor. "Architecture and Culture: Some Aesthetic Tensions in the Shaping of Modern New York City." In *Visions of the Modern City: Essays in History, Art, and Literature*, edited by William Sharpe and Leonard Wallock, 189–219. Baltimore: Johns Hopkins University Press, 1987.

Benjamin, Walter. *Charles Baudelaire: A Lyric Poet in the Era of High Capitalism*. Translated by Harry Zohn. London: Verso, 1997.

Benjamin, Walter. *The Arcades Project*. Edited by Rolf Tiederman. Translated by Howard Eiland. Cambridge, MA: Harvard University Press, 2002.

Blake, Angela. *How New York Became American, 1890–1924*. Baltimore: Johns Hopkins University Press, 2009.

Bowlby, Rachel. *Just Looking: Consumer Culture in Dreiser, Gissing, and Zola*. London: Methuen, 1985.

Brenner, Neil. *New State Spaces: Urban Governance and the Rescaling of Statehood*. New York: Oxford University Press, 2004.

Brenner, Neil, and Chistian Schmid. "Planetary Urbanization." In *Urban Constellations*, edited by Matthew Gandy, 10–3. Berlin: Jovis, 2012.

Brenner, Neil, and Nik Theodore, eds. *Spaces of Neoliberalism: Urban Restructuring in North America and Western Europe.* Oxford: Blackwell, 2003.

Breslin, James E. B. *Mark Rothko: A Biography.* Chicago: University of Chicago Press, 1993.

Brooker, Peter. *New York Fictions: Modernity, Postmodernism, the New Modern.* New York: Longman, 1996.

Brooker, Peter. *Modernity and Metropolis: Writing, Film, and Urban Formations.* London: Palgrave, 2002.

Brooks, Michael W. *Subway City: Riding the Trains, Reading New York.* New Brunswick, NJ: Rutgers University Press, 1997.

Brown, David P. *Noise Orders: Jazz, Improvisation, and Architecture.* Minneapolis: University of Minnesota Press, 2006.

Burden, Amanda M. "Reflection." In *The Greatest Grid: The Master Plan of Manhattan, 1811–2011,* edited by Hilary Ballon, 193. New York: Columbia University Press, 2012.

Burdett, Ricky, and Deyan Sudjic, eds. *The Endless City.* London: Phaidon, 2007.

Burdett, Ricky, and Deyan Sudjic, eds. *Living in the Endless City.* London: Phaidon, 2011.

Cahan, Abraham. *"Yekl," and "The Imported Bridegroom" and Other Stories of Yiddish New York.* New York: Dover, 1970.

Cahan, Abraham. *The Rise of David Levinsky.* New York: Penguin, 1993.

Caldwell, Mark. *New York Night: The Mystique and the History.* New York: Scribner, 2005.

Camus, Albert. "The Rains of New York." In *Lyrical and Critical Essays,* edited by Philip Thody, translated by Ellen Conroy Kennedy, 182–6. New York: Vintage, 1970.

Cather, Willa. "Behind the Singer Tower." In *Willa Cather's Collected Short Fiction, 1892–1912,* edited by Virginia Faulkner, 43–54. Lincoln: University of Nebraska Press, 1970.

Christie, John Aldrich. *Thoreau as World Traveler.* New York: Columbia University Press, 1965.

Coburn, Alvin Langdon. *Alvin Langdon Coburn, Photographer: An Autobiography.* Edited by Helmut Gernscheim and Alison Gernsheim. New York: Courier Dover, 1978.

Corkin, Stanley. *Starring New York: Filming the Grime and the Glamour of the Long 1970s.* New York: Oxford University Press, 2011.

Corner, James. "Lifescape – Fresh Kills Parkland." *Topos: The International Review of Landscape Architecture and Urban Design* 51 (2005): 14–21.

Crane, Stephen. *Maggie: A Girl of the Streets, and Other Tales of New York.* Edited by Larzer Ziff. New York: Penguin, 2000.

Crary, Jonathan. *Techniques of the Observer: On Vision and Modernity in the Nineteenth Century.* Cambridge, MA: MIT Press, 1992.

Crooks, Harold. *Giants of Garbage: The Rise of the Global Waste Industry and the Politics of Pollution.* Toronto: Lorimer, 1993.

Dasgupta, Sudeep. "Permanent Transiency, Tele-visual Spectacle, and the Slum as Postcolonial Monument." *South Asian Studies* 29.1 (2013): 147–57.

Davis, Mike. *Planet of Slums.* London: Verso, 2006.

De Certeau, Michel. *The Practice of Everyday Life.* Translated by Steven Rendell. Berkeley: University of California Press, 1988.

Debord, Guy. *Society of the Spectacle.* Translated by Donald Nicholson-Smith. New York: Zone Books, 1995.

DePalma, Anthony. "Landfill, Park...Final Resting Place? Plans for Fresh Kills Trouble 9/11 Families Who Sense Loved Ones in the Dust." *New York Times,* June 14, 2004.

D'Eramo, Marco. *The Pig and the Skyscraper*. Translated by Graeme Thomson. London: Verso, 2002.

Deriu, Davide. "The Ascent of the Modern *Plâneur*: Aerial Images and Urban Imaginary in the 1920s." In *Imagining the City: The Art of Urban Living*, edited by Christian Emden, Catherine Keen, and David Midgley, 189–212. Oxford: Lang, 2006.

Dibazar, Pedram, Christoph Lindner, Miriam Meissner, and Judith Naeff. "Questioning Urban Modernity." *European Journal of Cultural Studies* 16.6 (2013): 643–58.

Dikeç, Mustafa. *Badlands of the Republic: Space, Politics and Urban Policy*. Oxford: Blackwell, 2007.

Donald, James. *Imagining the Modern City*. London: Athlone, 1999.

Dos Passos, John. *Manhattan Transfer*. New York: Mariner Books, 2000.

Dowling, Robert M., and Donald Pizer. "A Cold Case File Reopened: Was Crane's Maggie Murdered or a Suicide?" *American Literary Realism* 42.1 (2009): 36–53.

Dreiser, Theodore. *The Color of a Great City*. Syracuse, NY: Syracuse University Press, 1996.

Dreiser, Theodore. *Sister Carrie*. Oxford: Oxford World's Classics, 1998.

Drew, Richard. "The Horror of 9/11 That's All Too Familiar." *Los Angeles Times*, September 10, 2003.

"Early Skeleton Construction." *Engineering Record* 40 (1899): 237–8.

Edison Film Company Catalog. c.1901. From the Library of Congress American Memory Collection. Digital ID: lcmp002 m2a36374.

Eeckhout, Bart. "The 'Disneyfication' of Times Square: Back to the Future?" *Research in Urban Sociology* 6 (2001): 379–428.

Eliot, T. S. *The Waste Land*. New York: Norton, 2013.

Elliott, Kamilla. *Rethinking the Novel/Film Debate*. Cambridge: Cambridge University Press, 2003.

Ellison, Ralph. *Invisible Man*. New York: Vintage, 1995.

Elsaesser, Thomas. *Metropolis*. London: BFI, 2000.

Engels, Friedrich. *The Condition of the Working Class in England*. Edited by David McLellan. Oxford: Oxford University Press, 2009.

Fagg, John. *On the Cusp: Stephen Crane, George Bellows, and Modernism*. Tuscaloosa: University of Alabama Press, 2009.

Fehrenbacher, Jill. "Interview: Architect James Corner on NYC's High Line Park." *Inhabitat*. Accessed October 4, 2013. http://inhabitat.com/interview-architect-james-corner-on-the-design-of-high-line/.

Ferriss, Hugh. *The Metropolis of Tomorrow*. New York: Princeton Architectural Press, 1986.

Fitzpatrick, Tracy. *Art and the Subway: New York Underground*. New Brunswick, NJ: Rutgers University Press, 2009.

Follini, Tamara L. "Habitations of Modernism: Henry James's New York, 1907." *Cambridge Quarterly* 37.1 (2008): 30–46.

Foucault, Michel. "Of Other Spaces." In *The Visual Culture Reader*, edited by Nicholas Mirzoeff, 229–36. London: Routledge, 1998.

Foucault, Michel. *Archaeology of Knowledge*. London: Routledge, 2002.

Freud, Sigmund. "The Uncanny." In *The Penguin Freud Library*. Vol. 14: *Art and Literature*, edited and translated by James Strachey, 339–76. London: Penguin, 1985.

Friedberg, Anne. *Window Shopping: Cinema and the Postmodern*. Berkeley: University of California Press, 1993.

Friends of the Highline. "About Friends of the High Line." Accessed October 4, 2013. http://www.thehighline.org/about/friends-of-the-high-line.

Friends of the High Line. "High Line: Team Statement." May 5, 2006. Accessed August 4, 2014. http://www.thehighline.org/james-corner-field-operations-and-diller-scofidio-renfro.

Friends of the QueensWay. "About Us." Accessed October 6, 2013. http://www.thequeensway.org/about-us.

Frisby, David. *Cityscapes of Modernity*. Cambridge: Polity Press, 2001.

Gandal, Keith. *The Virtues of the Vicious: Jacob Riis, Stephen Crane, and the Spectacle of the Slum*. New York: Oxford University Press, 1997.

Graham, Stephen. "Introduction: Cities, Warfare, and States of Emergency." In *Cities, War, and Terrorism: Towards an Urban Geopolitics*, edited by Stephen Graham, 1–25. Oxford: Blackwell, 2004.

Habermas, Jürgen. *The Structural Transformation of the Public Sphere: An Inquiry into a Category of Bourgeois Society* Translated by Thomas Burger. Cambridge, MA: MIT Press, 1989.

Hamann, Horst. *New York Vertical*. New York: teNeues, 2001.

Hamilton, William L. "A Fence with More Beauty, Fewer Barbs." *New York Times*, June 18, 2006.

Harvey, David. *Spaces of Hope*. Edinburgh: Edinburgh University Press, 2000.

Harvey, David. *A Brief History of Neoliberalism*. Oxford: Oxford University Press, 2005.

Hayden, Thomas. "Fields of Dreams: Turning 'Brownfields' and Dumps into Prime Real Estate." *U.S. News & World Report* 132.2 (2002): 62–4.

Henkin, David. *City Reading: Written Words and Public Spaces in Antebellum New York*. New York: Columbia University Press, 1998.

Hoffman, Katherine. *Stieglitz: A Beginning Light*. New Haven, CT: Yale University Press, 2004.

Horwitz, Howard. "*Maggie* and the Sociological Paradigm." *American Literary History* 10.4 (1998): 606–38.

Howells, William Dean. *A Hazard of New Fortunes*. New York: Modern Library, 2002.

Hughes, Robert. *The Shock of the New: Art and the Century of Change*. London: Thames and Hudson, 1991.

Huyssen, Andreas. *Present Pasts: Urban Palimpsests and the Politics of Memory*. Stanford, CA: Stanford University Press, 2003.

Huyssen, Andreas. "Introduction: World Cultures, World Cities." In *Other Cities, Other Worlds: Urban Imaginaries in a Globalizing World*, edited by Andreas Huyssen, 1–23. Durham, NC: Duke University Press, 2008.

Jackson, Kenneth T., ed. *The Encyclopedia of New York City*. New Haven, CT: Yale University Press, 1995.

Jacobs, Jane. *The Death and Life of Great American Cities*. New York: Modern Library, 1993.

Jacobs, Jane M., Stephen Cairns, and Ignaz Strebel. "Materialising Vision: Performing a High-Rise View." In *Visuality/Materiality: Images, Objects, and Practices*, edited by Gillian Rose and Divya Tolia-Kelly, 133–53. Farnham, UK: Ashgate, 2012.

Jacobs, Steven. "From Flaneur to Chauffeur: Driving through Cinematic Cities." In *Imagining the City: The Art of Urban Living*, edited by Christian Emden, Catherine Keen, and David Midgley, 213–29. Oxford: Lang, 2006.

James, Henry. *The American Scene*. New York: Penguin, 1994.

Johnson, James Weldon. *The Autobiography of an Ex-Coloured Man*. New York: Vintage, 1989.

Johnson, James Weldon. *Black Manhattan*. New York: Da Capo Press, 1991.

Johnson, Ken. "Walking the Walk, in a Rhapsodic New York Ballet: 'Street' at the Metropolitan Museum." *New York Times*, March 14, 2013. Accessed October 20, 2013. http://www.nytimes.com/2013/03/15/arts/design/street-at-the-metropolitan-museum.html.

Jordan, Shirley. "The Poetics of Scale in Urban Photography." In Lindner, *Globalization, Violence, and the Visual Culture of Cities*, 137–49.

Juhlin, Oskar. "The Automobile Flâneur." In *Social Media on the Road: The Future of Car Based Computing*, edited by Oskar Juhlin, 113–25. London: Springer, 2010.

Kern, Stephen. *The Culture of Time and Space: 1880–1918*. Cambridge, MA: Harvard University Press, 1983.

Kessner, Thomas. *The Golden Door: Italian and Jewish Immigrant Mobility in New York City, 1880–1915*. Oxford: Oxford University Press, 1977.

Kidder Smith, George E. *Looking at Architecture*. New York: Abrams, 1990.

Koolhaas, Rem. *Delirious New York*. New York: Monacelli Press, 1994.

Koolhaas, Rem. "The Generic City." In *S,M,L,XL*, by Rem Koolhass and Bruce Mau, 1238–64. New York: Monacelli Press, 1995.

Kostof, Spiro. *The City Assembled: The Elements of Urban Form through History*. New York: Brown, 1992.

Krauss, Rosalind. "Grids." *October* 9 (1979): 50–64.

Landau, Sarah Bradford, and Carl W. Condit. *Rise of the New York Skyscraper, 1865–1913*. New Haven, CT: Yale University Press, 1996.

Larsen, Nella. *Quicksand*. Edited by Deborah E. McDowell. New Brunswick, NJ: Rutgers University Press, 1986.

Larson, Gerald R., and Roula Mouroudellis Gerantiotis. "Towards a Better Understanding of the Evolution of the Iron Skeleton Frame in Chicago." *Journal of the Society of Architectural Historians* 46.1 (1987): 39–48.

Le Corbusier. *When the Cathedrals Were White*. Translated by Francis E. Hyslop, Jr. New York: McGraw Hill, 1964.

Lefebvre, Henri. *The Production of Space*. Translated by Donald Nicholson-Smith. Oxford: Blackwell, 1991.

Libeskind, Daniel. "Memory Foundations." *Studio Daniel Libeskind: World Trade Center Design Study*. Accessed August 19, 2004. http://daniel-libeskind.com/projects/ground-zero-master-plan.

Library of Congress Digital Collection. "Early Films of New York, 1898–1906."

Lindner, Christoph. *Fictions of Commodity Culture: From the Victorian to the Postmodern*. Aldershot, UK: Ashgate, 2003.

Lindner, Christoph. "London Undead: Screening/Branding the Empty City." In *Branding Cities: Cosmopolitanism, Parochialism, and Social Change*, edited by Stephanie Hemelryk Donald, Eleonore Kofman, and Catherine Kevin, 91–104. New York: Routledge, 2009.

Lindner, Christoph, ed. *Globalization, Violence, and the Visual Culture of Cities*. London: Routledge, 2010.

Lindner, Christoph. "The Postmetropolis and Mental Life: Wong Kar-Wai's Cinematic Hong Kong." In *The New Blackwell Companion to the City*, edited by Gary Bridge and Sophie Watson, 327–36. Oxford: Blackwell, 2011.

Lindner, Christoph. "Amsterdam–New York: Transnational Photographic Exchange in the Era of Globalization," *International Journal of Cultural Studies* 16.2 (2012): 151–68.

Lindner, Christoph, and Miriam Meissner. "Slow Art in the Creative City: Globalization, Street Photography, and Urban Renewal." *Space and Culture* (2014). doi: 10.1177/1206331213509914.

London, Jack. *People of the Abyss.* London: Pluto Press, 1993.

Loukaitou-Sideris, Anastasia, and Renia Ehrenfeucht. *Sidewalks: Conflict and Negotiation over Public Space.* Cambridge, MA: MIT Press, 2009.

Lowline. "Timeline." *TheLowline.org.* Accessed October 6, 2013. http://www.thelowline.org/about/project.

Lubove, Roy. *The Progressives and the Slums: Tenement House Reform in New York City, 1890–1917.* Pittsburgh: University of Pittsburgh Press, 1962.

Lukács, Georg. *History and Class Consciousness.* Translated by Rodney Livingstone. London: Merlin Press, 1971.

Lynch, Kevin. *The Image of the City.* Cambridge, MA: MIT Press, 1960.

Lyotard, Jean-François. "Scapeland." *Revue des Sciences Humaines* 209 (1988): 39–48.

Maffi, Mario. *New York City: An Outsider's Inside View.* Columbus: Ohio State University Press, 2004.

Marcuse, Peter, and Ronald van Kempen, "Introduction." In *Globalizing Cities: A New Spatial Order?*, edited by Peter Marcuse and Ronald van Kempen, 1–21. Oxford: Blackwell, 2000.

Marx, Karl. *Capital: A Critique of Political Economy.* Vol. 1. Translated by Ben Fowkes. New York: Penguin, 1990.

McNamara, Kevin R. *Urban Verbs: Arts and Discourses in American Cities.* Palo Alto, CA: Stanford University Press, 1996.

Meister, Sarah Hermandson. *Michael Wesely: Open Shutter.* New York: Museum of Modern Art, 2004.

Mickalites, Carey James. "Manhattan Transfer, Spectacular Time, and the Outmoded." *Arizona Quarterly* 67.4 (2011): 59–82.

Miller, Brian J. "The Struggle over the Redevelopment at Cabrini-Green, 1989–2004." *Journal of Urban History* 34.6 (2008): 944–60.

Miller, Robert K. "'Behind the Singer Tower': A Transatlantic Tale." In *Willa Cather's New York: New Essays on Cather and the City*, edited by Merrill Maguire Skaggs, 75–89. London: Associated University Presses, 2000.

Mitrano, G. F. "Sontag and the Europeans." *Women's Studies* 37.8 (2011): 908–20.

Monteiro, George, ed. *Stephen Crane: The Contemporary Reviews.* Cambridge: Cambridge University Press, 2009.

Mowll Mathews, Nancy. *Moving Pictures: American Art and Early Film, 1880–1910.* Manchester, VT: Hudson Hills Press, 2005.

Mulvey, Laura. "Visual Pleasure and Narrative Cinema." *Screen* 16.3 (1975): 6–18.

Mumford, Lewis. *Sidewalk Critic: Lewis Mumford's Writings on New York.* Edited by Robert Wojtowicz. New York: Princeton Architectural Press, 2000.

New York City Department of City Planning. *Fresh Kills Park: Draft Master Plan.* New York: City of New York, 2006.

Nye, David. *American Technological Sublime.* Cambridge, MA: MIT Press, 1994.

O'Connell, Shaun. *Remarkable, Unspeakable New York: A Literary History.* Boston: Beacon, 1995.

Orwell, George. *Down and Out in Paris and London.* New York: Mariner Books, 1972.

Page, Max. *The Creative Destruction of New York, 1900–1940.* Chicago: University of Chicago Press, 1999.

Page, Max. *The City's End: Two Centuries of Fantasies, Fears, and Premonitions of New York's Destruction.* New Haven, CT: Yale University Press, 2008.

Page, Max. "Introduction: More than Meets the Eye." In *Reconsidering Jane Jacobs*, edited by Timothy Mennel and Max Page, 3–13. Washington, DC: APA Planners Press, 2011.

Parsons, Deborah L. *Streetwalking the Metropolis: Women, the City and Modernity.* Oxford: Oxford University Press, 2000.

Pascal, Janet B. *Jacob Riis: Reporter and Reformer.* New York: Oxford University Press, 2005.

Poe, Edgar Allan. "The Man of the Crowd." In *Selected Writings of Edgar Allan Poe*, edited by David Galloway, 179–88. London: Penguin, 1967.

Pollock, Griselda. *Vision and Difference: Femininity, Feminism and the Histories of Art.* London: Routledge, 1988.

Pomerance, Murray. "Prelude: To Wake Up in the City That Never Sleeps." In *City That Never Sleeps: New York and the Filmic Imagination*, edited by Murray Pomerance, 3–17. New Brunswick NJ: Rutgers University Press, 2007.

Pound, Ezra. *Patria Mia.* Chicago: Ralph Fletcher Seymour, 1950.

Ramirez, Jan Seidler. *Painting the Town: Cityscapes of New York.* New York: Museum of the City of New York, 2000.

Ramirez, Jan Seidler, and Barbara Ball Buff. "Catalogue." In Ramirez, *Painting the Town*, 69–332.

Resina, Joan Ramon. "The Concept of After-Image and the Scopic Apprehension of the City." In *After-Images of the City*, edited by Joan Ramon Resina and Dieter Ingenschay, 1–22. Ithaca, NY: Cornell University Press, 2003.

"Remarks of the Commissioners, March 22, 1811." Reprinted in *The Greatest Grid: The Master Plan of Manhattan, 1811–2011*, edited by Hilary Ballon, 40–2. New York: Columbia University Press, 2012.

Richards, Thomas. *The Commodity Culture of Victorian England: Advertising and Spectacle, 1851–1914.* Stanford, CA: Stanford University Press, 1991.

Riis, Jacob. *The Battle of the Slum.* New York: Cosima, 2008.

Roess, Roger P., and Gene Sansone. *The Wheels That Drove New York: A History of the New York City Transit System.* Heidelberg: Springer, 2013.

Royle, Nicholas. *The Uncanny.* Manchester: Manchester University Press, 2003.

Sandeen, Eric J. "Looking After the Singer Tower: The Death and Life of Block 62." *Prospects: An Annual of American Culture Studies* 30 (2005): 597–621.

Sanders, James. *Celluloid Skyline: New York and the Movies.* London: Bloomsbury, 2002.

Sante, Luc. *Low Life: Lures and Snares of Old New York.* New York: Farrar, Straus and Giroux, 2003.

Schleier, Merrill. *The Skyscraper in American Art, 1890–1931.* Ann Arbor, MI: UMI Research Press, 1986.

Scobey, David. "Anatomy of the Promenade: The Politics of Bourgeois Sociability in Nineteenth-Century New York." *Social History* 17.2 (1992): 203–27.

Scott, William B., and Peter M. Rutkoff. *New York Modern: The Arts and the City.* Baltimore: Johns Hopkins University Press, 1999.

Sharpe, William Chapman. *New York Nocturne: The City after Dark in Literature, Painting, and Photography, 1850–1950.* Princeton, NJ: Princeton University Press, 2008.

Shields, Rob, ed. *Cultures of the Internet: Virtual Spaces, Real Histories, and Living Bodies.* London: Sage, 1996.

Simmel, Georg. "The Metropolis and Mental Life." In *The Blackwell City Reader*, edited by Gary Bridge and Sophie Watson, 11–9. Oxford: Blackwell, 2002.

Simpson, David. *9/11: The Culture of Commemoration.* Chicago: University of Chicago Press, 2006.

Small, Robert Grafton. "Dead Men Walking: From Baudelaire to Bauhaus and Beyond." *Consumption, Markets, and Culture* 5.1 (2002): 13–9.

Soja, Edward W. "Six Discourses on the Metropolis." In *Imagining Cities: Scripts, Signs, Memories*, edited by Sallie Westwood and John Williams, 19–30. London: Routledge, 1994.

Soja, Edward W. *Postmetropolis: Critical Studies of Cities and Regions.* Oxford: Blackwell, 2000.

Soja, Edward W. "Urbanizing the Globe, Globalizing the Urban." Lecture at Amsterdam Centre for Globalisation Studies, Univesity of Amsterdam, October 30, 2013.

Stalter, Sunny. "Farewell to the El: Nostalgic Urban Visuality on the Third Avenue Elevated Train." *American Quarterly* 58.3 (2006): 869–90.

Stieglitz, Alfred. "Six Happening I: Photographing the Flat-Iron Building, 1902–3." *Twice a Year* 14–15 (1946-7): 188–90.

Stoppani, Teresa. *Paradigm Islands: Manhattan and Venice: Discourses on Architecture and the City.* London: Routledge, 2011.

Suárez, Juan A. *Pop Modernism: Noise and the Reinvention of the Everyday.* Urbana: University of Illinois Press, 2007.

Tallack, Douglas. "City Sights: Mapping and Representing New York City." In *Urban Space and Representation*, edited by Maria Balshaw and Liam Kennedy, 24–38. London: Pluto, 2000.

Tallack, Douglas. *New York Sights: Visualizing Old and New New York.* New York: Berg, 2005.

Taylor, William R., ed. *Inventing Times Square: Commerce and Culture at the Crossroads of the World.* Baltimore: Johns Hopkins University Press, 1998.

Thomas, Piri. *Down These Mean Streets.* New York: Random House, 1997.

Thoreau, Henry David. *The Correspondence of Henry David Thoreau.* Edited by Walter Harding and Carl Bode. New York: New York University Press, 1958.

Trollope, Frances. *Domestic Manners of the Americans.* London: Penguin, 1997.

Veblen, Thorstein. *The Theory of the Leisure Class.* Edited by Martha Banta. Oxford: Oxford University Press, 2009.

Verrazano, Giovanni da. *The Voyage of John De Verrazano, along the Coast of North America, from Carolina to Newfoundland, A.D. 1525.* Translated by Joseph G. Cogswell. New York: New-York Historical Society, 1841.

Vidler, Anthony. *The Architectural Uncanny: Essays in the Modern Unhomely.* Cambridge, MA: MIT Press, 1999.

Virilio, Paul. "The Overexposed City." In *Rethinking Architecture: A Reader in Cultural Theory*, edited by Neil Leach, 381–9. London: Routledge, 1997.

Walkowitz, Judith. *City of Dreadful Delight: Narratives of Sexual Danger in London.* London: Virago, 1992.

Ward, David, and Olivier Zunz. "Between Rationalism and Pluralism: Creating the Modern City." In *The Landscape of Modernity: New York City, 1900–1940*, edited by David Ward and Olivier Zunz, 3–15. Baltimore: Johns Hopkins University Press, 1992.

Waring, George E. *Street-Cleaning and the Disposal of a City's Waste.* New York: Doubleday and McLure, 1897.

White, Morton, and Lucia White. *The Intellectual versus the City: From Thomas Jefferson to Frank Lloyd Wright.* Cambridge, MA: Harvard University Press and MIT Press, 1962.

Whitman, Walt. *Leaves of Grass and Selected Prose.* Edited by Lawrence Buell. New York: Modern Library College Edition, 1981.

Whitman, Walt. "Manhattan from the Bay." In *Walt Whitman: Complete Poetry and Collected Prose,* 822–33. New York: Library of America, 1982.

Whitzman, Carolyn, Crystal Legacy, Carline Andrew, Fran Klodwasky, Margaret Shaw, and Kalpana Viswanath, eds. *Building Inclusive Cities: Women's Safety and the Right to the City.* Abingdon: Routledge, 2013.

Wigley, Mark. "Insecurity by Design." In *After the World Trade Center: Rethinking New York City,* edited by Michael Sorkin and Sharon Zukin, 69–85. New York: Routledge, 2002.

Willis, Carol. "Drawing towards Metropolis." In Ferriss, *Metropolis,* 148–84.

Willis, Carol. *Form Follows Finance: Skyscrapers and Skylines in New York and Chicago.* New York: Princeton Architectural Press, 1995.

Wolff, Janet. "The Invisible *Flâneuse*: Women and the Literature of Modernity." *Theory, Culture and Society* 2.3 (1985): 37–46.

Woods, Mary N. "After-Images of the 'New' New York and the Alfred Stieglitz Circle." In *After-Images of the City,* edited by Joan Ramon Resina and Dieter Ingenschay, 183–208. Ithaca, NY: Cornell University Press, 2003.

Yerkes, Carolyn. "Reflection." In *The Greatest Grid: The Master Plan of Manhattan, 1811–2011,* edited by Hilary Ballon, 203. New York: Columbia University Press, 2012.

Zipp, Samuel. *Manhattan Projects: The Rise and Fall of Urban Renewal in Cold War New York.* New York: Oxford University Press, 2010.

Žižek, Slavoj. *Welcome to the Desert of the Real.* London: Verso, 2002.

Zola, Emile. *The Ladies' Paradise.* Translated by Brian Nelson. Oxford: Oxford University Press, 1998.

{ INDEX }

Figures are indicated by f following the page number.